DIGITAL CAMERA
C O M P A N I O N

DIGITAL CAMERA
C O M P A N I O N

Ben Sawyer
Ron Pronk

⊘ CORIOLIS GROUP BOOKS

	Keith Weiskamp
	Michelle Stroup
Cover Artist	John Kleinman, Digital Stock, Chris Marchetti
Cover Design	Gary Smith
Interior Design	Nicole Birney
Layout Production	Kim Eoff
Proofreader	Jeff Kellum
Indexer	Luanne O'Loughlin

The Coriolis Group, Inc.
14455 N. Hayden Road, Suite 220
Scottsdale, AZ 85260
Phone: (602) 483-0192
Fax: (602) 483-0193
Web address: http://www.coriolis.com

ISBN 1-57610-097-9 : $29.99
Printed in the United States of America
10 9 8 7 6 5 4 3 2

ACKNOWLEDGMENTS

This book has had a lot of friends all of whom deserve some mention and thanks. In no particular order I want to thank:

Leon Schiffman, who cheerleaded this idea when I asked him what he thought, Jean Padigian and Doug Howe at Olympus who loaned me their wonderful 200L and 300L cameras, Patricia Carasco at Casio who helped me get a review model of Casio's QV10A, Kerri Walker at Apple who loaned this project an Apple QuickTake 150 and helped arrange interviews with Apple's digital camera managers, and Anne Marie Walcyzk at Eastman Kodak who sent Kodak DC50 and DS20 cameras for our use.

Holly Fisher at LivePicture (previously at Metatools) who was one of the best and most responsive PR people we have dealt with. Other people who were immensely helpful were Patricia Pane and Sonya Schaefer at Adobe, Susan Taylor at Apple Computer, Kellie DiNaro at Walt & Company, Michael Pilmer at Alien Skin Software, Dave Pola at Equilibrium, Paulien Ruijssnaars at Fractal Design Corporation, Jim Brennan at Fuji, Krista DiGiacomo at Kaidan, Mark Law at Extensis, and Kimberly Mattis at Polaroid.

I'd like to thank all the companies that provided demos or software for the CD-ROM, especially Stephan Giauurdie at LivePicture, and David Gray for his awesome Jigsaws Galore program.

I'd also like to thank Jay York of Affordable Photo for letting me use his studio space and offering some technical advice on camera equipment and lighting, as well as Richard Berry for his camera tips and information about CCD Technology.

Finally I want to thank the people at Coriolis who've all gone the extra mile for this title, Denise Constantine, my original editor; Josh Mills who has gone out of his way to market this book like no other; Tom Kessner who mastered the CD-ROM; and Tony Stock who contributed some filter ideas. Not to be left out by any means is Nicole Birney for her work on the color section, Nomi Schalit and Kim Eoff for the production, and Jeff Kellum for the proofing. Thanks also to Tom Mayer and the sales staff, as well as Dave Friedel and Tony Potts, who always are a good sounding board.

Finally I'd like to thank the three people who helped me the most with this book: Ron Pronk who not only edited this book, but put together the second color section, as well as wrote several chapters; Dave Greely; who helped with some of the writing and early picture taking; and Michelle Stroup, who sheparded this project through to the end, an incredibly hard job that was handled with an amazing eye for detail and staying on task. I can't imagine this book getting completed without her.

CONTENTS

CHAPTER 14 CAMERA MANUFACTURERS: A REFERENCE GUIDE 305

FOREWORD

Digital photography is the next revolution in electronic imagery. As a reader of this book (and an owner or prospective owner of a digital camera), you too feel the energy that this exciting technology is creating.

The ability to digitally enhance and manipulate images—which is the real magic of digital photography—is not particularly new. For the past decade, professional graphic designers have been using expensive scanners, high-end software, and sophisticated imaging workstations. Only recently, however, has the power of digital imaging become available to consumers. This shows that a technology doesn't have to be "new" to catch on, what is required is a lucky event. In the case of digital photography, this event is the convergence of powerful image-editing programs, widespread use of home computers, and the dropping prices of digital cameras.

While I was president at Apple about 11 years ago, we were involved in the creation of desktop publishing, first by helping Apple get started and then by creating the LaserWriter, the first printer to use scaleable font technology. Looking back, it's easy to see that an idea enabled by great technology has created an entire industry: desktop publishing. CD-ROM is another technology that eventually created a market, when in 1992 Apple and a few other companies decided to offer computers with built-in CD-ROM drives at very reasonable prices. We chose to do it when the manufacturers could deliver double speed drives and when there were authoring tools to work with. This was exactly the catalyst that was required—suddenly a new market emerged.

When I first saw Live Picture's image-editing software in 1993, it looked like it had the same potential. And now it's evident that digital photography will be an explosive market. Photographers, graphic artists, and home users will soon have all the tools to create true photorealistic documents. Why is digital photography so hot these days? It isn't just that images can be digitized, or that digital cameras or printers are available that can produce photographic quality prints; rather, the convergence of revolutionary enabling technology, strategic pricing, killer applications and the collaboration of many companies is stimulating a new industry. This is happening now with digital photography, and as president of Live Picture, Inc., I am pleased to be in the center of it.

There are several other breakthrough technologies, which we have included in the Live Picture products, that will help realize our goal of creating a digital imaging experience that is completely phototealistic and fully user interative. The first technology, FlashPix, is a new image file format developed for sharing, viewing, and printing high quality images both on the desktop and over the Internet. The second technology, FITS, is a resolution-independent system for describing and rendering photos.

FlashPix, designed by Live Picture, Kodak, Hewlett-Packard, and Microsoft is an open industry standard that will enable photographers, designers, graphic artists, and home users to work with high resolution digital images on standard computers. Live Picture's products utilize FlashPix to allow users to browse, crop, scale, and rotate in real time at the highest quality.

The FlashPix file format is creating a digital photography revolution and the World Wide Web is the perfect medium for digitally showcasing and sharing these images. With FlashPix, it won't be long before we will be accessing the Web to view our vacation pictures, decide which photos we want printed and then send them as an email attachment to our friends and family.

We tend to believe that all innovation takes place exclusively within small companies today, but all markets are legitimized by larger companies. With the collaboration of highly respected companies, the digital photography market is soon to explode into an entire industry.

John Sculley, CEO
Live Picture, Inc.
January, 1997

INTRODUCTION

Ever since I've known Keith Weiskamp I've sent him a constant barrage of notes and email bearing ideas of all shapes and sizes. At the bottom of one lengthy email about some interesting development, I attached a small paragraph that mentioned that digital cameras were starting to look really hot and Coriolis might want to do a book about this technology that was suddenly hitting its stride. That note wasn't much different from hundreds of others I've sent him—except about a week later he sent back a note saying he liked this idea enough to move ahead on it. I immediately began some research to see if an initial hunch would prove viable enough—a few hours later, I had gathered enough articles to prove that the cameras were picking up steam.

The result of that early note—coupled with lots of phone calls, brainstorms, and hard work from myself and partner Ron Pronk resulted in this book, the first book about digital cameras. It certainly won't be the last.

One of the most interesting things about doing this book was watching as magazine after magazine and article after article from mainstream media to computer media raved about how hot digital cameras had finally become. During the creation of this book, these industry pundits have all spoken highly of the coming digital camera revolution: Bill Gates, John Dvorak, Bill Machrone, John Sculley, and George Fisher. This isn't bad company, and all of these people weighed in *after* we'd begun the planning of this project in late August of 1996. The fall revealed almost every major computer magazine sporting digital cameras on their cover. Almost every major consumer technology company from Microsoft to Sony to Kodak (and even Sega) promoted products geared toward digital cameras. Amazing still is the thought that this is just the beginning of a real revolution in picture taking.

The entire consumer technology revolution, especially for computers, to me, is based upon a simple premise—enhancing existing interests. Prior to the mid 1990's, computers and many other technologies did little to enhance existing interests that people had prior to this wave of chips and software now being heaped upon us. That's why most people who bought computers prior to now were lovers of computers and electronics. Today it's different, with programs like Family Tree Maker, Web browsers, or Green Thumb's line of gardening software and hardware like digital cameras, we're seeing a wave of technology that allows people to actually enjoy an interest they already have. Whether it's taking pictures, gardening, or researching the family history, today computers actually make it more interesting and more fun to do. This is the real revolution that computers will give us, and it is only going to continue—especially in the case of digital cameras.

Digital cameras give people a whole new way to think about pictures. A picture is no longer has to be the actual shot taken; the original image is now a starting point, and can be manipulated into a new image. With a digital camera, you don't just shoot pictures, but you develop them too, and with digital imaging, pictures aren't just developed—they're *changed*. The ability to change a picture is what makes it even more individual. This is what some experts (like the folks at Apple) are now calling "personal imaging." After all, a photograph or snapshot is by nature a very unique image, and the ability to manipulate the photo makes the image your very own.

And consider this: We are only just at the beginning of any piece of the personal computer, digital camera, Internet or personal imaging revolution. I am certain that 1,000 years from now, people will look back and say that many of the technologies they then take for granted will have been initially pioneered in the 1990's. Digital cameras will be one of those technologies and, as you will see with your own digital camera and this book, that idea isn't really farfetched.

A Digital Camera FAQ

1

Digital photography is the combination of film photography and computer imaging. Rather than generate an image by drawing it on the computer, an artist, photographer, or computer user like yourself starts with a photograph, which can either be scanned in or shot directly with a digital camera. After the image is in a computer-readable format, you can enhance the image, change it, size it, and much more.

After you complete your editing work with an image, you can output it on paper, load it on to a Web page, email it, animate it, or do whatever else comes to mind.

Prior to computers, photography involved the art of film exposure and developing, and involved using tools like X-acto knives and touch-up paints. But now, thanks to developments in computer hardware and software, incredible possibilities have been opened up to professionals and consumers alike. Digital photography is one of the most exciting technologies to emerge during the 20th century. More importantly, digital photography is available to both professionals and hobbyists. With the appropriate hardware and software (and a little knowledge), anybody can put the principles of digital photography to work.

What Are Digital Cameras?

Digital cameras are on the cutting edge of digital photography. Recent product introductions, technological advancements, and price cuts—coupled with the emergence of email and the World Wide Web—have helped make digital cameras the hottest new category of consumer electronics products. Figures 1.1 through 1.3 show several different digital camera models.

Digital photography has, for some time (especially at the low end of the market), relied exclusively on scanners and traditional film developing. For many people, it's too much of a hassle to take pictures, have them developed, see if they're any good, possibly have them redeveloped, scan the images, and, finally, process and edit the images until they look ideal.

Digital cameras cut a huge swath through that process. With a digital camera, you can shoot photos to your heart's content, and then download them in minutes—directly into your computer—for review and processing. Because digital cameras require no film, no developing, and provide a much easier and faster computer acquisition phase, they're becoming the tool of choice for those who work with photographs.

How Do Digital Cameras Work?

Digital cameras don't work the same as your garden-variety 35 mm camera. In fact, they're more closely related to computer scanners, copiers, and

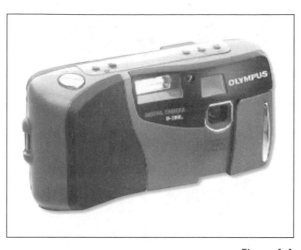

Figure 1.1

A low-end digital camera of the point-and-shoot variety from Olympus.

fax machines. Most digital cameras use a special, photo-sensitive chip called a *charged-coupled device (CCD)*. This special chip reacts to light and can translate the strength of that reaction into a numeric equivalent. By passing light through red, green, and blue filters, the reaction can be gauged for each separate color spectrum. When the readings are combined and evaluated via software, the camera can determine the specific color of each

Figure 1.2

A mid-range 35 mm digital camera from Polaroid.

Figure 1.3
A high-end digital camera from Dicomed.

segment of the picture. Because the image is actually a collection of numeric data, it can easily be downloaded into a computer and manipulated.

The key here is that the light has to be strong. Digital cameras, especially the less expensive cameras, hate low-light situations. The brighter the light, the better (although obviously there can be too much light).

After a CCD chip has created an image of a photo, it sends the data to another chip within the camera. This second chip converts the data to the camera's internal storage format, usually in some compressed graphics format like JPEG. The camera then stores this data in its internal memory. Most cameras use a special form of RAM called *static RAM* or *SRAM*, which can hold its internal data even without an electrical current (which other forms of RAM require).

This entire process takes a few seconds on most cameras—it's not instantaneous—which is why you can't keep clicking after taking a photo. As digital camera technology improves (and prices come down), expect to find cameras that do this process in less than a second, rather than the typical four to five seconds currently required. Cameras will also get smarter and be able to compensate for lower light conditions and blurriness, and will be able to take several shots in a row or generate automatic panoramas.

How Do Digital Cameras Compare With Traditional Cameras?

Film photographs have immeasurably higher resolution (millions of pixels versus thousands or hundreds of thousands) than digital cameras. Film-based cameras are also more expensive to maintain, because even though digital cameras may cost more, they don't use any film.

There are many more subtle comparisons to be made between digital cameras and their film-based counterparts. For many users, the more appropriate way is to say they don't compare at all. Not only do digital cameras use a different type of photographic technology, they're designed for a different use. That is, digital cameras are designed specifically to capture and input computer images—something other cameras can't do (at least not without the help of a scanner). In this sense, neither digital cameras nor film-based cameras are "better." If you want high-quality photos to pass around at the office, then you want a film-based camera. If you want images that will be loaded into your Web page, you want a digital camera.

However, there are some situations where it does make sense to compare and evaluate the two types of cameras. If you're a professional graphics artist, or in magazine or newspaper publishing, you'll have to decide whether the convenience of a digital camera is worth the lower resolution you'll get—even with the most expensive digital cameras.

Consider the members of the Associated Press photojournalism corps. Many of these professionals shoot with digital cameras, while others use traditional, film-based cameras. And many graphics artists have both types of cameras. Even many hobbyists and professional photographers recognize the tradeoffs in the two types of technologies and consequently use both.

What Types Of Digital Cameras Are Available?

Not all digital cameras are created equal. There are several types of digital cameras, as well as several different price points and features to consider. In the early years of digital photography, two basic types of cameras were available: fully integrated cameras and cameras that attached to traditional-lensed cameras. But a new class of digital camera is evolving—one that is more closely related to video cameras. These new cameras feature a sophisticated still-shot system that can be used just like a digital camera. Other digital cameras, like one sold by Ricoh, actually capture brief bits of video (several seconds) instead of a single still.

Another way to classify digital cameras is by price. There are three levels of digital cameras and three price ranges. The first level encompasses consumer, or low-end, cameras that cost under $500, typically offer low (400×300 or less) resolutions, and have few bells and whistles.

The next level, mid-range cameras, are aimed at computer design and development professionals or more serious consumers. These cameras are priced between $500 and $2,000 and sport resolutions of 640×480 to 1024×768 (or slightly better). They also tend to have added features, like zoom lenses, support for PCMCIA memory cards, and LCD screens.

Beyond the $2,000 range lie professional-level cameras with high resolutions (4096×4096 and better). These cameras can cost thousands of dollars (more than $30,000 in some cases). Many use 35 mm-compatible lenses or are compatible with off-the-shelf 35 mm cameras. These cameras are for serious photographers and organizations that can justify the cost.

WHICH CAMERA IS THE BEST?

The best camera will always be the one you choose to buy. Seriously, there is no "best" digital camera. While we certainly have opinions and personal favorites, our choices have been made based on personal needs and desires, and we're sure you'll have your own personal set of standards.

However, you *will* need to be armed with information so that you know what you're buying. Perhaps we should amend our statement, then, and say: The best digital camera is the one you buy *when you make an informed purchase*. In each camera category, you'll find that a few stand out. So how do you decide? If you do the right homework (and we'll show you how in later chapters), you're sure to purchase a camera that will give you the results you expect.

Basically, when you consider the purchase of a digital camera, you'll need to consider the price/performance ratio first. In other words, how much do you want to spend in order to achieve the photograph results you desire? When you approach a potential purchase in this way, cameras stack up quite differently. For instance, the photo quality of a low-end camera is significantly inferior to a high-end camera, but that's mostly because they're completely different classes of cameras. High-end cameras generally cost more than $1,500 and the low-end ones sell for around $300. For the money, buying a low-end camera will allow you some incredible functionality, but if you're really looking for the features available with a mid-range camera, you're going to be disappointed. After you review the entire range of cameras in terms of price and features, you can boil down your choice to an informed and intelligent one. Again, we'll provide some detailed purchasing criteria in later chapters.

WHAT'S THE DIFFERENCE BETWEEN SCANNING AND DIGITAL PHOTOGRAPHY?

If you don't have a digital camera, the easiest way to convert photos into a format that can be understood by your computer is to use a scanner. Scanners actually use some of the same CCD-based technology of digital cameras, but nevertheless they're *not* digital cameras—they're just a tool to get printed photos into a computer. In addition, a scanner can't accurately input anything but the flattest of surfaces. Digital cameras, on the other hand, can produce an image of anything—surfaces need not be flat because a digital camera is designed to deal with a 3D world, just like film-based cameras.

However, even low-end scanners can transform a high-quality photo into a resolution higher than a low-end digital camera can muster. But at the high end, some digital cameras have amazing resolution capability—at very reasonable prices to boot. For the most part, though, scanners offer better resolution than digital cameras, but less overall functionality. Digital cameras also do a poor job at reproducing existing photos in newspapers or magazines. For that kind of job, scanners provide better results.

A new class of scanners provides a compromise between traditional scanners and digital cameras—in fact, this kind of scanner is specifically aimed at the digital photography consumer. These *portrait scanners* are small scanners built specifically to scan typical 3×5 photographic prints produced from film-based cameras. Hewlett-Packard is actually integrating these scanners directly into their PCs, much like a hard drive or other peripheral. There are also special Advanced Photo System scanners (which we'll discuss later in this chapter) that can directly scan developed Advanced Photo System film and input the results directly into a computer. These hybrid systems provide excellent bridges between scanning photos from traditional cameras and digital cameras.

Before digital cameras became popular, the scanner was the king of image acquisition. But, as digital photography has evolved and camera resolution has increased, scanners are being used more for optical character recognition and for scanning existing photographic prints and other published materials. Digital cameras are beginning to emerge as the major form of photographic image acquisition for PC users. But it's probably also true that digital cameras will not replace scanners completely. Both devices will have a job to do. It's just that much of what scanners used to be responsible for will be replaced by digital photography.

WHAT IS THE ADVANCED PHOTO SYSTEM?

In the previous section, we briefly mentioned the *Advanced Photo System (APS)*, which is a revolutionary new photo format that we suspect most digital photographers will be using in a few years. When the world's major film and camera companies noticed the strong emergence of digital photography, they collaborated to develop the APS, which updates film and 35 mm photography with a host of features that are quite significant for people in the digital photography movement.

APS is designed to treat film almost like a floppy disk. In other words, the film is designed to store images as well as other magnetic data—such as date-and-time stamps, text annotations, and camera setting information. Images can be taken and stored in multiple formats, including 3.6×6, 4×7, 3.5×5, 4×6, and panoramic sizes like 3.5×8.5 and 4×11.5. Cameras that support the APS format are able to rapidly switch between formats *on the same film*. In addition, the film can be replaced and reused even in the middle of a roll. The film cartridge advances and rewinds to and from the latest snapped shot, without exposing the film.

And here's perhaps the greatest feature of APS: With traditional film, you snap pictures, then develop the film and create negatives to later turn into prints. With APS, the film *is* the exposure. After the film is developed, it's wound back into the cartridge. Consumers can then pick and choose from a thumbnail sheet to determine which photos to develop. And with special equipment like Fuji's AS-1 Filmscan shown in Figure 1.4, you can even take the developed cartridge back to your house to scan the film directly into your computer. We'll discuss extra equipment more in Chapter 2. Instead of relying on prints from your local photo developing store, you can do it directly at home and then have the computer manipulate it just as you would a digital camera photo.

APS still requires the use of an outside developer, so digital cameras will probably become the main device that many use to capture pictures into their computers. The APS system, however, promises to blur the line between film-based technology and filmless cameras. In general, the rise of APS technology indicates that, regardless of whether a photographer uses film or takes a filmless route, the move is toward digital and computer-based photography.

WHAT IS PHOTO CD?

Photo CD is a special digital photography format created by Kodak. Originally heralded as the future of digital photography, Photo CD is now best

Figure 1.4
With Fuji's AS-1 Filmscan-it you can scan film right into your computer.

thought of as a good bridge technology between traditional photography and the new era of digital camera photography. Actually, Photo CD is both a file format and a film scanning technology that allows photographers to transfer traditional film shots, in full color, onto a CD-ROM. Photographers send their film to a Photo CD service bureau (unless they can buy the expensive scanning equipment themselves). The service bureau then returns to the consumer a CD, packed with the photos, for digital use. Photo CD may eventually become less of a standard as digital cameras and the newer (and less expensive) Advanced Photo System technology evolve and become more popular. Currently, though, Photo CD is still widely used and will probably remain as a digital processing option for many years.

WHICH COMPANIES MAKE DIGITAL CAMERAS?

Digital photography is such a hot medium that dozens of companies are making digital cameras. Digital photography is also such a new medium that many digital camera manufacturers are not traditional camera companies at all. In fact, some of the earliest entries into the marketplace come from companies that are more typically considered to be part of the computer industry. Among these companies are Apple, Epson, AGFA, Leaf, Phase One, Sony, and even Sega.

Of course, some of the major manufacturers of digital cameras are, in fact, the traditional camera companies. Kodak is one of the leading manufacturers of digital cameras. Fuji, Polaroid, Nikon, Olympus, and Minolta have also introduced digital cameras. It's clear that digital photography is a rapidly growing industry, whereas the film-based camera industry has already matured and is fairly static. So, it's in the best interest of traditional camera companies to go digital.

WHAT IS THE APPLE IMAGE CAPTURE PLATFORM?

In May of 1996, Apple Computer, a pioneer in the digital camera industry, announced the creation of a technology designed to usher in a new wave of digital camera hardware. Cameras that use this technology, which Apple calls the Apple Image Capture Platform (AIPC), should be appearing on the market in 1997 and beyond.

AICP is actually a combination of technologies. It makes use of a new microchip for digital cameras—the Motorola MPC823—and a special digital camera operating system that Apple has developed. The combination brings a new suite of functions to cameras. First, the cameras are much easier to program, which means developers can create new programs or easily integrate existing programs with digital cameras. Second, the technology makes the cameras themselves smarter. With the AIPC technology, cameras can run a program script to take a series of photos over a specified amount of time, automatically send images over the Internet, perform in-house stitching sessions, and much more.

AIPC is still an emerging platform. However, when it matures, this technology will allow software, hardware, and camera developers to accelerate the creation of new products that will continue to revolutionize the field of photography.

WHO'S USING DIGITAL CAMERAS?

We've already mentioned that many professional photographers use digital cameras, even though they offer lower resolution than film-based cameras. Other types of professionals, such as desktop publishers, Web developers, and multimedia producers, often don't require the highest quality for their images. For these users, low to mid-range digital cameras make a lot of sense. Many Web developers and desktop publishing professionals are using Apple QuickTake, Fuji, Polaroid, and Kodak DC40/DC50 cameras—all of which cost between $700 and $1,500—to produce good-quality photos (resolutions of 640×480 and better). Depending on your needs, you too might likely find that digital cameras can contribute to your job or business. Digital cameras don't require film, which makes the images they generate so versatile. The fact that these cameras don't use film also means lower operational costs over traditional cameras. These two factors make digital cameras useful for a wide range of situations, including many where regular cameras would be a major hassle. For example, insurance adjusters use digital cameras to inspect and assess damage scenes quickly. Imagery is stored instantly in a database and can be emailed to other experts for quick analysis and cost estimation. Security guards can use digital cameras to instantly take a picture of anyone entering a sensitive checkpoint. And many newspaper photographers, as we've already mentioned, now carry digital cameras to reduce the delay in reporting breaking news.

WHAT TIPS CAN YOU OFFER IN TAKING DIGITAL PHOTOGRAPHS?

First and foremost, taking good photos requires following some basic photography tips, some practice, and eventually acquiring a trained photographic eye. Beyond these basics, though, there are certainly some specific tips that apply to digital photography. Most of these tips are covered in Chapters 4 and 5. In fact, helping you to improve your digital photography skills is one of the major goals of this book. So, you'll find tips included in just about every chapter.

CAN I SELL MY DIGITAL IMAGES?

Yes and no. Many people feel that a substantial market will emerge for stock art and photography when self-publishing (especially on the Web) explodes in popularity. Bill Gates has even started a separate company, Corbis, to build a huge digital image archive from which he licenses imagery to magazines, Web sites, and other publishers and artists. In addition to Corbis, other stock archives—like Art Today and PhotoDisc—are doing much the same. Depending on the quality of the imagery you produce, it is possible for you to earn money selling digital imagery. However, because you're competing with professional image archive companies, the likelihood that you can make money hand over fist is slim unless you're a consummate professional with a skilled eye and excellent digital processing skills.

Even if you're not a pro, there are many opportunities to make a bit of money from your images. We'll focus on these opportunities in Chapter 13.

WHY MUST I WAIT BETWEEN SHOTS?

As we already mentioned briefly, most digital cameras have slight delays before and after the shutter button is pressed. In time, as the technology advances, the delays should be eliminated. For now, though, most photographers will have to learn how to work with these delays. The first delay is caused by the camera clearing the CCD chip and setting all its internal systems to take the photo. Typically, this delay is a little less than a second.

In the instant after a picture is taken, the camera may take as many as several seconds to render the picture internally, compress it, and then store it in the camera's internal memory. After the compression and storage processes have been completed, the camera is ready to take another shot. Again, as memory sizes in cameras increase and the compression technologies inside the cameras get faster, this delay will get much shorter or will be eliminated altogether.

Since most digital cameras currently require these delays, it's difficult to shoot fast-moving objects. Some existing higher-end cameras can take several successive frames at once. So in some unique cases, stop motion or successive photos of a moving object is possible.

WHAT ABOUT OTHER DIGITAL CAMERA HARDWARE?

Many hardware options are available for use with your digital camera, so it's important to know what's available and how to decide whether you need these options. Most importantly, you need to think carefully about the kind of PC to use. You probably already have a PC, but if you're new to digital photography, you might eventually want to upgrade to a system that can better handle digital imagery. In Chapter 2, we'll answer your questions about matching the right computer hardware with your digital camera.

There are many other hardware items to consider. For instance, Fuji, Hewlett-Packard, and Epson are among several major manufacturers that make printers specifically designed to output digital photographs. DC-PRO and Kaidan are two accessories companies that sell special lenses for many types of digital cameras, as well as an assortment of tripods, including ones for creating panoramic shots.

Storage is also a major hardware concern. Many people use Photo CD systems to store images on CD-ROM, and then there are high-capacity removable storage systems like iomega's Zip drives. Digital photos can quickly fill up your hard drive. If you become serious about digital photography, even as a hobby, we heartily recommend that you buy a Zip drive (or other high-capacity removable storage device). Otherwise, you'll find yourself discarding images you might otherwise have wanted to keep.

How Do I Decipher The Digital Photography Jargon?

As is true with any technology, digital photography has its own set of technical jargon that you'll have to learn. The following paragraphs explain some of the basic terms that are important to learn.

- *ISO/ASA* is a ranking used to describe how sensitive and clean the imagery is. The lower the reading, the less likely it will be that the camera will introduce noise or graininess into the imagery.

- *Bit depth* is a computer graphics term used to describe how many colors a graphics technology can reproduce. Eight-bit depth means that the total color range a graphic can reproduce is 256 colors. Every digital camera in existence has a bit depth of 8 bits *per color*, since color is decided by a mix of red, green, and blue. That equals 256×256×256, which is 16.7 million colors. This level is known as 24-bit depth (or 8bits * 3).

- *TWAIN* is another common term used in digital photography. TWAIN refers to a special piece of software that allows your camera to be easily used by TWAIN-compatible software. For instance, Paint Shop Pro, the top shareware imaging package, works with TWAIN devices. So, you can access and work with your digital camera directly from within Paint Shop Pro. TWAIN-compatible devices include scanners, fax machines, and, of course, digital cameras, to name a few.

- *Megapixel* refers to cameras that produce very high-resolution photos (greater than 1000×1000 pixels).

There is more terminology, of course, but as is true for the few just described, most terms are fairly easy to understand. To help, we've included a glossary of common terms, acronyms, and phrases at the back of the book.

WHAT IS FLASHPIX?

FlashPIX is a new graphics format created specifically for digital photography. FlashPIX was created by an alliance among Kodak, LivePicture, Microsoft, and Hewlett-Packard, and is based on a graphics format called IVUE, which stores imagery in a way that allows the image to be manipulated extremely rapidly. IVUE also allows users without super-fast equipment to work with complex photos. In addition to the features of IVUE, FlashPIX maintains a lot of other image information—such as captions, capture device information, camera settings, and more. The format is also designed to work well over networks and on the World Wide Web. Because images can be manipulated so fast and with little memory overhead, FlashPIX might very well become the dominant photo format for the Web. Users will even be able to look at and process images directly on a Web page. You can read more about FlashPIX in Chapter 6.

WHAT ARE PCMCIA AND COMPACTFLASH CARDS?

Except for the high-end cameras, most digital cameras have some form of local storage capacity. Some of these cameras (but not all) enhance their local storage with special memory cards you can swap in and out of the camera. This makes it easy to have lots of storage—if you need more pictures just buy more cards.

Digital cameras currently use three types of memory cards. The first type, PCMCIA cards, are divided into two categories: those that offer memory through a special set of RAM chips called static RAM (SRAM), and those that give cameras memory by being mini-hard drives that plug into the cameras. The SRAM cards are commonly called Type I or II PCMCIA cards, sometimes referred to as FlashFilm. A third type, which are actually mini-hard drive cards, are known as Type III PCMCIA cards. These cards are slightly thicker than their flash RAM cousins and are used mostly in cameras that capture images of 3 MB to 5 MB. The third type is a new flash RAM standard called CompactFlash. These work almost exactly like PCMCIA RAM cards, but their smaller size makes them better for smaller devices like digital cameras.

Depending on manufacturer and price, you can find cards with 2 MB to 80 MB in flash RAM and, up to 350 MB plus on the Type III PCMCIA hard drive cards. You can also find readers for the cards that plug into your desktop computer, to easily transfer the images without going through the camera.

Look for CompactFlash to become a major standard for digital cameras. PCMCIA cards will be used on mid-range systems that might need higher RAM counts for their increased image size.

WHAT SHOULD I USE TO MANIPULATE MY PHOTOS?

Digital cameras have only recently come into widespread use. However, the software that lets you expertly improve or manipulate digital photographs has existed for many years. This fact means that there are many different software tools you can use to process your digital images.

Most of these programs will be covered in detail later in this book. You might already be familiar with such widely used programs as Photoshop and Kai's Powertools, but we'll also introduce you to lesser known programs like Kai's Power Goo and LivePicture. And you'll also learn about Digital Expressions' Art Song, which lets you create music from your digital photos.

Regardless of whether you use your digital camera for work, fun, or as a hobby, you'll dramatically improve the use of your camera if you have quality software that allows you to manipulate the images you capture. Some of the software packages we showcase in this book are expensive, but many of the products are extremely affordable. Paint Shop Pro, for instance, is a nice shareware image processing and editing product available for only a $69 registration fee.

WHAT ARE LIVEPICTURE AND PHOTOSHOP?

Photoshop and LivePicture are high-end digital imagery editing and processing programs. Photoshop is the granddaddy of digital imagery products and is now in its fourth revision. LivePicture is a more recent package but has a feature set that's on par with Photoshop.

Since these tools are so powerful and are widely used by top designers, digital professionals, and developers, you'll often hear about them. Most consumers and occasional digital photography users will most likely stick to simpler editing products like Adobe's PhotoDeluxe or Microsoft's Picture It!, which pack a lot of power even though their feature sets are more limited. However, if you're looking for top-of-the line imaging power, Photoshop and LivePicture are the tools the pros use.

WILL DIGITAL CAMERAS MAKE ME A BETTER PHOTOGRAPHER?

Yes and no. As we'll demonstrate in later sections of this book, a trained photographic eye will always take a better photo than an untrained eye. There *are* some things that even technology can't correct. However, because digital cameras give you rapid access to your photos, and because you can easily work with a variety of cool imaging software, you can improve your photos after you've taken them. If a photo is too dark, you can lighten it. If a photo has too much border space, you can crop it. In these instances, digital camera technology can make you a better photographer because you cannot only learn from your mistakes, but you can correct your mistakes at will. Even so, the better you get at taking raw photos with your camera, the better your photo will be—no matter how much image processing you perform.

CAN I CREATE ANIMATION WITH MY DIGITAL CAMERAS?

A digital camera is no substitute for a video camera, but you can do many things to meld digital photography and animation. One approach is to take various stills of a subject in different positions—much like stop motion photography—then page-flip those images to create a simple animation. Another technique is to take two or more different photos and use a program like Kai's Power Goo to create high quality animated morphing movies with your photos. Several projects in this book demonstrate in greater detail how to do such work.

Is Digital Photography Better Done On A Macintosh Or A Windows PC?

In almost every way, Mac and comparable Windows computer platforms are equal when it comes to digital photography. Both platforms offer identical or similar major programs for working with digital photographs, including Adobe PhotoDeluxe and Photoshop, LivePicture, Web tools, email, desktop publishing, and more. All the major cameras include connections and software for both Mac and Windows systems. Some might say that the Macintosh, which has a strong history in the publishing and graphics processing industry, is a better system for heavy users of digital cameras. But available software and hardware for Windows systems are just as powerful and versatile as the software and hardware available to Macintosh users.

Is There Software To Help Me Organize My Pictures?

As you take more and more pictures in pursuit of your new digital photography hobby, your hard drive will eventually look like the digital equivalent of the proverbial shoebox of traditional photography notoriety. Thankfully, there are a host of cool products—like JASC Media Center, Media Minds' Photo Album, and more—that can help you store, back-up, organize, and administer your digital photo collection. We'll cover all of these packages and give you tips for maintaining your digital photograph collections in Chapter 8.

Can I Email My Pictures And Post Them On The Web?

One of the coolest things you can do with your digital camera is to quickly snap and send photos to friends and family via email or by posting them to your own Web site. The sheer speed with which you can share long-distance events is truly compelling. Photograph your kids opening presents on Christmas day and send the images the same day to grandparents a thousand miles away. Take a two-week vacation and, instead of the traditional postcard, send over a dozen images back to the hometown crowd, showing where you've been as little as 30 minutes ago.

If you're not yet up to speed on the Web, or if you're not yet using email, we've include specific chapters in this book that will get you up and running. We'll also explain which hardware and software you'll need to get on the Internet. Emailing a photo is really easy; posting images to a Web site is a little more complex, but not terribly difficult. Posting files to a Usenet newsgroup requires a bit of additional trickery, but we'll explain how to do this and much more later in the book.

WHAT ARE QUICKTIME VR AND SURROUND VIDEO?

QuickTime VR and Surround Video are top of the line in terms of what computer software represents for the future of photography. QuickTime VR, developed by Apple (the VR stands for "Virtual Reality"), and Surround Video, a Microsoft Windows technology, allow users to navigate through 360-degree environments that are essentially a series of stitched-together photos or 3D-rendered scenes. Imagine taking a 360-degree panoramic shot, taping the ends together, blowing it up to life size, and then standing in the middle of the photo and watching it revolve around you. Essentially, that is what QuickTime VR and Surround Video let you do. The computer scrolls the entire photo, showing the user a specific viewing portion of it at one time. Panoramic photos tend to have perspective problems, so the software instantly corrects these distortions on the fly so that, to the user, the entire scene is perspectively correct.

Both QuickTime VR and Surround Video have been built for use on CD-ROMs and on the Web. QuickTime VR even includes such features as hotspots and animated objects.

Can I Connect My Camera To My TV To View Pictures?

Some digital cameras have a video output capability, so that you can connect the camera to your TV. With such a camera images can be viewed on a TV set via a video-out cable similar to a cable used with a VCR or camcorder. Not every camera has this feature, though. So, if you want to output images to your TV, make sure you buy a camera that supports this capability.

Will My Color Printer Provide Quality Output Of My Photos?

If anything has paralleled the development of digital cameras, it would have to be the quick ascendancy of new color printing technologies, both for home use and for use by large service bureaus.

We'll take a close look at output options in later chapters. Many people have very good ink jet color printers in their homes. These printers can do a decent job printing out digitally captured photos. Although early ink jet printers were initially laughed at by graphics professionals due to their poor resolution and color quality, these printers are now so sophisticated that most can print digital photographs with very nice results. However, quality prints from home ink jet printers only come when the printer is performing at peak conditions—such as with special ink jet paper and with an excellent ink supply.

Color laser printers are also readily available and affordable now, as are dye-based printers. Both are a step up in quality from ink jet printers. A new and exciting output option is coming from companies like Fuji and Hewlett-Packard, which have debuted printers specifically designed for printing digital photographs.

If you need even higher resolution output, or have special needs like poster printing or simply can't afford a high-end color printer, don't fear. In almost every major metropolitan area in the U.S. and internationally, you'll find what are commonly referred to as "service bureaus." These companies own high-quality printers, and typesetting and imaging equipment, and offer a wide range of output services for customers. Many are a combination of film-developing, image-processing, and desktop publishing companies. Customers can submit images via disks, via modem, or via the Internet, and can specify the desired output (such as image quality, color scheme, size, paper type, and so on).

Typically, service bureaus provide extremely high quality output (1270 dpi), and output poster prints, color separations, and more. In Chapter 10, we've included an extensive section that details all the image processing services a good service bureau can perform for you. We also included tips on how to work with these companies, cost-comparison charts, and information on several national bureaus in case you want to work with one remotely.

Purchasing A Camera
And Other Equipment

2

With the advent of digital cameras, some people are already forecasting the "death of film." Let's not be so hasty. You'll probably always find a use for your 35 mm camera, but it's undeniable that digital cameras represent the most significant part of the future of photography. About 278,000 digital cameras were sold worldwide in 1995. In the first three months of 1996 alone, that number jumped to 400,000.

The industry is projecting sales of 5.58 million by 1999. Remember, however, that the technology is still just a few years old, even at the professional level. So, the quality of cameras will continue to increase dramatically, while prices will fall in an equally rapid fashion. Currently, the price range of cameras runs from about $500 to $40,000 and over. Remember when calculators, VCRs, and compact disc players were major investments? No longer. The same price/performance transformation will be true of digital cameras.

Because the movement toward digital photography is happening so rapidly, the first question you might ask yourself when considering the purchase of a digital camera is, "Do I need one now?" A lot of people, of course, already have answered "yes" to that question. However, if you've bought this book because you want to explore *before* you buy, or if you're waiting for prices to come down a bit more and for image quality to improve, it's a good question to consider.

If you expect a digital camera to be a suitable replacement for film prints, you'll be disappointed unless you buy a top-of-the-line $40,000 camera. However, as we explained in Chapter 1, there are many reasons—beyond image quality—to purchase and use a digital camera. For example, if you spend a lot of money on film processing for photos that you actually use on your computer, a digital camera is a time and money saver.

Assuming you do need (or at least want) a digital camera now, there are a myriad factors to consider, and questions to ask yourself and your camera dealer. What will you be using the camera for? How much money do you have to spend? Is your home computer powerful enough to deal with memory-consuming image files? Will you need a printer or other accessories? This chapter is intended to help you answer these questions and to become a smart digital camera equipment consumer.

Here are some of the major topics that we'll address:

- The class of camera that's best for you

- Camera features and how they affect price and performance

- Computer needs

- Other equipment and accessories to consider

WHAT IS YOUR PRICE RANGE?

"What will you use your camera for?" and, "How much do you have to spend?" are closely related questions. Be forewarned, though: No matter what you are going to use a digital camera for, you will need to spend at least several hundred dollars to purchase the camera alone—and accessories, better computer equipment, spare batteries, and so forth can increase your overall digital photography expenses.

If you use a digital camera often enough, it will eventually pay for itself in eliminated film and film processing costs. If you're not sure whether you'll use a digital camera frequently enough to justify the cost, you could begin by renting a camera. Also, by renting, you can pick up enough experience to better help you choose a camera. You should, however, already know what level of camera you can afford. There's no sense test driving a Ferrari when you know you can only afford a Taurus.

Tip We've found several places that rent digital cameras. Check your local area camera shop or nearby stores that rent computers. We can't make a specific recommendation, so make sure you feel comfortable with a store before you rent.

Most of the Kinko's outlets have a Kodak digital camera on premises to use in their PC/Mac production departments. Check out Kinko's at http://www.kinkos.com.

Low-End Cameras

If you are a casual shutterbug, a designer who doesn't need resolution higher than 1024×768, or simply on a budget, then you should focus on the low end of the digital camera price range. This category includes the Apple QuickTake, the Kodak DC50, and similar products from the likes of Casio, Olympus, and Chinon. These cameras generally offer resolutions of about 640×480 pixels (though newer ones like the Olympus 300L achieve up to 1024×768) and cost from several hundred dollars to over $1,000. Cameras at the extreme low end cost about $500 and offer about 400×340 resolution. These cameras are a great deal of fun, but you shouldn't expect professional-quality work. They are fine choices if you just want to include photos with your email messages or add photos to your personal Web page.

Here are a few examples: Let's say that you live in California and you (or your wife) have just had a baby. Wouldn't be nice if Grandma and Grandpa in Maine could see what the little one looks like as soon as you have a chance to hurry home and download the photos? Holidays, weddings, big games, or any special event can be quickly captured and sent to friends and relatives who are unable to be there in person. Entry-level cameras are quite useful for these purposes. But for desktop publishing and more serious Web development, you will need a camera that offers resolution of at least 640×480, which is still within the low-end range. Real estate and insurance agents will also find that entry-level or other low-end cameras work well for documentation purposes.

Mid-Range Cameras

Desktop publishers with a budget of about $2,000 to $5,000 are typical candidates for mid-range digital cameras. Graphic artists without large-scale budgets also should consider this category.

Most mid-range cameras work directly as attachments to 35 mm field cameras. This setup not only provides increased resolution but also provides the user a range of lens attachment abilities. If you already own and use a 35 mm camera, this solution gives you additional functionality within familiar hardware.

Many newspapers are beginning to convert to digital cameras in the mid-range to high-end category. This eliminates the time and cost of film processing—in the newspaper business, speed and financial savings are critical to meeting deadlines or beating the competition. And news media companies are increasingly launching Web sites to accompany the paper versions of their products. For these companies, a digital camera becomes almost a necessity for ease of use and speed.

High-End Cameras

High-end cameras are currently limited to professionals or hobbyists who have deep pockets. Not convinced? These cameras cost at least $5,000 and can cost as much as $50,000. For a professional, they can be quite worth the cost. For everybody else, they aren't.

At the high end, one of two types of system is used—charged coupling device (CCD) chips or scanning camera backs, which attach to a conventional 35 mm or (at the highest end) a traditional 4×5 camera. Making the transition from traditional cameras to scanning backs is more difficult for the experienced photographer. Because the image is formed one line at a time and requires as much as 12 minutes to scan at high resolution, traditional lighting does not work. Production time is also quite slow. However, the resulting image is of phenomenal quality; some of these cameras achieve resolutions of 7000×7000 pixels at 150 lines per inch. For an idea of how large that is, consider that an image from a PhaseOne or Dicomed camera can easily be 140 MB to 170 MB in size. That's over 100 times the size of a typical image shot with a Kodak DC50. These storage requirements, of course, require a large-capacity computer hard drive and backup system.

Due to this large image size, most high-end cameras aren't portable. They're studio cameras that require the computer to be directly attached to the camera at all times. Of course, for a camera costing thousands of dollars, you don't want to take it to some rugged part of the world where you might drop it.

Breaking Down The Digital Camera Technologies

We've talked in general about the types of cameras out there, but now we need to get technical—at least a little. There are five specific technologies you will encounter when considering cameras. Most of these apply to high-end products.

Liquid Crystal Tunable Filter (LCTF)

This newer technology is being used for the first time in the Dicomed Big Shot, a $50,000+ camera that supports stunning resolution. The Liquid Crystal Tunable is a "front of lens" filter that cycles rapidly through red, green, and blue as the shot is being taken and reads it into the computer.

Scanning back

Scanning backs are typical in the higher end of the digital camera market. They run through the photograph one line at a time (hence the scanning name), which means the capture time is long but yields very high quality.

Striped array

A CCD chip is divided into partitions that are each dedicated to one of the three color spectrums. This is an easy and cheap solution, however, often the color of the final output contains "interpolated" data, which results in lower quality and can cause artifacting.

Three-chip

This is the most popular scheme used in video cameras and digital cameras. (In fact, many use the same chips as those used in camcorders.) In this scheme, one chip is dedicated to one color—or, more commonly, a single chip is divided between red and blue, and two chips are used for the green light spectrum.

Three-shot color

Each color spectrum is given its own exposure, which results in awesome color quality but lengthens capturing time.

Understanding Digital Camera Features

Digital cameras, like conventional 35 mm cameras, include a variety of features that influence price, versatility, and image quality. Again, consider what you will use the camera for and chose the equipment with the features that best suit your needs. Do you need zoom capability? Wide angle? Selective deletion? The ability to expand memory? The following sections explain the major features that are included with various digital cameras.

Resolution And Photo Capacity

As you climb the price ladder, the resolution (photo quality) available with digital cameras increases. A low-end camera might allow you as little as 320×200 pixels in order to store more than just a handful of images. If you want higher quality photos, the number of images you can store decreases.

For example, the Apple QuickTake 100 will allow 32 images at 320×200 resolution, but only 8 images at 640×480. Those low-end numbers are fine for screen display and are generally acceptable for prints no larger than 4×5 inches. Enlarging the images beyond that will result in a loss of detail. But if you simply want paper photographs, you are better off buying a $10 disposable camera. The digital camera has numerous other advantages and uses that we'll discuss later.

At the high end, camera systems such as the AGFA Actioncam or the Minolta RD-175 can produce a 24-bit, 1528×1146 pixel image. It's also important to consider whether a camera can switch between different resolutions and, if so, how this ability affects the number of pictures the camera can store. Some low-end cameras are limited to one resolution—others provide multiple resolutions. The Kodak DC50, for example, has low, medium, and high resolution options. Be sure to ask about a camera's ability to change resolution within the same photo session—in other words, can the camera take a couple of high resolution photos, a few more at medium resolution, and several at low resolution before the stored images are downloaded. Note that some cameras, can switch resolutions but not within the same session.

Tip

Remember: Storage capacity isn't only valuable when taking high-quality shots. It is an equally important factor for taking several decent photos during one session.

PCMCIA Cards

One way to augment limited memory is by adding PCMCIA cards, which expand your camera's image storage capacity. Some cameras, however, use only internal memory. For those cameras that accept PCMCIA cards, such as Kodak's DC50, the addition of one of these removable cards provides the ability to take a large number of photos during one session. Another advantage of a memory card is the ability to group photos by category—unlike film, which can't be removed and reinserted. For example, you can keep all of your son's baseball games on one card, all of your daughter's softball games on another card, and images of the dog playing Frisbee in the yard on a third card—before downloading the images. In general, the ability of a camera to increase memory through the use of PCMCIA cards,

Figure 2.1
A PCMCIA card from the Pretec Electronics Corp.

such as the one shown in Figure 2.1 from Pretec Electronics Corp., is a good solution if you need to store a large number of images before you download them into a computer. PCMCIA cards generally cost from $80 for 2 MB to $300 for 16 MB.

CompactFlash

Many newer, consumer-oriented cameras use a newer form of static RAM (SRAM) cards called CompactFlash, such as the one seen in Figure 2.2 from CompactFlash inventor, SanDisk. For example, Kodak's new DC25 camera uses the CompactFlash standard. CompactFlash cards work just like PCMCIA cards, but are smaller—about one-half to one-third the size of a standard PCMCIA card.

Selective Deletion

Unlike film cameras, most digital cameras allow the user to delete unwanted images. However, not all deletion schemes are the same. Most allow you to delete only the most recent shot. Some go a step further, and allow *selective deletion*, which means you can delete non-sequential images. Conversely, some provide the dreaded "all or none" deletion method. With this system,

Figure 2.2
CompactFlash's main advantage is its smaller size.

if you want to delete a bad shot, you need to sacrifice every other shot in the camera's memory.

Most cameras, though, are more advanced than that. In fact, the selective deletion method will soon become standard. It's a feature that gives you more options. For example, suppose you reach the end of your camera's memory, but suddenly find yourself with a shot you can't possibly pass up. By selectively deleting an earlier image of less importance, or one that can be reshot later, you can clear enough memory to capture a one-time opportunity, like a hawk perched on a tree limb during your walk through the local park.

LCD Screens, Video, And Sound

Some cameras—such as the Fuji DS-220 and the Olympus 200L—include an LCD screen that allows the photographer to instantly review pictures. Some cameras can even double as a video camera and record a limited amount of sound. The Ricoh RDC-1, for example, is capable of recording 10 seconds of sound and can even be used as a video camera for a few minutes.

Make sure, though, that a camera advertising an LCD screen has an actual picture-viewing LCD screen. There are two types of LCD screens—the kind for reviewing photos and one that simply displays camera settings, such as images remaining, flash setting, and choice of low, medium, or high resolution.

Bundled Software

Some digital cameras are sold with image processing software, while others aren't. Find out what software is included and determine if it is all you will need. The package is most likely also sold separately, and the manufacturer and product can be investigated on the Web. In general, most of the packages that accompany the low-end cameras aren't enough. The simpler packages usually target the casual user—if you're planning high-end work, you should consider upgrading to more hefty image-editing programs, like Photoshop or LivePicture.

Zoom

Some cameras at the lower end of the price range have zoom lenses. High-end digital cameras work with traditional photo equipment, so it's easy to attach a zoom or other lens. But if you want this capability at the low end, you can buy it built in. Kodak's DC50 is a good example of a low-end camera that includes a zoom feature. Other cameras, like Epson's PhotoPC, can work with optional accessory attachments that provide zoom capability, but these aren't as flexible. A zoom feature, of course, adds cost to a camera. Also, most of the zoom lenses we've seen on point-and-shoot digital cameras were really built to work at shorter distances, and didn't really provide telephoto capabilities. On the DC50, for instance, the zoom feature is really better for positioning close-up objects at just the right size rather than for capturing distant images.

TV Viewing

Do you want to be able to view your images on your television? Some companies—Casio, in particular—offer this as an option. With this feature, you just plug in a special cable that outputs a standard NTSC video signal. Then, simply view the pictures directly on the TV. In the future, we expect some cameras to add a range of transitions for even greater impact.

Connections

Make sure the camera you're buying has the proper connection kit for your computer. Most cameras include proper cabling for both PC and Mac, but not always. Also, look for newer connection technologies like infrared transfer systems, which allow users to transfer imagery from the camera to the computer without cabling. Some of Sony's new line will sport this feature.

Tripods

Most, but not all, digital cameras can be mounted on a standard tripod. One interesting project requiring a tripod involves shooting several side-by-side images and "stitching" them together on your computer to form a panoramic image. Without a tripod, your picture would be uneven and unconvincing. Only the very low-end models are not tripod-ready. Some tripods are specially designed for compiling stitching sessions. These tripods are covered in more detail later in this chapter.

Camera Settings

With some cameras, you can't adjust the settings unless it is attached to a computer. Such cameras can usually take low-or high-resolution photos, but to change from one setting to the other, you must connect the camera to your computer and then run the software that changes the setting. These cameras have obvious limitations.

Portability

Do you need a portable camera? Some of the high-end studio cameras are not portable—and needn't be. Portability doesn't refer to just the size of the camera. Storage space, battery life, and the ability of a camera to work without being attached to a computer all affect a camera's portability.

BUYING THE RIGHT COMPUTER FOR DIGITAL PHOTOGRAPHY

Cutting and pasting high-resolution, 24-bit graphics takes some horsepower and memory. If you have decided to purchase a digital camera, be sure your computer is powerful enough to handle heavy graphics processing and storage. Otherwise, you'll need to make an additional financial commitment to upgrade your computer system.

First, consider the photo-processing software you wish to use—Photoshop, LivePicture, or PhotoDeluxe, for instance—and find out its systems requirements. In other words, the software you choose will also determine your hardware needs. Storing a lot of photos can fill up a 600 MB hard drive quickly. If you plan to store a large number of images, consider purchasing a backup/archiving device, such as the iomega Zip drive. We'll run through all the computer equipment involved and explain what types of issues you should consider.

CPU

Processing high-resolution digital images takes power. If you're already doing heavy Web or desktop publishing, you probably have a computer with adequate capabilities. However, if you're buying a digital camera for use on a lower-end machine like a 33 MHz 486, you'll find it difficult and time consuming to use some of the more advanced image processing options. We recommend at least a 100 MHz Pentium or Power Mac computer. The more sophisticated the image processing you plan to do, the faster the Pentium or Power Mac you should have.

Memory

Memory capacity is probably more crucial than any other hardware requirement. To handle memory-hogging graphics, you will probably need at least 8 MB of RAM, although 16 MB is probably a more realistic minimum. If you're going to do a lot of work with Photoshop or with high-resolution pictures, you should consider upgrading to 32 MB or 64 MB of memory. This level of memory capacity is especially useful when working with multiple images.

Graphics Card And Monitor

The graphics cards used in most computers today are capable of 1024×768 resolution with 24-bit color which is essential for digital photographs because looking at a digital picture in 256 colors isn't acceptable. If you have an older graphics card, you should consider upgrading your video card to at least this standard. If you're going to be viewing lots of photos or are contemplating working with some really high-end imagery, you might want to consider a high-end card with at least 4 MB of VRAM (video RAM), and support for higher resolutions (some reasonably priced cards achieve up to 1280×1024). The more powerful your video card, the faster your system will be able to redraw photos as you move them about the screen. As a final note, make sure your monitor can support the resolution of your card if you do decide to upgrade.

Modem Connection

If you want to email your photos, you obviously need a modem. A 28.8 Kbps modem or faster is recommended due to the time necessary to send photos—even when they are compressed. Newer modems are available that support speeds of 33.6 Kbps and even 56 Kbps. These modems are especially fast at moving many graphics rapidly across the Internet.

Printer

Outputting digital images is such a complex topic that we decided to devote an entire chapter to outputting options, Chapter 10. For now, though, we'll just briefly mention some basic printer options. The basic color printers are either a standard ink-jet printer or a higher-end color laser printer. Beyond these two options are a couple of derivatives, such as newer ink-jets specifically tailored for photo printing by home users and some higher-end thermal dye printers that create laser-like quality color prints with a glossy finish. Most users will opt for the basic ink jets, which cost around $300. The output quality is actually quite good. For more special printing needs, it's simple enough to take your digital images to a service center for higher-quality output. These service centers are discussed in Chapter 6.

ACCESSORIES

As is true with any technology, digital photography involves numerous optional accessories you can purchase to add functionality or quality to your camera—especially at the low end.

Some Overall Accessory Resources

Before we delve into the specifics of various accessories, we should explain that there are two catalogs you should take a look at. DC-Pro is a catalog company devoted to selling accessory lenses, filters, carrying cases, and other equipment for digital cameras. Digital Distributors also handles lots of accessories for cameras (like Casio's QV series). Calumet is the leading catalog for general photography equipment. Many of the items mentioned hereafter can be found for sale by these three companies.

DC-Pro
9 Sammis St.
St. James, NY 11780
Phone: 516-434-8800
Fax: 516-434-9238

Digital Distributors
150 20th St.
Brooklyn, NY 11232
Phone: 718-832-3456
Fax: 718-832-3764

Calumet Professional Imaging
520 West Erie St.
Chicago, IL 60610
Phone: 312-440-4920

Tripods

Two basic types of tripods are available for digital cameras. The first type is simply a standard tripod that you would use with a 35 mm camera. The leading tripod supplier is Bogen Tripods. The second type of tripod is designed specifically to help you take panoramic VR photos. These tripods help you position and turn the camera perfectly to take the right series of pictures for use in QuickTime VR or Surround Video Development (see Chapter 12). One of the leading manufacturers, Kaidan, offers two unique tripods. The first, shown in Figure 2.3, allows the camera to take a 360° photo of a scene, and the second, shown in Figure 2.4, is an object VR stand that allows the camera to revolve around a specific object to create a 3D VR scene of that object. Both of these attachments will be explored more in Chapter 12.

Bogen Tripods
Bogen Photo Corp.
565 East Crescent Ave.
P.O. Box 506
Ramsey, NJ 07446
Phone: 201-818-9500
Fax: 201-818-9177
Web address: http://www.manfrotto.it/bogen/

Figure 2.3
Kaidan's M-1000, a new motorized object rig, to be available in 1997.

Kaidan

703 East Pennsylvania Blvd.

Feasterville Business Campus

Feasterville, PA 19053

Phone: 215 364-1778

Fax: 215-322-4186

Web address: http://www.kaidan.com

Kaidan makes a line of motorized tripods for using digital cameras to make QuickTime VR and SurroundVideo scenes.

Figure 2.4
Kaidan's QuickTime VR panoramic rig attaches to your tripod.

Lights

Depending on the quality of photos you expect, you might want to have better control over your lighting. Tota-Light, made by Lowel, is an excellent light for the casual photographer. It's designed to be portable and sells for about $110.

Tota-Light
Lowel-Light Mfg., Inc.
140 58th St.
Brooklyn, NY 11220
Phone: 718-921-0600
Fax: 718-921-0303

Reflectors

Sometimes you'll want to reflect light back on to a subject to illuminate a larger portion or add illumination to the entire subject. This is especially useful in outdoor lighting situations. For these situations, photographers use reflectors. In many cases, all you really need is a piece of white foam board, which you can find at any art supply store or good office supply store. If you want to go a step further, you can buy professional, collapsible reflectors. Calumet and other large photo supply catalogs sell Flexfill reflectors, which are widely used. The cost for these reflectors varies based on their size and whether you want to add an arm to it. But overall, the price range is about $50 to $75.

Lenses And Filters

Many digital cameras accept a range of filters and lenses. The low-end cameras don't offer much lens variety, but you can find varying focal lengths. Using the appropriate focal length will help clarify your pictures, so consider before buying: Will I take more close-ups or long-distance photos? Some low-end cameras are built to accommodate snap-on lens attachments and filters, as seen in Figure 2.5 and Figure 2.6. The mid-range and high-end cameras do offer different lenses and also support attachments.

Some cameras, like the Epson PhotoPC, accepts attachments that work with any 37 mm video camcorder. For other point-and-shoot cameras,

Figure 2.5
DC-Pro makes a variety of lens filters for low-end digital cameras that you can use for close-up and lighting adjustments.

you need to get special lens attachments from the manufacturer or from a third-party supplier like DC-Pro or Digital Distributors. In Chapter 5, we'll cover a range of lens filter suggestions. They tend to fall into three categories:

- Light Filters and Covers: These types of attachments help you adjust the light entering the lens. You can use red, green, or blue to separate one of the spectrums, or you could use a color-warming filter to enhance skin tones. Finally, some owners of cameras with exposed lenses might want to consider a cover.

- Close-up Lenses: When working close up, point-and-shoot cameras sometimes have problems adjusting their focus correctly to handle a small focal point. Close-up lenses help you reduce the focal length so that you can work quite close to your subject.

- Conversion Lenses: These lenses actually change the perspective of your subject. Whether it be for telephoto or wide angle, for example, conversion lenses give you many more options for fitting a desired image into your camera's viewfinder.

Figure 2.6
Depending on the model, DC-Pro and Kaidan make several different lenses, such as telephoto, for various low-end digital cameras.

Carrying Cases

The king of the carrying-case market for digital cameras is DC-Pro. Their catalog (mentioned earlier) offers carrying cases for almost all the major, uniquely styled cameras around. See Figure 2.7 for an example.

Batteries And Power Supplies

Digital cameras eat batteries for lunch, especially alkaline batteries. Make sure you've got a good supply of batteries around and consider using lithium batteries—they cost more (around $12 to $15 for 4), but last significantly longer. Some cameras have optional battery booster packs that work like portable power supplies; if you'll be away from power outlets for long periods of time, you should investigate these devices. Finally, make sure that when traveling to other countries, bring along a power supply that works with that country's current.

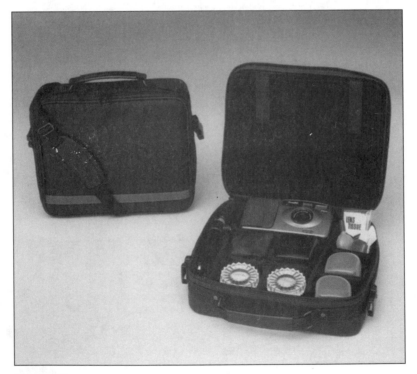

Figure 2.7
The only way to travel with your digital camera.

PCMCIA Cards And CompactFlash Cards

Many companies manufacture PCMC
IA cards and CompactFlash cards for digital cameras, but the companies
mentioned below stand out:

Microtech International
158 Commerce St.
East Haven, CT 06512
Phone: 203-468-6223
Fax: 203-468-9447
Web address: http://www.microtechint.com

Microtech International manufactures a line of cards and readers with a
specific focus on digital camera needs. For example, their Digital
FlashFilm PCMCIA cards are engineered for high speeds, which makes
the delay in saving the image much shorter than for a standard PCMCIA
card. A standard PCMCIA card will probably be cheaper, but you might
find the extra speed of the FlashFilm cards to be worth the extra money.
One note: There is no quality difference with FlashFilm branded cards—
just speed improvement.

Microtech makes cards up to 80 MB in size, which helps you store a lot of
pictures on lower-end cameras and is enough memory to store pictures on
higher-end cameras.

Some of the high-end cameras use PCMCIA hard drive cards, which
Microtech also makes under the DPA drive brand name. If you are interested in Microtech's products, here's a quick rundown of their product line.

Digital PhotoAlbum

The Digital PhotoAlbum is a PCMCIA card reader that comes in several
versions. First is the basic Digital PhotoAlbum product, which reads Type
I (memory) cards and Type III (hard drive cards). This is available as an
internal or external product. A second popular version of Digital
PhotoAlbum is a portable PCMCIA card reader that only accepts Type I
cards. All the readers ship with Microtech's CardFORCE software, which
most importantly can read the specialized file formats that the different
cameras use. You can use other, lower-costing PCMCIA card readers, but

if you do, you must also use the specific reading package that comes with your camera. CardFORCE is a great option if you use a variety of cameras and encounter different formats. A final note: These are SCSI drives that will need to plug into a SCSI card on a PC. While SCSI is faster than IDE, most PCs aren't equipped with it. You'll probably have to buy a SCSI card separately. All Macintoshes already have a built-in SCSI port.

DPA Drives

Some higher end cameras that generate large photos use, as their removable storage option, Type III PCMCIA cards that are actually miniature hard drives. Microtech manufactures a line of these, called DPA drives. Sizes range from 170 MB and up.

Digital FlashFilm

As described earlier, this is a speed-enhanced PCMCIA card that speeds up the time required to save an image. Sizes range from 2 MB to 80 MB. Ballpark pricing, as of 1997, was around $50 a megabyte, so you pay a little more for the speed than a vanilla PCMCIA card.

SanDisk Corporation
140 Caspian Ct.
Sunnyvale, CA 94089
Phone: 408-542-0500
Fax: 408-542-0503
Web address: http://www.sandisk.com

SanDisk manufactures Type II and Type III PCMCIA cards for a wide range of uses. They are a supplier of PCMCIA cards to Sony for Sony's digital camera. SanDisk also makes card readers as well. More importantly, SanDisk is the creator of the CompactFlash card standard that will be debuting on many new cameras throughout 1997 and beyond.

Here are two other companies that are major producers of PCMCIA and CompactFlash cards and card readers:

Pretec Electronics Corp.
48521 Warm Spring Blvd., #314
Fremont, CA 94539
Phone: 510-440-0535
Fax: 510-440-0534

Adtron Corporation
3050 South Country Club Dr., Suite 24
Mesa, AZ 85210
Phone: 602-926-9324
Fax: 602-926-9359
Web address: http://www.adtron.com

DO I REALLY NEED ALL OF THIS?

At this point, your head is probably spinning with all of the equipment you can buy. And we haven't even touched on software, which involves an entirely different list of products. Of course, you don't need all of this hardware. Most accessories, like tripods, lens attachments, reflectors, and even a state-of-the-art PC aren't requirements; they're just enhancements. The sheer amount of stuff that's available shows how important and popular this technology has become. As long as you stick to your budget, buying optional equipment can help make your digital camera more fun and more rewarding.

The Basics Of Digital
Photography And
Digital Cameras

3

If you're a first-time user of digital cameras,

you'll appreciate this chapter, which

explains the basics of taking pictures with

digital cameras and some basic issues

about digital photography. If you've already

mastered taking photos, downloading them

into your computer, and manipulating and

editing them, you'll still find that this chap-

ter provides you with plenty of new tips

and some interesting discussions about the

overall possibilities of digital photography.

THE MANY USES OF A DIGITAL CAMERA

After you've purchased a digital camera (or even before), you'll want to find out what you can do with it. The following sections provide some excellent examples to help get you started.

Create Digital Photo Art

One of the more popular uses for a digital camera is simply to create cool pictures and photographic art. With digital-imaging programs (like Photoshop), a digital camera, and your imagination, any work of art is possible—you can create photographic collages, turn cool photos into line art, place people within weird surroundings,—whatever you can think of. With a little ingenuity and experience, anyone can create cool pictures. The great thing about digital photography is that you're not limited to the photos that you shoot with the camera. After inputting the photos into your computer, the creative process begins. Take a look at Figure 3.1 for an example of a piece of art created using a digital camera and editing software.

Create Insurance Records

Many people neglect to take photos of their personal property for insurance purposes. It can be a hassle to take 300 shots of different items—including multiple shots of an item at several different angles—or to properly document your house, car, and other insured items. The film and developing costs on this sort of work can be several hundred dollars. But with a little time and a digital camera, you can create insurance photos literally in a snap. In fact, on the CD-ROM with this book, we've included a simple database program to help you organize all your insurance photos. Figure 3.2 shows a screen shot of this application.

Create Morphing Animations

Several software products allow you to morph photos into other objects or even other photos. Morphing is a lot of fun. A company called MetaTools has created the ultimate in digital photographic morphing—a product called Kai's Power Goo. Kai's Power Goo, as shown in Figures 3.3 through

Figure 3.1
Creating works of digital art is probably one of the best reasons to own a digital camera.

3.5, lets you do all sorts of funky stuff with your pictures. Morphing animations can be saved in standard digital video formats for later playback or for placement on the Web. In addition, morphing, especially Goo's many variations of it, provides great entertainment anytime.

Create Web Graphics And GIF Animations

Creating graphics for the Web is a laborious process for many people (even good artists), but the process is made a little easier with a digital camera. In seconds, you can create cool banners, buttons, backgrounds, and more with your digital camera—and you can place great photos, too. Beyond some of the more obvious contributions a digital camera can make to Web production or a home page, you might want to consider some more advanced ideas. For instance, you might set up a special program to turn your digital

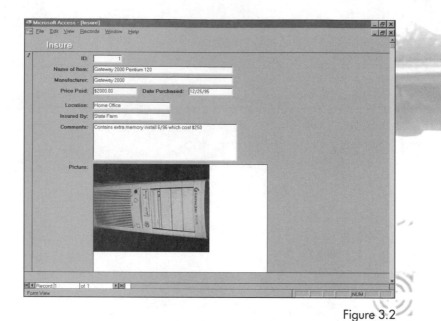

Figure 3.2
*If you were to shoot your insurance photos with a film-based camera,
you could spend a lot for film and developing alone.*

camera into the creator of a Web picture gallery. Program the camera to
download to your site a new picture every few seconds. When users log on,
they can see a nearly live picture of whatever is happening in the camera's
eye. Actual examples that have already appeared on the Web include

Figure 3.3
Start with a simple, innocent picture.

Figure 3.4
Add Goo.

continual images of freeways to show traffic levels in congested areas and beaches to show the current tides. One family even rigged a camera to a crib to provide photos of their newborn baby, updated on their Web site every 30 seconds.

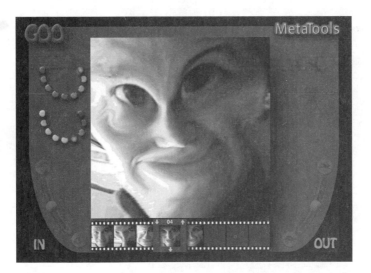

Figure 3.5
Create cool morphing pictures and animations!

Another approach is to create special animations with the help of your camera. Using a special format called GIF animation and a little creativity, you can create a very lively looking Web page. GIF animations are comprised of a single graphic file packed with many different images, all of which are cycled through by the Web browser after they're downloaded. This type of animation, commonly referred to as "page flipping," is very easy to produce with a digital camera. Figure 3.6 shows the images used in creating a fun, animated GIF.

Make Panoramic Stitched Photos

A friend of mine travels the world quite frequently, and displays panoramic shots on his refrigerator. He creates them with his simple point-and-shoot camera by taking a dozen side-by-side photos and simply taping them together to make a big, panoramic picture. You can easily do the same (and with much more accurate and impressive results) with your digital camera. This book includes a specific step-by-step project that demonstrates how to paste together multiple photos into a collage-like panorama. Figure 3.7 shows a simple stitched photo.

Figure 3.6

Animated GIFs can easily be created with a camera, and when done placed on a Web page.

Figure 3.7
A photo created by "stitching" together several consecutive photos.

Create Virtual Reality Tours

You can extend the concept of stitched panoramic photos by using formats called QuickTime VR and Surround Video. These advanced formats actually take a large panorama (even one that is 360 degrees) and turn it into a live, moving interactive scene. This approach requires some very precise photographic skills and some special equipment to help take the right photos, but the finished product is nothing short of spectacular. When a special VR (which stands for Virtual Reality) developing program is run and the author precisely stitches together the photos, the VR runtime software can play back the scene and can also correct any perspective problems, on the fly. Using the keyboard or mouse, you can move left and right through the scene as if you were standing inside it. Both Surround Video and QuickTime VR support their files when they're placed on the Web. You can even turn sections of the photo scene into links to other content as well.

Create Walking Tours

With a digital camera, you can have a lot of fun creating virtual walking tours. It's sort of like a digital slide show. Take a camera with you on a walk through your town or neighborhood, and take a series of shots every 100 feet or so. Create branching tours by first traveling in one direction from one spot, then returning and traveling in another direction. You might also record local sounds with a tape recorder (some digital cameras can record sounds as well). Compile all of this material on your computer and then create a multimedia file using a product like Macromedia's Director or Strata's MediaForge, or just use basic HTML to create a visual tour. This project is great for showing people a house for sale, or can even help illustrate what a local area has to offer to visitors. You can get really creative and transform the photos into sort of a choose-your-own-adventure game concept. Figures 3.8 through 3.10 show a few shots of a walkthrough made for the Web.

Figure 3.8

Shoot a collection of photos in a walking sequence.

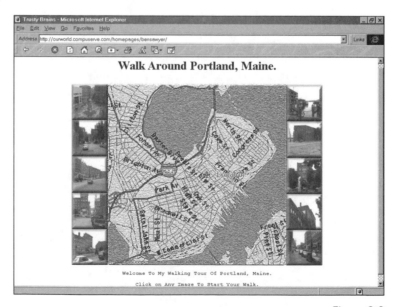

Figure 3.9

Organize the photos into a map and add descriptive captions.

Figure 3.10
Add the map to a Web site and offer virtual walkthroughs.

Create Photo Business Cards

If you've ever seen a business card from a Kodak employee, you already know the impact of including a photo on a business card. All of Kodak's business cards have a portrait photo of the person who handed you the card. You don't necessarily have to put a picture of yourself on the card, but you could include a photo that shows your product or service, or that depicts your business concept. You certainly could do this with any camera, but with a digital camera you can do the entire process yourself. This book will show you how. Figure 3.11 shows a photo business card.

Figure 3.11
Want an unforgettable business card? Add a photo.

Generate Computer Clip Art And Fonts For Web And Desktop Publishing

Just about everybody who owns a computer knows what a font is. And if you've ever bothered to look at any of the sample clip art that came with your typical presentation, graphics, or word processing program, you were probably disappointed with the selection. With a digital camera, you have a great opportunity to spice up both the text of your documents and your clip-art collection.

Take your camera with you on an outing some weekend and snap as many pictures of different letters and fonts as you can find. Concentrate on diverse typefaces, like traffic signs, text on manhole covers, graffiti, and business storefronts. Collect as many different variations of the alphabet as possible. Then, from these pictures, create a series of clip-art letters. You can later use these for drop cap situations like the one shown in Figure 3.12, or you can combine different letters into cryptograms that can be great for Web banners. In Chapter 9, we include a step-by-step project to perform this technique. Chapter 9 also describes some great tips for creating your own funky font collection.

Figure 3.12

The ability to create your own funky fonts is just one way that a digital camera can enhance your desktop publishing efforts.

You might also consider creating your own digital stock photo archive. As you travel with your camera, look for imagery that you might use for your Web pages or for desktop publishing purposes. Many times, these are simple pictures of common objects—like signs, doors, furniture, interesting people, textures, buildings, cars, and animals. But such common images can be used in interesting ways to portray concepts and links on a Web page. Stock photography is something that a digital camera excels at creating because the cost of producing each photo is so low. And by adding a simple archiving peripheral to your computer system, like iomega's Zip or Jaz drives, you can create a large stock photography archive without taking up precious hard disk space.

Generate Textures And Objects For 3D Graphics Programs

The film *Jurassic Park* proved to the general public that 3D modeling and animation has become a major technology. Computer graphics no longer look like they were done on a computer. In fact, the computer-generated 3D graphics industry is considered to provide one of the fastest growing and most promising career opportunities in the U.S. In California alone, 3D graphics jobs are being created at a clip fast enough to help alleviate the unemployment created by the downsizing of the aerospace industry there. Colleges and art schools are packed with students learning 3D graphics and modeling.

Your digital camera can actually be a key component for creating 3D graphics and animation. Ask any 3D artist what his or her most prevalent need is and he or she will probably tell you it's for textures and surface maps. After an artist creates a 3D model, he or she needs to apply textures and other surface maps to give a lifelike skin to that model. There's probably no easier way to create a horde of textures and cool surface maps than with a digital camera. Figures 3.13 and 3.14 show some sample textures taken with a digital camera.

You can also create 3D models directly from your photographs. A product called PhotoModeler helps you assemble a wire frame 3D model from digital photos. Another approach: Take 2D pictures of such objects as doors or

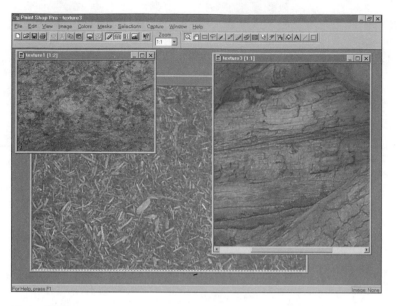

Figure 3.13
With a digital camera you can capture an array of textures.

fronts of TVs and turn them into 3D objects simply by adding depth to them. In this book, we'll cover some of the crossroads between digital cameras and 3D graphics.

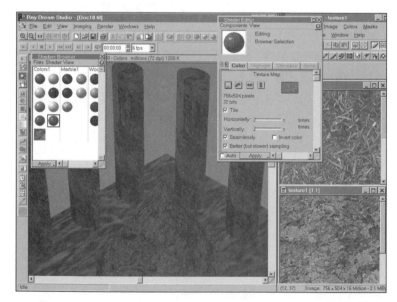

Figure 3.14
Capture full 2D objects as textures, too.

Email Photos To Friends And Family

Email can become photomail with the aid of a digital camera. More and more people are forming long-distance relationships or are living far apart from friends and family. A digital camera adds something special to email for people who rarely get to see each other. Take photos of yourself, products, and other business focal points. Or you can take photos of family events and other important events and instantly transfer them around the world. Many consumer experts believe the number one use of a digital camera will be to send images to friends and family via email. In this book, we'll cover that concept and take it a step further: We'll show you how to create even cooler digital postcards, that combine a series of photos, sounds, and text into a compact format that can easily be attached to an email message.

WHAT MAKES A PHOTO GOOD?

This is an excellent question. Most people know a good photo when they see one. Expert photographers, especially, can spot a fantastic piece of photography with their trained eye. However, the authors of this book have adopted the premise that a digital photo is different from a traditional photo. So the better question is: What makes a photo a good *digital* photo? Read on for a few important rules....

Rule 1: Good Digital Photos Begin With Good Raw Images

When you take a picture with a digital camera, you're most likely going to improve it later by using photo-imaging software. However, many digital photographers make the mistake of treating that software like a crutch rather than a tool. "I can take a lousy photo now because I can fix it later." This is a weak approach to digital photography. Consider this: If somebody hands you a lump of clay and tells you to create a work of art, you'll have a lot of sculpting to do—and there's no guarantee that the finished result will be any good. But if somebody hands you an excellent wet clay sculpture that just needs a little touching up, you'll have an easy time of it.

Digital cameras take unique pictures and, depending on the make and feature set of your camera, there is a lot you can do to take the best raw image possible. The best enhanced photos come from the best raw photos. This rule will be repeated throughout the book—live those words.

Rule 2: Maximize The Resolution Of Your Images

When using a digital camera, you are dealing with photos that will have a very finite resolution—even at the high end, and especially at the low end. At the low- to mid-range of the digital camera spectrum, the resolution of photos is from 350×300 to 800×600 dpi. That is not a very high-resolution range when compared to what you can achieve with traditional cameras. But when you compare these resolutions to common resolutions available with graphics on a PC, they aren't bad. In fact, most Web graphics are less than 640×480 dpi. By that yardstick, the resolution available with a digital camera is quite good. However, regardless of a digital camera's feature set, the resolution you can achieve will be finite.

This fact suggests the importance of adjusting your shots to compensate for limited resolution. Depending on what you're shooting, traditional photography instructs you to frame a shot perfectly. In other words, if you're taking a photo of a person, you should balance the body by including part of its surroundings in the frame. However, with digital photography, you'll often take pictures of a scene, only to cut away excess surroundings during editing. This means we should buck conventional photography wisdom and fill the entire frame as much as possible with only the image we plan to use. So, if you're taking a digital photo of a street sign, try to fill the viewfinder with *just* the street sign. This is what is meant by maximizing the resolution. In Chapter 5, this topic will be explored in more depth.

Rule 3: Think In Terms Of The Desired End Result

Rule 2 is actually derived from Rule 3. With traditional photography, the idea is to capture perfectly a single image with the camera's eye. However, in digital photography, you'll often be creating composite works from a variety of sources. Or you may be shooting to create clip art or with some other purpose in mind—simply because there are so many different ways you can use digital photos. Therefore, it's important to think precisely about what sorts of shots you need to create the final imagery you have in mind. A good photographer sees the actual picture at the time the picture is taken; however, a good digital photographer often has to create a conceptual image of the final photo, and then imagine how the current shot will fit into the final result. We'll explore this concept more in later chapters.

Rule 4: Take Digital Photos With A Purpose In Mind

With a digital camera, it's very easy to take photos for no real reason. Aside from the time required and the price of batteries, there is very little cost associated with taking pictures with a digital camera. Because it's easy to get into the habit of taking really bad or worthless pictures, you need to keep your guard up when you use a digital camera. You have to consciously avoid filling your hard drive with lots of garbage. Part of taking a good photo of any type is to take it with a purpose in mind—this is even more true in regards to digital cameras.

Rule 5: Keep In Mind The Fundamental Rules Of Photography—Even If You Don't Follow Them

Again, the authors of this book believe that the rules of traditional photography don't always apply to digital photography. However, many people who buy a digital camera don't have any fundamental picture-taking skills. The best way to build good digital photography skills is to develop an understanding of the fundamentals of good picture taking in general—and then learn what adjustments you'll need to make to create good digital photos. In other words, you need to learn the rules before you can know when to break them. Once you've learned basic photography rules, making the adjustments mentioned in this section (and elsewhere in this book) is easy. The next chapter covers many general rules about taking good pictures.

A Typical Digital Photography Session

Throughout this book, you'll find different projects that include detailed steps for you to follow. As a preview, let's run through the simplest of projects—a typical digital photography session.

Step 1   *Gather your equipment and decide on a purposeful subject*

Before you begin a digital photography session, determine your purpose. Before taking your camera on the road with you, or setting it up at work or at home, take a few minutes to think about the types of photos you need to suit your purpose. Also, consider any special equipment you'll need. As you'll see in other parts of this book, there are many accessories—including special lens filters, tripods, and even extra batteries—that you'll want to consider. Digital cameras eat batteries for lunch; few things match the frustration of being in the middle of a gorgeous series of mountain-top shots only to have the batteries go dead.

Step 2   *Think about the camera settings and then shoot*

As you'll learn, most digital cameras tolerate nothing but perfect lighting conditions. Look for the best lighting possible before snapping a picture. Also, many cameras have settings for such things as light sensitivity, flash, focus, and more. On most point-and-shoot cameras, if the camera goes into sleep mode, any custom settings will revert back to their original defaults. Unless you need to rush, always check the camera settings to make sure they're still the way you want them. Then, shoot your photos.

Step 3   *Connect the camera to a computer*

Often, the most frustrating part about using a digital camera occurs the first time you have to connect it to your personal computer. Many of the low-end cameras have poor manuals and configuration software, so connecting the camera successfully for the first time can be a trial-and-error process. The camera itself tends to be the biggest problem. Most models connect to a serial port, which can create a conflict with another device that's already using that port. Another problem occurs when a cable is plugged in improperly. Once you've worked through the connection process for the first time, though (and don't be afraid to call technical support), subsequent connections will simply involve plugging in the cable between the camera and the computer.

Step Download the pictures and save the best ones

4

After you've plugged the cable in, turn on your computer and run the software to download the pictures. There are several ways to do this, depending on the software that came with your camera. Not all cameras use the same software package, or driver software approach, so it's difficult to be specific here. In general, most downloaded software displays a series of thumbnail graphics that represent the images stored in the camera. You then choose the set you want to download from the camera. After opening the set of images with the camera, you can either make modifications and save it to a file or simply save the images "as is," and make modifications later. Many downloading packages allow you to modify the photos in a variety of ways, but not all of these packages provide the same number of modification options. So it might make more sense to simply download the images to disk and then make any modifications later.

Often, It's best to save a raw file, downloaded "as is." You never know when you might want to rework from the original images. By downloading and saving raw images before you make any changes, you maintain a set of the originals.

Step Modify the imagery

5

Examine your images. For each image, examine it visually and perhaps take some notes, as a critic might do. Is the image too big, too dark, too light, too blurry? After you've determined the photo's deficiencies, systematically work with an image processing package to improve the final imagery—one problem at a time. Every photo won't require this much effort, of course. However, almost every photo will require some effects to make it the best it can be. Experiment and work until you get the image just right—then save it.

First, become experienced with your image processing package. Also, consider doing things gradually. For instance, don't apply effects that require a setting to be made in broad sweeps or with abrupt differences; use small increments (or decrements) to gently reach the best setting.

Step Apply the imagery

6

Remember to *do* stuff with your pictures. This isn't as trite as it might seem. Digital photography, unlike film photography, lets you change images and provides you with new ways to use imagery. The most you can do with film photographs is to put them in a frame, in an album, on a slide, or in a shoebox. Digital photographs can be morphed, stitched, shaded, lightened, collaged, and a lot more. Make sure you take advantage of these possibilities. That *is* why you bought a digital camera, isn't it?

DIGITAL PHOTOGRAPHY ISSUES

Even though digital cameras provide great possibilities, there are several disputes regarding them. Before going any further and considering all the great things you can do with your digital camera, you should take some time to consider some of the issues that are being debated by photography experts and computer users alike.

Will Digital Cameras Replace Film Cameras?

Someday, it may be possible to replace film cameras with digital cameras. That day is a long way off, however. From both a cost and technical standpoint, there are reasons why some people should *not* use a digital camera. If you just want to snap photos of family members and family events to keep as momentos, you don't need a digital camera. Until digital cameras become much cheaper and as easy to use as film-based cameras, film will remain a better alternative for many people.

Toys Or Tools?

At the low-end range of digital cameras, many professionals are questioning whether these are worthwhile. Are these toys or tools? Can a $400 camera with a resolution of 640×480 dpi be taken seriously? Should a major Web developer use these? The answers lie in the level of quality you need or find acceptable. Low-end digital cameras can work both as fun "toys" and as serious tools. The role they take is dependent on the user's expectation, not on the product.

Raw Vs. Retouched

Is a good digital photographer one who can snap perfect images or one who can take "so-so" images and transform them into works of beauty? Perhaps a picture has been perfectly image-processed so that lots of poor photography work has been shredded away. On the other hand, isn't the ability to manipulate and edit digital photos the most important reasons for using a digital camera? The answer can go either way. Most people tend to side with the "garbage in, garbage out" philosophy. However, there is a favorable case to be made that no picture is complete until it is complete. Whatever state an image is in at the beginning isn't nearly as important as the final image.

Ethics, Anyone?

In 1995, *Time* magazine got into a lot of trouble by publishing a digitally altered cover photograph without telling its readership the image had been altered. In 1996, Virginia Senator John Warner's campaign was embarrassed when his media consultant created an ad that showed his opponent shaking hands with an unpopular former governor. However, the photo had been doctored to create the image. Both of these instances illustrate the most important issue facing digital photography: For all the fun and promise digital cameras and digital imaging offer us, they can also help us create very misleading images. Even in cases in which the intent might be to have fun and to be creative, the result can still be wrong. For instance, taking a person's picture on the street, then publishing it on the Web, seems fairly harmless, but it could be considered an invasion of privacy depending on what the image shows and where it's published.

Digital cameras are extremely powerful tools, and when you combine them with other powerful computer tools, like email, the Web, and desktop publishing, they truly shine. Just make sure that, as you take, modify, and present digital photos to friends, family, and the world, you have permission to do so, that you identify photos as altered when it isn't obvious, and overall you do so with a proper purpose in mind.

Most Of All, Have Fun

Digital cameras are lots of fun, something that people can tend to forget when they get wrapped up in trying to create the "perfect" image. Tens of millions of people use computers, but many people view them simply as work tools; they aren't viewed as being cool or fun. However, show people a digital camera, demonstrate Kai's Power Goo, or include a photo in an email to a friend, and the reaction is almost always one of delight. Try taking a friend's picture with a digital camera and then display the photo on the screen 10 seconds later. Your friend is almost certain to be impressed.

For more than 100 years since photography was invented, photographs have seemed like magic. Arthur C. Clarke, the great science fiction writer, once said that amazing technology is indistinguishable from pure magic. As wondrous as film photographs can seem, digital photography can seem even more amazing, and as Arthur C. Clarke would say, that's magic. Magic for the next 100 years.

Top Tips For Taking

Good Pictures

4

Taking pictures is easy; taking *good* pictures

isn't. And owning a digital camera doesn't

automatically make you a good photogra-

pher; in fact, it poses some special challenges.

This chapter is devoted to some fundamen-

tals of taking good pictures. Most of these

ideas are fairly easy to remember and are

basic photography rules; the like can often

be found in photography guides and

text books.

Why is this chapter important? Remember, a digital photo or piece of digital photo art—even after hours of cutting, pasting, and image processing—will always be better if the original photo is shot in the best light, at the best resolution, with the best framing, and with the right focus.

Experiment With Every Aspect Of Your Camera

Consider how important it is to be thoroughly familiar with your digital camera's capabilities. Even at the low end, there are quite a few features to learn. Test your camera under various conditions to find out how it reacts to light, different colors, and other conditions. (See Chapter 5 for a step-by-step discussion of this process.) If you know these detailed aspects of your camera, you'll take better pictures.

 Some of your camera's best features might only be accessible via the software that shipped with your camera. For example, two weeks after we started shooting with an Epson PhotoPC, we discovered that the accompanying software enabled us to see an almost instant preview on our screen of the camera's eye. This made it much easier to line up head shots because we could preview the actual result on the screen.

Focus On The Subject

Many amateur photographers lack what is commonly called a "photographer's eye," and a common pitfall is to take photos that don't zero in on the subject. Every time you take a picture, work to focus on the subject. Zoom in or get as close as you can to the part of the picture that you most want to have in the picture. This is very critical for digital cameras due to their limited resolution.

Get in the habit of asking yourself every time you take a picture, "What is the one subject of this photograph?" Also, try this experiment: After you've taken a picture in which you have successfully focused on the subject, take the same picture again, but this time pull back from the subject. Examine the differences. The mental image you'll form from this experiment should help you intuitively determine when an image is in focus.

If you can afford it, consider buying an array of lens and filter attachments for your camera. The added features you'll have will improve your creativity and increase the types of photos you'll be able to take.

GET THE EXPOSURE CORRECT

Exposure is important to taking good pictures, especially digital ones. Not all cameras offer exposure settings, but some, like Kodak's DC50, do. Digital cameras love light. The best pictures we took with the DC50 were shot with the exposure on the lightest setting. Do some experimenting. In different types of weather and under various lighting conditions, take pictures with different exposure ratings and evaluate the results. Although image processing software can improve exposure mistakes, this problem is better corrected by getting the exposure right in the first place.

REDUCE BACKGROUND DISTRACTIONS

Sometimes a photographer will focus so intently on the primary subject that he or she ignores what is in the background. It's a common mistake to take photos with too much happening behind the primary subject. This is especially a problem with digital pictures, because a cluttered background makes it difficult for the software to properly adjust the foreground imagery, or it even may cut out the foreground object. It also makes for a lousy shot.

When shooting moveable objects that you plan to use as clip art or in photo collages, consider photographing them using a white backdrop. You can buy a large piece of white foam board at any good art supply store.

WHEN TO USE A FLASH

Many digital cameras have built-in flashes. They usually have three settings: always flash, never flash, and flash when the camera determines extra light is needed. In many cases, flashes can ruin a perfectly good photo or create errors that can be difficult to clean up later.

Of the point-and-shoot cameras we tried, most automatically used the flash on cloudy days. We achieved better results by turning the flash off and then opening up the exposure to let in more light. The flash wasn't as controllable as the exposure—the light from the flash tended to bounce off nearby objects and create flares.

BE AWARE OF LIGHTING

Light, light, light—we can't stress its importance enough, especially with digital photography. The key is to be aware of where light is coming from—especially with sunlight. Why? Well, light reflects. Depending on where light is coming from, it could very well reflect off your subject. Where light hits a subject incorrectly, it can cause the a color to vary greatly in tone or wash out other colors nearby. All of these problems can make for some time-consuming clean-up chores when you're back at the computer.

Professional photographers work hard to get just the right lighting, while amateurs tend to just point and shoot. Finding the right lighting takes time. Be patient. You might also want to revisit Chapter 2 to consider the value of purchasing a Tota-Light, some foam board, or a FlexFill reflector. Your control of lighting will increase dramatically, and, as you learn how to master lighting, your digital photos will increase in quality.

TAKE MULTIPLE SHOTS, NOT SINGLE SHOTS

Digital cameras limit the number of pictures you can take during one session—unless you carry a laptop or use a camera with memory cards. Even so, don't use this limitation as an excuse to take only one photo of a good subject. Remember: You don't have to pay for film. Many times, you'll find that taking several photos of a subject will yield only one good picture—and many times it'll be the one you didn't expect much from!

EXPERIMENT WITH ANGLES

It's common for beginning photographers to want to shoot everything "dead on." However, the frontal approach doesn't always yield the best shot. For example, sometimes light can reflect badly. It's always a good idea to look for different angles of subjects. You can combine this approach with the previous tip. That is, take multiple shots of the same subject but at different angles.

Try taking pictures of recognizable objects or places in ways you don't naturally view them. This technique often results in a unique and interesting photo. Even though the subject is familiar, the novelty comes from the viewpoint.

TIPS FOR TAKING THE BEST PICTURES WHEN TRAVELING

Consider purchasing a laptop: Digital cameras are limited in the number of images that can be stored at one time—often fewer than 50. If you're traveling, especially on an extended vacation, you'll probably want many more photos than that. But it also can be difficult to find a computer that you can use to download your images. And even if you do find a computer, you'll need dozens of diskettes to store your images—if they even fit on diskettes.

If your camera accepts PCMCIA cards, you're covered. Simply buy enough cards to store the images you plan to capture during your trip. If your camera doesn't have a PCMCIA slot, your best bet is to buy a laptop that you can bring with you to download images periodically. The laptop doesn't even have to be very powerful. As long as it accepts the cable to your camera and has plenty of free hard disk space, it will do fine. Later, when you get home, you can transfer the images to your PC for editing and processing.

Plan your travel and "schedule" photos: When traveling and taking pictures, consider sketching out a plan on a piece of paper.

Think about the shots you want to take on your trip and schedule your photo sessions to improve the likelihood of getting these shots. Include time to download the images to a computer (if one is available) and consider buying extra storage cards and batteries.

Tell a story with your pictures: The best travel pictures will tell a story of your trip. Look for photos that recall interesting events, people you met, and places you visited in a way that will allow you to later organize them into a photo journal. Look for pictures that are off the beaten path, but can still remind you—and tell the story to others—of where you've been.

Keep a journal: As you travel, keep a written journal of the photos you've taken and the places you've been. Each photo can represent a unique story; that story is best remembered right after the photo was taken.

Have your camera ready at the airport: Try to download your pictures before going through airport security. Digital cameras may appear suspicious to airport security because there is no film cartridge to verify that it is a camera. You might be told to run the camera through the x-ray machine. Remember to first remove your storage cards if they have images!

Be careful about electricity: Remember that not all foreign countries use the same electrical standard. Don't plug your digital camera into an outlet in a foreign country before checking that the electrical voltage is compatible with the camera.

Backup is critical: When traveling, you don't have time to return to places in order to recapture lost photos. Whenever possible, download pictures and back up those images. Few things are as aggravating as discovering that your laptop died and you have no backups of your 500 pictures.

ADD ACTION TO A SUBJECT

Most of the objects you shoot won't be moving, but that doesn't mean you can't create movement in your pictures. Try to position yourself and your subject in such a way as to create displacement—either by finding an actionable angle (such as an off-center shot) or by being above or below your subject. Think of displacement as a way to suggest a direction that an object could move. The viewer will look at the photo and cognitively fill the picture with movement.

SHOOT PEOPLE NATURALLY

One of the cardinal sins of photography is to take pictures of people who are posing for the shot. The best shots of people are taken when they are behaving naturally, as though the camera isn't there. Think about it. Why are sports photos often so powerful? Because these scenes capture people in natural movement. The occasional posed shot is fine, but you'll be amazed at how many interesting photos you can get when you rely more on natural movement.

SHOOT SOME UNIQUE IMAGES

You can use the tips presented in this chapter to start experimenting. Of course, if this is all new to you, you might want to pick up some photography guides to help you get the basics down. The most important step to taking good pictures is knowing the ins and outs of your digital camera—you want your images to look unique, but first you want them to be of the best quality. With the technological information presented in other chapters, combined with some of the basic photography tips presented here, you're ready to go out and view the world from a new angle.

A Guide To Shooting With

Digital Cameras

5

When it comes to shooting with a digital camera, you'll learn something new every time you take a picture and work with imagery. We've talked to many people who have digital cameras in order to find out what most people want to learn, and we've included two sidebars that detail some issues and innovative uses of digital cameras for photographic work. Basically, this chapter is meant to help you really dig in and take great photos!

WHY DIGITAL?

The first thing to ask yourself when it comes to digital photography: Why should you be using a digital camera in the first place? High-end models are great, but quite expensive. Low-end cameras allow you to take decent photos, but until recently, you couldn't even get a 1024×768 picture unless you bought a camera at $1,000 or more. With a regular film-based camera and a good scanner, you can easily create a nice digital image, and there are photography and print shops that can put your film imagery directly on a Photo CD for you. So why are so many people buying and using digital cameras?

- Convenience. Nothing in the entire image-capture universe beats a good digital camera for convenience. A video frame grabber requires a computer and a video camera. Still video cameras are good, but a strong digital camera can produce a higher-resolution still. With a digital camera, you simply shoot your images and download them into your computer. All of the lower-end cameras we've used took less than 10 minutes to download a few shots once we knew the process.

- Price. On the higher end, some comparisons have shown that there's an even cost between conventional photography and digital photography. In time, as digital cameras come down in price (see more on this later), they'll probably be cheaper than a good 35 mm camera. On the lower end, especially for people who are capturing imagery for the memories and for sharing (more so than for resolution), a digital camera can be an exceptional money saver. Film developing costs money and takes time. By contrast, a digital camera's upkeep is mostly just the price of replacement batteries. If you have an AC adapter and do mostly indoor shooting, even that cost can disappear. If you enjoy taking pictures of family outings, special events, and vacations, a good digital camera is more than worth its price because the number of photos you can take—for free—is virtually unlimited. In fact, with a digital camera, you'll probably discover that you take more pictures than you ever would with a conventional film camera.

- Animation. It's easy to create nice stop-motion animations with your digital camera and a tripod. Try doing this with conventional photography! (You'll experience hours of frustration simply trying to align photos correctly on the scanner.) And digital video doesn't work well with stop-motion animation. Also, you would have to deal with the lower resolution question plus the extra expense of a frame grabber.

WHAT MEDIUM?

The next big question to ask: What medium will I be outputting my digital images on? Essentially, there are three main digital photography media:

- Screen output

- Printed output

- Professional-quality output

Screen output is the most popular use for digital cameras because the resolution of most consumer, lower end cameras is perfect for screen-based imagery. Cameras like the Olympus 300L, which shoots at 1024×768, or the Kodak DC50, which shoots at 756×504—and many of the cameras like the Epson PhotoPC, Apple Quicktake, and Casio, all of which shoot at 640×480—are perfect for Web pages and multimedia applications because 90 percent of computer screens don't display any higher than 1024×768 resolution.

Printed imagery is the second most popular medium for digital photo output, but here's where the resolution issue begins to make a difference. With a good photo-quality ink-jet printer, you can actually get some nice results from a 640×480 image. But don't fool yourself into thinking that image will be better than what you would get with a regular, film-based camera. It won't. Once you've accepted that fact, though, and especially if you strive to shoot crisp, clean imagery, you'll find that digital cameras—even low-end ones—can be very useful for generating printed photos for personal or low-end professional use (such as a company newsletter).

When it comes to professional imagery, digital camera photography requires one thing above all else: money. You can't produce four-color separated, high-quality work without a top-of-the-line digital camera, like Kodak's DCS4XX series, a Leaf, or a Dicomed Big Shot, to name a few. These cameras produce imagery that, while still not the same quality as that produced by top-of-the-line film cameras, provides acceptable quality for many professional uses. An increasing number of photographers—from AP reporters to graphic arts photographers—are converting to digital format. Of those whom we spoke to, we received a consistent message: Few of them considered digital photography to be a replacement for film, but it does provide an alternative approach (although some photographers do work exclusively with digital cameras). In addition, many explained that they had developed strong digital photography skills in the areas of lighting, the post-production process, and color correction. If you're thinking about striving for professional-level output with digital photography, read the session "What's A Professional Photographer To Do?" that appears at the end of this chapter.

Developing A Digital Camera Philosophy

Many of the following ideas are geared toward the use of low-end digital cameras, but many are applicable to all levels of digital photography. I'd like to thank Rich Berry, who builds his own digital cameras specifically for taking astronomy shots (see the color section), for donating several of these ideas. Rich offers a wealth of expertise about CCD technology and also experiments on his own with an Epson PhotoPC.

Accentuate The Advantages, Ignore The Deficiencies

If you can't see it in the viewfinder, don't shoot it. Don't fight low resolution; instead, exploit it as much as you can. Fill the viewfinder with your subject as much as possible. Don't aim at distant objects—your photo will not have the detail you want. Also, take multiple shots of the same image and stitch them together. When you are shooting a long-distance photo, shoot for an interesting shape (such as an interesting horizon) or for the colors (a sunset, for instance). You'll be much happier if you strive for photographic results instead of detail.

In addition, think about the unique pictures you can take with a digital camera, such as stop-motion animations or playing with Goo (see Chapter 9) during a children's party. These types of activities can help you realize the unique traits of a digital camera.

Be Artistic

The major reason for buying and using a digital camera is that you can modify your images in almost unlimited ways. True, sometimes a nice picture is just that—a nice picture. However, you can do a lot when you begin with a nice photo and then manipulate it to create more artistic results. Look at some of the examples in the color sections. Using filters in programs like Photoshop, Fractal Design Painter, and LivePicture, you can create some exciting and artistic images. For instance, by cutting out different images and creating a collage from them, you can tell an entire story in one picture.

Remember: Some people are better artists than others, but everyone is an artist to some degree. Art is not just about producing a fantastic final image—it includes the fun, creativity, and exploration you experience when you work with photos. Playing with digital photos is at times a therapeutic process—we've seen normally rambunctious children sit at the computer for hours playing with color corrections on photos. The point is: Don't settle for point-and-shoot. Remember to manipulate and change.

SHOOTING IDEAS AND TIPS

The following ideas are intended to help give you a set of principles that you can use to become a better digital photographer. Although some of these concepts hold true for film-based photography as well as digital photography, most of these ideas are unique to digital photography. You'll find out why as you read on.

Capture The Best Raw Imagery First

The key to a good digital image is to create the best raw image possible. Even the best color correction or image-processing software is not going to do for your image or artwork what a great, clean, original photo will.

There are two basic points here: Find a good digital subject, and then take your time so that you get the shot and conditions just right.

Good digital photography subjects can be of any object, event, person, or group of people. In any event, images that have lots of saturated colors, good and even lighting, and clear contrast work best. Landscapes work well, but try to find ones that have good, clear contrasts—such as a body of water against a shoreline or a nice skyline against the afternoon sky. Emphasize the colors in landscapes by taking pictures of sunsets and sunrises (see the color section), when you can get some awesome colors and cool cloud lines.

You'll need patience for good digital camera pictures. Spend time finding good lighting and positioning. Use a tripod when you can to control the positioning of the camera. If you travel without a laptop or don't have a way to download your images, conserve your shots and wait for something that grabs you as unbelievably interesting. Don't shoot moving images, because most digital cameras don't have the shutter speed to keep up.

Working Backwards Toward A Plan

When you shoot with a digital camera, it pays to think backwards through what it is you want to create. For example, if you want to create an awesome but simple shot, then your attention to every aspect of the picture you're about to take is of paramount importance. However, if you plan to create some interesting photo-collage or are going to cut out a subject, then that probably means trying to fill the viewfinder with only the desired part of an image—regardless of how bad the photo itself might look.

Or, if you're trying to create an interesting line-art image, you'll need to maximize your photo to extract the lined imagery from it. This might mean using a backdrop and different lighting. The fact is that digital cameras open up so many interesting possibilities with image processing that you'll want to learn how to create the optimal synergy between the photo you're about to take and the final result that you want to achieve.

Lighting Greatly Affects Digital Photos

To say that lighting affects a digital camera's images is a major understatement. Conventional film is affected by light as well, but the tonal and color qualities of film-based photography make it less reliant on lighting conditions. Digital camera is thoroughly rooted in light. Too much lighting in areas of your digital camera photo will create banding effects, which is difficult to correct without putting in lots of work. Darkness, on the other hand, can kill a digital photo. Even just slightly too little light will demonstrably reduce the clarity of your picture. Even with a flash (which brings its own set of problems), dusk-level lighting can be too poor for a digital camera. Higher end cameras with more sensitive CCD chips are significantly less hampered in this area.

Another factor in digital photography: Certain types of light affect different cameras differently, which is true of conventional photography as well. It's key, though, that some lighting situations will affect digital cameras differently than conventional cameras—so you'll have to experiment. Fluorescent lighting can create brightness and color problems; for best results, use commercial video lights. In one session, though, we were using a camera at a friend's studio and he suggested Tungsten lamps. Later, when we looked at the photos on the computer, we were amazed at the orange tint that was severely added when the camera was positioned so that the light cut across (rather than behind) the lens.

For low-end cameras, natural daylight is really best. Using desk lamps and camera lamps is fine, but expect to manipulate them for direct-on light. Why? Because the light and low resolution of your camera will fight your efforts to get a nice, continuous tone. To maximize the use of daylight in taking photos of objects without having to go outdoors, we set up a table with a backdrop made of white posterboard and positioned it next to a large window that receives an immense amount of light most of the day. Solid or partly clouded sunlight is by far the best source of light for a digital camera.

Watch Those Reflections

The combination of light and shiny objects leads to reflections. This can be a curse or a blessing, depending on what it is you're looking for in your photo. One morning, I awoke to an amazing sunrise and rushed out with my camera to take photos of boats heading out for lobstering against the Portland waterfront. It was around 5:50 a.m. and the sunrise was at its peak. I stood on a wharf taking photos of various sailing vessels (one of which appears in the color section after we processed it to create a silhouetted effect). When I downloaded the image, I discovered that the sun's reflection on the water was a little bit stronger than I thought. While a conventional photo might have better handled the reflection and provided more color variation and detail, my digital photo washed that area of the photo into one large continuous flat color area—which had its good and bad points. But either way, the result wasn't what I had expected.

Although reflections can be desirable, digital cameras can capture reflections *too* well. Be especially aware that a reflection can flatten the color. What do we mean by "flat color?" There is very little gradation between the brightest spot of your image and the rest of the picture (where light isn't being reflected back).

Also, when you shoot outdoors, direct or reflected sunlight can cause recorded images to take on a greenish tinge. You can minimize this effect by opening up the camera's aperture, if that's possible with your camera.

Buy Lenses For Variety

Some cameras, like Epson's PhotoPC and the Kodak DC40, easily accept a variety of different lens attachments. You'll find that these attachments can be well worth the investment, especially using the close-up lens for shooting small objects or subtle textures. Most low-end cameras are of the point-and-shoot variety, so the addition of such lenses can greatly increase the flexibility and usability of your photos. For more information, check out the accessory companies mentioned in Chapter 2.

Shoot In Black And White

In doing the research work for this book, we had a nice conversation with Rich Berry (see the sidebar in this chapter, "Digital Camera Photography For Astronomers"), who passed along the idea of "shooting in black and white for a few days." We tried it, and discovered that it's a great way to learn and a useful idea for image generation.

When you download a batch of photos next time from your digital camera, convert them all to grayscale photos. When you look at a digital image as a black-and-white photo, you can learn a lot about the way tone works with your digital camera. You also can see more about how the contrast in a digital photo works.

Taking this idea further, you might also convert some images to two-color (black and white only—no gray) images as well.

Shoot On Wet And Cloudy Days

After a rainstorm can be a great time to use your digital camera. Colors come out crisper after a soaking rain cleans surfaces and makes then bright and shiny. Although you have to be cognizant of reflections, wet and shiny surfaces generally look great in digital images.

Shoot Anything—Exercise Reckless Abandon

With digital photography, what comes in isn't exactly what comes out. This is a strength. To some, the best feature of digital camera photography is that you can shoot without much regard to cost. So here's a good exercise that costs you nothing: Look for pictures you might not normally take— cracks in the road, a dry leaf on the ground, or a building you like—even if these things look ordinary. After all, you're not wasting film; you're not wasting anything, really. Shooting unconventional images can yield some interesting imagery—especially when you use odd images as a starting block to create some form of digital art. For example, a shot of that leaf might yield an incredible texture to be applied to something else. Or, perhaps by cutting out a piece of it, you might discover that it makes an interesting piece of clip art for desktop or Web publishing.

Always Download Everything

Thumbnail images do not always tell the truth about how well a photo has turned out. In addition, a picture that looks lousy in a thumbnail may have a portion that is interesting or useful. Before you discard photos, download images from your camera and view them on your hard disk.

Turn Off The Flash

When you take photos on cloudy days or at dusk or sunrise (when you might have borderline lighting conditions), turn off the flash. Infrared light from a flash can affect the image because it's processed by the CCD chip. For example, red areas might be recorded as greenish. When you photograph indoors, create enough light for a no-flash photo, or see if the results without the flash are good enough. To see the difference, take the same photo with the flash on and then with the flash off. More often than not, the flash doesn't help your photo. Learn to work without it.

Don't Trust The LCD Display

If your camera has an LCD display, you'll discover that it's a great feature—but don't trust it. Most LCD displays are backlit and thus pictures can look much better on them than they will once they're displayed on your computer—especially in the areas of color saturation and brightness. LCDs are best used for positioning issues—checking for that thumb or index feature—and for simple viewing. However, be forewarned: The LCD screen is not an exact representation of the final shot. When we took some pictures with a camera that had an LCD screen, we later discovered that the lighting was all wrong, and half the shots were worthless.

Take Extra Batteries

With digital cameras, battery life might as well be called half life. These cameras eat batteries for lunch. We use lithium-ion batteries for extended power and order them through the mail. When you're preparing for extended trips away from the AC adapter, pack extra batteries. Some companies offer battery booster packs that can load in a bunch of batteries and output them to the AC adapter port. If you use such a device, make sure that the power output perfectly matches your camera's needs.

Think About Cutouts

When you're shooting with a digital camera, think about looking for cool objects to cut out. Remember: Your raw image is not necessarily the final result.

Maximize Image Resolution Area

When it comes to shooting objects and other items, image resolution is key. Digital cameras have a finite resolution. A good digital photographer knows how to get the most out of the limitations of resolution. The are a couple of points that follow that are important to keep in mind when you consider image resolution.

Composition Or Object?

If you're shooting a typical photo composition, all of the basic photography rules apply. However, if you're specifically shooting a single object, then all the rules for framing a shot, adding action, and so forth go out the window. Instead, you want to fill the frame as much as possible with only the object—even if it creates a horrible shot—solely to devote as much resolution as possible to the object.

Turn The Camera At Various Angles: The Hypotenuse Trick

One way to maximize your camera's resolution (especially when shooting objects) is to experiment by taking photos at weird angles. Try lining up the camera vertically along the hypotenuse of the object. Do this when the image is too tall to fit in the viewfinder either horizontally or vertically. This is a great way to take pictures of buildings and other tall objects, like statues and trees. Later, you can rotate the picture and then cut out the excess. See Figures 5.1-5.3.

Use A White Board For Objects

As we've mentioned elsewhere, build a solid backdrop for shooting objects. White foamboard works best. You can create a really strong backdrop with three pieces of foamboard. Using tape and push pins, put together two of the boards into a simple L-shaped backdrop. Then, use the third piece as a base (if you'll be shooting down on an object). If you'll be shooting a very light object, you might find some other colored board to create contrast for the object.

Figure 5.1
Some objects are too tall for your camera lens, even if you hold it vertically.

Watch Those Settings!

Most digital cameras offer a variety of settings. One of the most common setting is for image resolution—many cameras offer both high and low settings. However, as we've discovered with numerous cameras, most have a default setting that will re-activate if you don't use the camera for a while (even for as little as 20 minutes). Thus, you need to keep in mind the resolution setting you want every time you take a photo. I learned this the hard way one night when I replaced the batteries in the middle of a concert. I was taking pictures of the band for a Web site that the band wanted to create. I had to discard some excellent shots because they were too low in resolution—even worse, some shots were taken at great angles and showed some truly funny moments.

Figure 5.2

Holding your camera diagonally will sometimes give you the extra height you need.

Always Shoot At High Resolution

Many cameras offer you the opportunity to switch between different resolutions "on the fly," thus allowing you to conserve memory (and take more shots). With the exception of functional shots, such as ones you might take to provide insurance records, always shoot at the highest resolution. You can always reduce the resolution of an image later, but you can never increase its resolution.

Shooting For Textures

When shooting for textures, take several pictures at different distances, and be aware of the focal length. We found that, when creating 3D pictures, we

Figure 5.3
You can cut out the angles later in an image-editing program.

were able to achieve good results by shooting the same images at different distances and then overlapping them to create a 3D effect. Consider the examples shown in Figure 5.4.

Figure 5.4
Shooting a surface at different distances can produce a different pattern.

DIGITAL CAMERA PHOTOGRAPHY FOR ASTRONOMERS

As we were researching this book, we discovered an amazing group of amateur astronomers who have built their own digital cameras specifically for taking photographs of the cosmos. (See the color section for some examples.) While that's a little more advanced than what you will probably be shooting, it's still based on the same CCD digital technology and processing capabilities.

Essentially, all of this work started when avid astronomers and CCD experts Viekko Kanto, John Munger, and Richard Berry wrote a book titled *The CCD Camera Cookbook*, which explains how to build a very sensitive home-made camera that can take pictures through amateur telescopes.

The cameras are built with off-the-shelf technical parts. (Some people, accessible on the Web, will even put one together for you.) The typical cost is as little as $250, but you can increase the quality by spending more for better CCD chips, which will enhance the image resolution.

The cameras run software programs that specially process the pictures and control the camera. Many people who use the Cookbook camera run the software on notebook or laptop computers so that they can cart the camera to a remote field, away from city lights.

Cookbook cameras can produce exceedingly amazing imagery (as the Web sites listed at the end of this page and the photos in our color gallery section will attest). However, imagery is usually captured not in split-seconds, but over the course of 30 seconds to several minutes while the CCD array intensely scans the scene.

To build a camera, first order *The CCD Camera Cookbook* ($29.95) from:

Willmann-Bell, Inc.

P.O. Box 35025
Richmond, VA 23235

Phone: 804-320-7016
Fax: 804-272-5920
Web address: www.willbell.com/cookbook.htm

The book contains a diskette with software that tests the camera's circuits and runs the camera.

The cameras built with the Cookbook take pictures from 192×65 to 378×242 pixels. The Cookbook camera produces images in the NASA-sponsored FITS file format that is widely used in both amateur and professional astronomy today, so you can process images from the Cookbook camera with virtually every software package made for astronomy.

Camera developer Richard Berry offers two software programs that offer linear and nonlinear brightness scaling, unsharp masking, cropping, resampling, script-based batch processing, and allow you to save processed images in standard TIFF format. The programs, called AIP245 and CB245, were developed specifically for the Cookbook camera. Ordering information for these programs can be found on Richard Berry's Web site located at twvi.com/~rberry/.

According to Berry, over 1,000 cameras have been built and many more are being constructed. You can also order an upgrade from Willmann-Bell, Inc. for $19.95, which includes new software and tips on improving the camera's output.

Here are a couple of highly recommended Web pages set up by Cookbook digital camera enthusiasts. Many also contain cool technical discussions of CCD chips and CCD photography, which can be interesting to any digital camera owner:

Richard Berry's Photo Gallery

wvi.com/~rberry/images.htm

Al Kelly's CCD Astrophotography Page

http://www.ghgcorp.com/akelly/

Al Kelly's page has some awesome photos that have to be seen to be believed. You'll also find a great set of links for exploring the works of other Cookbook camera users.

Shooting 2D And Copy Work

If you plan to capture text from a page for artistic purposes, you'll want to think about getting a simple copy stand from a photo catalog. Low-end cameras don't work well for this purpose, though. Before you decide whether you would benefit from a copy stand, experiment first by focusing a camera on a page of text or some other simple, flat piece of copy work. You might also invest in a close-up lens, if that is available for your camera. For the most part, though, this task is best left to a scanner, which excels at this type of work.

Calibration May Be Required

If you're a high-end camera user, talk to your sales or manufacturing representative about camera calibration. CCD chips can actually get "lazy" and require some calibration to perform continually at peak performance. This is especially true of cameras that are used repeatedly under the same conditions, such as being used for a stop-motion animation process. For low-end camera owners, there is no need to worry about this problem.

THE NEVERHOOD: DIGITAL CAMERAS FOR CUTTING-EDGE, STOP-MOTION ANIMATED GAMES

In November of 1996, Dreamworks Games released The Neverhood, an innovative computer game that features stop motion Claymation characters and sets. We had the opportunity to talk with the creator of The Neverhood, Doug TenNapel, for an article on the product for *Game Developer Magazine*. While talking to TenNapel about the process, Ben was amazed to learn that they had used a digital camera for the entire process.

Here are some details, which may interest you if you would like to experiment with your own Claymation or stop-motion animation work:

Neverhood developers used a fairly high-resolution camera, the Minolta RD-175, which features 1100×1400 pixel resolution. Frames were then crunched down to a common palette using Equilibrium's DeBabelizer super palette function. Using Autodesk Animator, all the individual frames were assembled and sound effects were added and synchronized. When those steps were complete, the .fli files created by Autodesk Animator were run through RAD Software's Smacker, which specializes in compressing .fli animations. The resulting animation ran at 15 frames per second, which is about 3 frames superior to conventional Saturday morning animation.

The sets and some characters were built with clay. The developers used Van Akin and Harpets clay, imported from England. Harpets clay was used to create the characters Wallace and Gromit, and Will Vinton used the Van Akin clay for the California Raisins commercials.

Most of the main sprites in the game are actually created in latex, which, when shot, actually looks like clay. These latex puppets are supported by a metal exoskeleton, which they use to set the poses during animation. Bolts on the skeleton are loosened so that a new pose can be created, and then the bolts are re-tightened. Small slits in the latex at every joint, which are invisible to the eye, give the puppeteers access to the skeleton. When the characters are positioned, they're actually bolted to the set for the shot. Characters that leave the floor are positioned on poles or with string, which is later edited out.

To avoid as many palette problems as possible, characters were kept simple, with little detail, and broad color choices were used. One of the biggest problems for this technique was with lighting. Two 30'×30' light racks were brought in to allow for the perfect capturing of imagery. (This level of lighting accuracy was necessary because the game was intended to be a major retail product.) Recalling the problem, TenNapel said, "We had to find a way to make consistent light; we had to redo all of the power in our building." A peer power source was brought in to keep the lights from fluctuating. Bulbs were changed often and the cameras were reserviced and recalibrated to make sure the CCD chips weren't getting oversensitive to certain lighting conditions.

In the end, Neverhood shipped to well received reviews and featured a style of animation never before seen in video games— and never before attempted with a digital camera. Judging by the success of The Neverhood project, one can expect many more stop-animation films to be done with digital cameras.

For more information on doing stop-motion animation with your camera, check out the following sites on the Web:

The Neverhood: www.neverhood.com

Autodesk Animator: www.autodesk.com

Game Developer Magazine: www.gdmag.com

DeBabelizer: www.equilibrium.com

Smacker: www.radgametools.com

WHAT'S A PROFESSIONAL PHOTOGRAPHER TO DO?

When it comes to digital photography and taking great digital pictures, professional photographers have the most questions and worries—because their jobs depend on their cameras. An immense amount of a photographer's picture-taking skills are built solely through extensive experience, but digital photography requires a new set of technical skills.

Let's cover some of the more distinct technical and specific topics that are required for digital photography at the professional level. This is meant more as an overview, since we assume you're just starting to investigate the process. The best advice we can give you is to scan the Web and other sources to find a few photographers who work with digital images and who discuss their experiences—especially the computer side of image processing.

Does It Save Money And Time?

Many high-end photographers are at first attracted to digital photography for the promise of cost and time savings; however, on the high end of the market, cost savings aren't apparent when you switch to digital. Why? Well, equipment costs are still very high—especially when you factor in the cost of a top-of-line Mac or PC loaded with extra RAM, a large archiving device (like a read-write CD-ROM), and color-correction and calibration equipment. When it comes to time, if you're not a technical expert, you're going to have a considerable learning process to work through, or you're going to have to hire someone who already has these skills. At the high end, the post-production skills required to really exploit products like LivePicture or Photoshop are considerable.

However, if you can get over the hurdles of technical setup and operation, and you expect enough work (new or otherwise) because you can serve clients' requests for digital work, over time you might easily justify the costs and time investment. For more about the potential costs of digital photography, check out *Desktop Publishers Journal*'s article on this subject. You can find this article on the Web at http://www.dtpjournal.com/dtpjournal/9611F1.shtml. It's highly recommended reading.

Color Calibration

When it comes to professional digital photography, color is a king-sized problem. Screens don't display color the same way print does, and lighting is different with CCD-based cameras. These and other obstacles need to be combated with color correction devices and software that can help calibrate your monitor so the screen colors of an image closely match the final, printed colors. Calibration also pertains to your clients' computers. If your clients will be looking at images on their machines for proofing, you might want to work with them to make sure they understand this issue (most will), and you may even work to arrange calibration of their machines as well. Many photographers also invest in cutting-edge dye sublimation printers for proof preparation.

Image Processing Software Skills Are A Must

Even though high-end cameras take excellent photos, there is still a need for image processing. Many clients will expect you to be a total provider, which involves taking the photos and performing the touch-up work to adjust color, improve sharpness, and remove dust and scratches. This means you need to invest in software like LivePicture and Photoshop, and you should take the time to learn them. These software programs have many powerful features to become familiar with. Consider investing in one or more books to take you through tutorials, which can be a great way to learn. Additionally, as you'll see from some of the software described in this book, there are a lot of interesting and useful packages that can be used to edit your photos. Professionals will want to focus on acquiring a range of software to open up as many digital darkroom capabilities as possible.

Work With Dealers And Manufacturers

At the high end of the digital camera market, you'll find a dedicated group of sales and marketing people—we talked with many of them and they were all extremely helpful. At companies like Kodak, AGFA, Dicomed, Leaf, and PhaseOne (the chief players in the high end of the market), you'll find a lot of help and knowledge about how digital cameras can be applied to the professional marketplace. Many might even visit you with their wares (if you're a bona fide prospect) to show you how the process works and how you can justify the costs. Later, when you buy your camera, you'll also want to consult with these professionals to find out how to get the most from their products. At the super-high end of this market, a lot of cutting edge, custom built technology is available, so the information and knowledge that a camera or other digital device manufacturer can offer are critical. You might also consider attending Viscom, a leading trade show for desktop graphic artists, where most of the high-end camera companies display and demonstrate their wares.

Digital Camera File Formats

6

In terms of computer display and storage, the biggest difference between text and graphics is size. For instance, the complete text of this book fits on one 3-1/2" diskette. The graphics—photos and screen shots—used in the book barely fit on a 100 MB iomega Zip drive.

Why are graphics so big? Start your word processor and then open a text document. Take a close look at the content of the screen. You'll notice that, even though the screen might be "filled" with text, the actual text only takes up a fraction of the screen. Interestingly enough, most of the screen is actually blank—that is, it contains only your word processor's background color (probably white).

Now open a graphics image (preferably a photograph) and display it full size on your computer screen. The first thing you'll notice is that the image doesn't have any "holes." In other words every pixel in the picture is being used to help display the image. If the image is in color, different-colored pixels have to be mixed carefully to produce the precise colors. All of this color information has to be stored, in addition to the image itself, in memory and on your hard disk. The bottom line is that a color photograph can easily take up more than 1 MB of memory or hard-disk storage. Some high-quality images can take up 20 MB or more.

The disk storage and memory-hogging nature of graphics have led to the development of dozens of different file-storage formats. Most of these formats were developed with the same basic goal in mind: to store the most graphics information in as little space as possible. Almost all of the file formats that we'll describe in this chapter achieve this goal (some better than others) by using *compression* schemes. As the name suggests, compression is a technique for reducing the original size of a file.

Understanding the details of file compression and graphics file formats is a pretty technical business. Fortunately, as a digital photographer, you don't really need to know these details; you'll do fine if you simply try to understand some basics about file formats and compression. But it is important to learn the basics. As we already mentioned, there are dozens of possible formats that are used to store graphics on a computer. But each format has different benefits and drawbacks, and each format uses a different compression scheme. When you choose a file format for storing your digital images, you'll need to decide which format is best for the intended purpose of your images.

THE FUNDAMENTALS OF FILE COMPRESSION

Although there are dozens of different techniques for compressing digital images, there are only two basic approaches:

- Run-length encoding

- Lossy compression

In the next few paragraphs, we'll tackle both approaches. The terms might sound a bit intimidating at first, but you'll be surprised to learn how simple these concepts really are.

Run-Length Encoding (Lossless Compression)

The actual compression of an image is handled by the digital-processing software that you use to download your images to your computer or the software you use to manipulate and edit the images. Most image-processing programs can store and read a variety of file formats, which means they understand the storage and compression scheme that each file format uses.

Run-length encoding (also called *lossless compression*) is really a fancy way of saying that identical color information only needs to be stored once. The software that compresses the image first determines which areas of the image are the same and which are different. Images that contain repeated data (such as a blue sky) can be compressed so that only the starting and ending points of the sky need to be recorded. (This is oversimplified, of course, since there are different shades of blue and the sky will probably be interrupted periodically by a tree, mountain, or other object. But for now, we'll keep things as simple as possible.)

Essentially, the software says, "Start the color blue at pixel 47 and repeat it until we reach pixel 2112." This concept is illustrated by Figure 6.1. The actual algorithm that handles this compression is more complex than this, of course. But you get the idea: Essentially, the software can "throw out" the portion of the image from pixel 48 to 2112, which significantly reduces the size of an image when it's stored on disk. However, run-length encoding doesn't reduce the size of an image in memory. Why? When the image is retrieved from disk, the software "fills in" the missing pixels with the appropriate color information. To reduce the size of an image in memory, we need to use a different approach.

Figure 6.1

In this image, the sky would be the easiest portion of the image to compress with a lossless compression scheme because several thousand pixels would be identical.

Lossy Compression

Lossy compression provides a way to reduce the size of an image in memory without significantly degrading the appearance of the image when you view it on screen. Lossy compression is based on the principle that the human eye more easily detects changes in light than changes in color. Imagine that you walk into a dark art museum. Even though dozens of beautiful and colorful paintings are hung on the walls, all you can detect are a few dark blobs. In this sense, the light is far more important to what you can see than the colors used in the paintings.

With lossy compression, then, some data is deliberately removed to achieve a better compression ratio. And the data is never put back in. Specifically, a lossy compression algorithm keeps gradual changes in color but deletes portions of an image that have abrupt changes in color. The human brain "fills in" the missing color with the closest nearby color. For example, imagine a tree against the backdrop of a blue sky. A lossy compression scheme would delete portions of color around the edges of the tree. When you look at the image on screen, your brain fills in the missing color definition with the color that it *does* see in the tree.

COMMON GRAPHICS FILE FORMATS

Now that we've explained a bit about file compression, we can continue with a discussion of the file formats themselves. We're not going to discuss every format under the sun; that would be a waste of your time. Instead, we'll focus on the file formats that are widely used for digital graphics and a few that are growing in popularity.

Before we begin, we'll reiterate why it's important to understand these file formats: The file formats that you elect to use to store and process your images will vary depending on the ways in which you want to use the images. Are you going to print the images on a high-resolution printer? Are the images primarily going to be used for display on your Web site? Is it important that your images take up as little hard-disk space as possible or is it more important to reduce the size of your images in memory? The answers to these and other questions will help you determine which file formats to use. Table 6.1 provides you with a quick overview of the different file formats we'll discuss in this chapter.

TIFF

TIFF, which stands for *Tagged Image File Format,* was originally created by Aldus Corporation for use in storing and editing high-resolution grayscale images created with scanners. Although TIFF has been around longer than most other popular graphics file formats, it has held up remarkably well—chiefly because the TIFF specification has been revised and improved several times.

The current version of TIFF supports high-resolution color and divides different portions of an image into *tiles,* or separate blocks of data. For each tile, the software stores a tag that provides information about the way

Format	Supports high-resolution display	Supports high-resolution printing	Compression format	Royalty free	Supported by Web browsers
TIFF	Yes	Yes	Lossless or None	Yes (v. 6.0)	No
GIF	No	No	Lossless	No	Yes
PNG	Yes	Yes	Lossless	Yes	Yes (Netscape and Explorer 3.0)
JPEG (JFIF)	Yes	No	Lossy	Yes	Yes
EPS	Yes	Yes	None	Yes	No
FlashPIX	Yes	Yes	Lossy	Yes	Yes (predicted)
PICT	Yes	Yes	Lossless	Yes	Only on Macs
BMP	No	No	None	Yes	No

Features and drawbacks of common graphics file formats.
Table 6.1

the tile should look. The advantage of tiles is that software packages that support the TIFF format only need to store the portion of an image that's currently being viewed on screen. Tiles that aren't being viewed can remain on hard disk and then loaded into memory as needed. This is an important feature if you're editing a very large, high-resolution image.

TIFF Tradeoffs

If you're using a low-end camera, storing images in TIFF format can be a waste of firepower, and might not even be an option. Simply put, there's no point in using a format designed for high-resolution images if your camera can only capture low-resolution images. However, if you own a mid-range or high-end camera, and if the resolution of your images is important, TIFF is an excellent storage format. One benefit of TIFF is that most image-processing packages support it and allow you to convert TIFF images into other formats, which can be especially important if you plan to use your images for multiple purposes.

For instance, suppose you want to take photographs of your newborn son. Later, you plan to take the photos to a service bureau for high-quality color output. For this purpose, TIFF makes an excellent storage format. You also want to place one or two of the photos on your personal Web page. Many Web browsers don't support TIFF. In addition, the initial resolution of your TIFF images might be so high that it significantly slows down the loading of your Web pages. For this purpose, it makes more sense to convert the images to JPEG, which supports a lower-resolution, lossy compression and display format. Most programs that can process TIFF images provide you with the option to store them either uncompressed (best for fast loading and storing of images) or in a run-length encoded compressed format.

GIF

GIF, which stands for *Graphics Interchange Format*, was originally developed in the mid-1980s by the CompuServe online service. At the time, modem speeds of 9600 and slower were common. GIF was intended chiefly to provide a way to compress graphics so that they could be transported more quickly via a modem. When the Web began to grow in popularity, GIF was adopted quickly by Internet users as *the* standard graphics file format.

GIF Tradeoffs

Although GIF is still a widely used format, especially on the Web, it has one important drawback. First, the GIF format only supports 8-bit graphics. On monitors that can display 16-bit and 24-bit color, GIF images seem overly limited, especially for large and high-resolution images. The LZW compression algorithm used with GIF images was originally designed to compress text, not graphics. However, for inline icons, clip art, and other low-resolution graphics displayed on the Web, GIF is still a good choice. In general, the higher the resolution of your original image, the more likely it is that you'll want to store it as a JPEG, rather than a GIF, format for use on a Web page. By the way, virtually all Web browsers support the GIF format.

The major advantage of GIF images stems from some additions that were included in its latest revision. The original official GIF specification was called GIF87a, named for the year in which it was released. The more current specification, released in 1989, is called, appropriately enough, GIF89a. The differences between GIF87a and GIF89a are small, but significant.

GIF89a adds support for *interlaced* graphics. If you've spent any time on the Web, you're probably already familiar with interlaced images. Under this approach, a Web browser displays only every eighth row of an image on its first pass through the image, then every fourth row, then every second row. Interlaced graphics help reduce the frustration that can occur while waiting for a graphics image to be transferred and displayed with your Web browser. A portion of the image is displayed quickly, then additional portions of the image are filled in until the complete image appears.

GIF89a also gives you the change to create simple animations, which are commonly called *animated GIFs*. Nothing is changed about the format of the graphics data except that a single GIF file contains an entire sequence of GIFs, which are then cycled through once the file is loaded. By changing the look of each frame slightly, you can create "page-flipped" animations rather easily. In Chapter 11, we'll show you how to create your own animated GIFs using a digital camera and some simple software.

PNG

PNG, which stands for *Portable Network Graphics*, is the direct successor to GIF. For many years, the GIF format could be used freely by software developers. However, in 1994 Unisys, which owns a patent on the LZW compression algorithm, stunned the online world by announcing they were going to begin enforcing the patent. This means that any developer who uses the GIF format has to pay a royalty fee to Unisys.

Software developers responded by collectively designing the PNG specification, which is similar in format to GIF, but does not use the LZW compression formula. In fact, the compression format that PNG *does* use is more powerful than LZW and supports 24-bit graphics to match the power of today's monitors and video cards. Like GIF, PNG offers an interlace derivative format—except instead of loading the graphic in successive waves of lines, it loads it in successive waves of pixels.

PNG Tradeoffs

Perhaps the most significant drawback of PNG is that it is *too* new. Some of the older Web browsers and digital processing software packages don't support PNG, simply because it didn't exist at the time. However, current versions of both Netscape and Internet Explorer, by far the most widely used browsers, do support PNG. Consequently, you can expect to see PNG used more frequently as a graphics file and compression format.

The most obvious advantage of PNG is that it is royalty free. Anybody can use the PNG format free of charge. PNG also supports the major improvements made in GIF89a, including interlaced and transparent images. However, PNG uses a run-length compression scheme. If your major consideration is to reduce the size of images stored in memory without degrading the appearance of an image, you're probably better off saving your images in JPEG's lossy format.

JPEG

Like PNG, JPEG was created by a consortium of software developers, so it isn't "owned" by any single company. This fact ensures that JPEG (which stands for *Joint Photographic Experts Group*) will remain a royalty-free file format. Unlike PNG, however, JPEG uses a lossy compression format, which makes it ideal for displaying images rapidly and at good resolutions. For this reason, JPEG is likely to emerge as the standard Web graphics format, rather than PNG—at least for a few years.

JPEG Tradeoffs

Some of the companies that defined the JPEG standard are also among the major developers of image processing software packages. Consequently, most desktop publishing programs and graphics software packages support the JPEG format. One advantage of JPEG is that it supports multiple compression levels. For instance, when you save a Photoshop image as a JPEG graphic, Photoshop gives you the option of saving it in Low, Medium, High, or Best resolution levels. As you might guess, the lower the resolution, the *lossier* the image will be—that is, more image data will be removed from the file.

The advantage of multiple resolutions is that you can experiment by saving an image at different resolutions until you reach an ideal file size/resolution ratio. If it's more important to you for your Web site visitors to have rapid access to your Web pages, then you might want to save your images as low- or medium-resolution JPEGs. If it's more important for your images to appear sharp, even if that means that your Web site visitors have to wait while images load, then you might want to save the images as either high or best-quality JPEGs.

There is one specific JPEG derivative, known as *Progressive JPEG*. When Progressive JPEG files are created, the data is arranged so that graphics display as they are loaded, initially displayed very blurry and then progressively sharper as the data is loaded.

The major disadvantage of JPEG is also its greatest advantage. That is, the lossy compression scheme limits JPEGs to a display format. If you want to print your images, especially if you want high-quality prints, TIFF is a more suitable format.

EPS

EPS, which stands for *Encapsulated PostScript*, was developed by Adobe as a way to embed a PostScript file within other files. It's easy to confuse EPS files with the PostScript language. PostScript was designed by Adobe as a way to print a file to any printer that supports the PostScript language. An EPS file is simply a PostScript file that includes some header information that makes it possible for other applications to embed it within documents. An EPS file also enforces some restrictions that do not apply to a standard

PostScript file. Chiefly, these are rules that ensure the EPS file can be inserted into a different file without corrupting the file. For instance, in Microsoft Word, you can embed an EPS file into one of your Word documents. One of the most popular uses for EPS files is to embed them into desktop publishing files, especially those created in PageMaker or Quark XPress.

EPS Tradeoffs

Because an EPS file is actually a collection of PostScript language code, it can be printed in a variety of ways on a PostScript printer. The software package that creates or edits an EPS file can define specific size, resolution, fonts, and other formatting and printing information. That information is embedded into the EPS file, then read and processed by the printer. Hundreds of printers support the PostScript language, including virtually all image setting systems used in the publishing business. As a result, EPS is the preferred file format for professional publishing and printing businesses.

EPS was intended to be used as a format for printing. The PostScript language code that is embedded in an EPS file provides for some great printing definitions, but it also bloats the size of the file. In addition, the cost and memory overhead required to build a PostScript engine into a software package is high. Consequently, most Web browsers do not support EPS files, nor do most shareware and freeware graphics viewers. For these reasons, EPS is not an option for displaying graphics on your Web site.

FlashPIX

FlashPIX is a new file format developed collaboratively by Eastman Kodak Company, Hewlett-Packard Company, LivePicture Inc., and Microsoft. As is true for PNG, the developers of the FlashPIX format are making it an open, royalty-free specification, so it can be used freely by all software developers. Because FlashPIX is supported by such industry giants as Kodak, HP, and Microsoft, you can be sure that it will be adopted as a graphics file format standard. For instance, Microsoft plans to build the format into their Internet Explorer Web browser. That means that Netscape will have to follow suit.

A FlashPIX file contains the complete image plus a hierarchy of several lower-resolution copies within the same file—making the FlashPIX file function like a small file when users want it and like a big file when users need it. FlashPIX uses a lossy compression format similar to JPEG to store and display multiple-resolution versions of an image. Applications can quickly access a low-resolution image for on-screen or online use, or employ a high-resolution image for higher-quality output. FlashPIX tools for software developers will promote the creation of FlashPIX-optimized applications that automatically select resolution levels, and make the substitutions transparent to the end user. Images at each resolution also are divided into rectangular tiles, which enable the application to minimize the amount of image data processed to access, display, or print a portion of the scene content.

FlashPIX Tradeoffs

A significant benefit of FlashPIX is its ability to store large, high-resolution images while simultaneously displaying low-resolution images that don't require much memory. This means, for example, that the same image can be printed at high resolution on a color printer and displayed at low resolution on a Web page. Users who have PCs or Macintosh systems with limited memory can open either a low-resolution version of the image or simply a portion of the high-resolution image.

About the only drawback to FlashPIX is that it is still a promise. Throughout 1997, you can expect to see and hear announcements about FlashPIX. If FlashPIX delivers on its promises, expect it to replace many other file formats for image processing, Web display, and high-quality printing.

Other File Formats

Two other file formats are worth mentioning, chiefly because you'll probably encounter them at some point. However, neither of these formats is very useful for digital image editing, display, and printing.

The first, BMP, is Windows' standard bitmap graphics format. Because any Windows application can save or open BMP files, you'll encounter these graphics scattered about on the Web. However, BMP images do not resize well. Also, the compression schemes that BMP supports are archaic. In general, avoid storing your images as BMP files.

The second format, PICT, is the standard graphics format for Macintosh computers. Most PC applications cannot read PICT files, although there are several utilities available for converting PICTs to more popular formats, especially JPEG. PICT graphics are powerful because the underlying Macintosh operating system directly supports this format. However, a PICT file on a PC is like a fish out of water. Unless you want to limit your images to a Macintosh viewing audience, it's best to avoid storing your images in PICT format.

ARCHIVING FORMATS

Archiving programs are also called compression programs. However, to avoid confusion with the internal compression schemes used by graphics file formats, we'll stick to the term "archiving programs." Archiving programs differ from compression programs chiefly in the way in which they are used. Compression routines operate at runtime. That is, a graphics image is compressed whenever you save it, and it's uncompressed whenever you open it.

Archiving programs, however, compress and uncompress files on demand only. Archiving programs also allow you to combine multiple files into a single compressed file, and you can combine text, graphics, and even program files into the same compressed file. Archiving your digital photos is useful for two reasons:

- Long-term storage: If you want to store images on your hard disk or a removable cartridge, and don't plan to view or edit the images for a while, you can group the images into a single Zipped or Stuffed file to reduce the amount of space they occupy. Archiving routines often can reduce the size of graphics files even though they are already compressed.

- Uploading to an Internet site: If you want to load your images into an FTP or other file archive on the Internet, you'll need to archive them first.

The two most popular archiving programs are PK Zip (and WinZip) and StuffIt. PK Zip and WinZip are used on PCs, while StuffIt is used on Macintosh systems. In Chapter 8, we'll explain more about WinZip and StuffIt, plus we'll provide some projects for working with WinZip.

PK Zip And WinZip

PK Zip and WinZip both archive files using the same format. That shouldn't surprise you, since both programs are created by the same author. However, PK Zip runs directly in DOS and is rapidly becoming obsolete. WinZip runs directly in Windows. Shareware and commercial versions of WinZip are available. Both versions are available from the WinZip Web site at **www.winzip.com**.

You can easily identify a Zipped file on the Internet, because it will have a ZIP file extension. To open a Zipped file, you must run PK Zip or WinZip after you have downloaded it. Cross-platform versions of PK Zip are also available for the Macintosh and for Unix. Figure 6.2 shows a Zipped file that contains six TIFF images and one Microsoft Word document. Notice that WinZip reduced the TIFF images by about 25 percent, while the Word document was reduced by about 70 percent. You'll get less space savings when you archive graphics than you will with text files, simply because the graphics usually are already partially compressed.

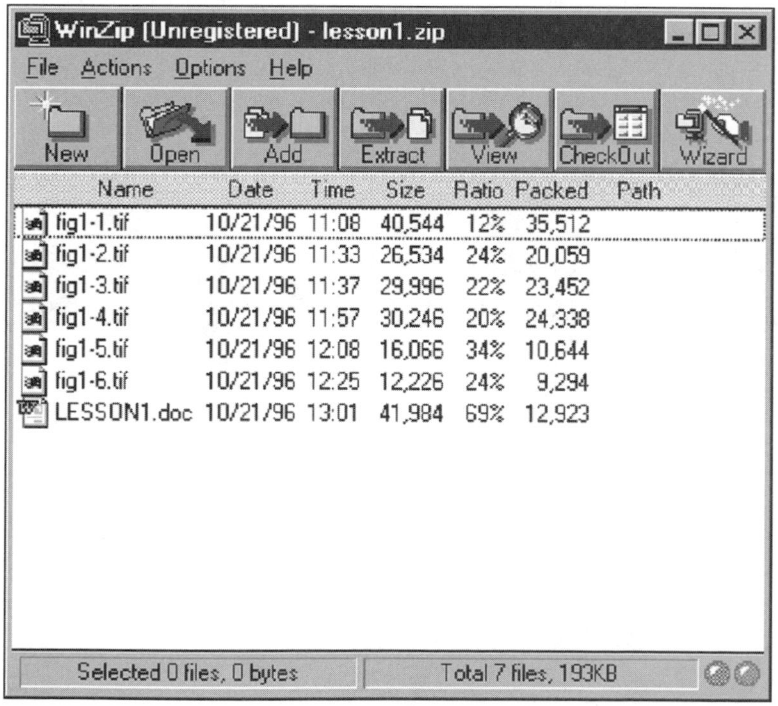

Figure 6.2

Seven files that have been archived into a single file using WinZip.

StuffIt

StuffIt is a product sold by Aladdin Systems and only runs on Macintosh computers. You can identify Stuffed files on the Internet by looking for either the SIT or SEA file extension. To unarchive a file that has the SIT extension, you can use a freeware package, called StuffIt Expander, which is available on the Web at **www.aladdinsys.com/index.html**. If you are running Windows on a PC, you can still unarchive SIT files by downloading an Aladdin program called Windows StuffIt Expander.

To create archived files on the Macintosh, you will need to purchase StuffIt 4.0 or StuffIt Deluxe. You can either create SIT (StuffIt) files or SEA (Self-Expanding Archive) files. A SEA file is slightly larger than a SIT file because it includes a small program that unarchives the file automatically, so users don't need StuffIt expander to open a SEA file—a Macintosh, though, is still required. If you choose to archive graphics on a Macintosh for distribution on the Internet, it's generally better to archive them as a SIT file. Not only is the file smaller than a SEA file, but Windows users who have downloaded Windows StuffIt Expander can also open and view your graphics files. If you archive the files into a SEA file, only Macintosh users will have access to your files. Figure 6.3 shows an archive that contains eight Stuffed files. StuffIt indicates that the space savings is 52 percent total for the eight files.

UUencoded Files

If you want to upload one or more graphics files to a Usenet newsgroup, you must encode them into an ASCII text format called UUencoded.

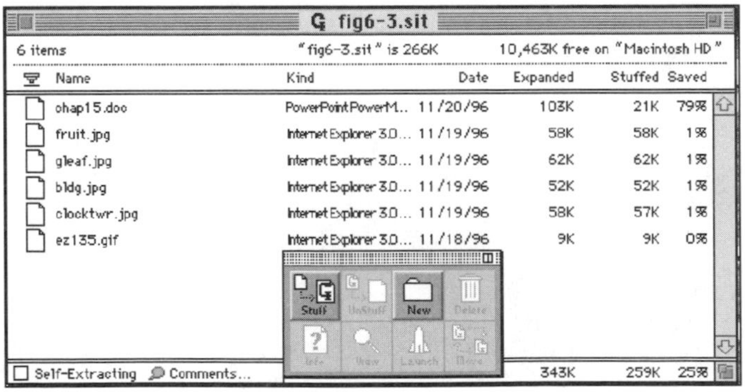

Figure 6.3
A folder that has been Stuffed using StuffIt Deluxe.

Almost all newsgroups only accept text files, and UUencoding provides a way to convert a graphics image into a plain text file. Several freeware and shareware programs are available for UUencoding files on both the PC and Macintosh platforms. Some Web sites you can visit to download UUencode and UUdecode programs are provided in Chapter 8. Also, if you use your Web browser to search for the string "UUencode," you'll probably uncover several other programs available for download.

Decoding UUencoded files used to be quite a headache, because UUencoding supports several different options that aren't always compatible with different UUdecode programs. However, this problem has all but disappeared, since both Netscape Navigator 3.0 and Internet Explorer 3.0 (and 2.1 for the Mac) automatically decode these files whenever you view them. So it's now easier than ever for Internet users to access and open UUencoded files.

READY, SET, PROCESS

In this chapter, we've given you an overview of common graphics file formats. Along the way, we've explained the basics of file compression and archiving. You'll no doubt encounter other, less-used formats. But the ones we've explained here are the ones you'll encounter and use most. Now that you know your options for saving your images, you're ready to process your images with confidence and display them on your Web site if you want.

Working With Raw Images

7

If you own a digital camera, you're probably interested in instant gratification—at least where your photos are concerned. After all, isn't one of the chief benefits of a digital camera the ability to almost instantly download and begin working with captured images? When you combine the speed and flexibility of digital cameras with any of the multitude of image editing packages that can be used to improve and transform your photos, you step into a whole new world of art and imaging possibilities. This chapter takes three basic ideas and merges them into perhaps the most important chapter in this book. The three crucial concepts are:

1. *Understand the most useful tips and techniques available for improving and working with raw imagery downloaded from your digital camera.* Actually, we probably could have filled this entire book with nothing but image-processing tips. But your library and local bookstore already have complete tomes dedicated to image processing tips—so we've ventured to offer you more. In this chapter, we'll present the most important image-processing tips—the ones that are most likely to make your photos look good.

2. *Understand what happens to a photo when you apply a specific image-processing technique.* In our view, it's not enough to say, "You use a sharpen tool to sharpen things." To manipulate your photos with precision, you need to know exactly what it is that a sharpen process does to the pixels in an image to create that sharpened look. By the end of this chapter, you'll know exactly what each image-processing technique really does to your photos. The better you understand how a specific image-processing tool works, the more your ability to effectively use the tool will increase.

3. *Understand all of the options that are available in the most widely used image-processing products.* The image-processing package that came with your camera (if any) isn't the be-all and end-all in digital photo image editing and processing. In fact, it's probably just the beginning. There are more than a dozen software products that will provide you with image-processing techniques that aren't available with the software that came with your camera. Do you *need* all of these commercial software products? When you total their purchase prices, you would have to shell out several thousand dollars to buy all of these products. In fact, the most popular half-dozen features can provide you with all of the tools that you really need. So, do you really need a half-dozen image-processing software packages? After we review these products in this chapter, you might find that a particular package offers you something you really want to be able to do. As you get more heavily involved in editing your images, you'll want to have more image-processing options. Over time, you might even build your software library to the point where you own most of the packages we describe in this chapter.

You might be wondering if some of the popular image-processing packages overlap in terms of the features they offer. In terms of basic features, they do. Most packages let you do basic photo-imaging techniques, such as sharpen, blur, mask, rotate, flip, and so on. However, software developers are competitive, and so are the products they create. Each image-processing package we'll discuss manages to offer features that its competitors don't have. The more you want to do with your images, the more you'll be tempted to purchase a new image-processing package—assuming you know what capabilities it offers. Finally, you might find that the interface and the way a particular product works gives you more control or just "feels better" for the way you work. For example, I prefer the interface in Kai's Convolver from MetaTools over the traditional sharpen-and-contrast tools available in Photoshop. They are both, however, excellent and tried-and-true options.

By the end of this chapter, we want you to understand all of the main features of the major products available for working with raw imagery, and the unique features available in each package. With that knowledge, you can add to the chest of software tools that will help you build creative, stunning, and unique images. See the color section of this book for a look at the cool effects you can create using the filters described in this chapter.

A REVIEW OF THE PRODUCTS

What follows is a brief introduction to some important applications. This will give you a general familiarity with the programs when you encounter them in future chapters.

Adobe Photoshop 4.0

Photoshop is the most widely recognized name in photo image-processing software. With the new version, 4.0, it is now perhaps the most widely used product of its kind. Photoshop provides a wide range of commands for cropping, color-correcting, rotating, and other image-editing options.

Adobe PhotoDeluxe

Realizing that the digital camera market was growing rapidly, Adobe created a "consumer" version of their Photoshop product to package with cameras and sell separately. The product has many features similar to those offered in Photoshop, but overall, it's aimed at home users, and certainly isn't as powerful or feature-filled as Photoshop. Adobe also packages a similar version called Photoshop LE.

Fractal Design Painter

Fractal Design Painter is more than just a paint program, which is what it is popularly used for. With FDP, you can simulate your photos so that they appear in such traditional media as charcoal, watercolor, or oil painting. FDP also contains a lot of image-processing power.

KPT Convolver

KPT Convolver is Kai's novel take on many common and some not-so-common image-processing filters, like blur, sharpen, and lighting. The product operates as a standard Adobe Photoshop plug-in and requires a host program, such as Photoshop, Fractal Design Painter, or Paint Shop Pro.

Kai's Power Goo

This standalone product, which we'll cover in detail in Chapter 12, is an extensive image-morphing package that can be used to create wild imagery as you push, smudge, and smear an image into a world of its own.

Kai's Power Tools

KPT is an extensive package of awesome Photoshop plug-ins that has become almost as popular as Photoshop itself. The product is especially loved for the many different types of image-processing functions it brings to Photoshop plug-in-compatible programs.

LivePicture

The new LivePicture is similar to Photoshop, but offers some additional functions that make it a top-of-the-line package for image processing. It is particulary useful for large files thanks to fast image-processing speed. LivePicture Overdrive is a stripped-down version of the full-featured package and sells for about half the price of its big brother.

Micrographx Picture Publisher

Picture Publisher from Micrographx is a basic image-editing package from this well known Windows developer. Picture Publisher is shipped in a reduced form with some cameras and can use Photoshop plug-ins.

Paint Shop Pro

This is a popular shareware package from JASC. In version 4.0, Paint Shop Pro includes lots of the basic features you'd expect to find in a solid image-processing package.

PhotoTools 1.0

Here's another top Photoshop plug-in product from Extensis, a new software company that has created a variety of graphical effects packages.

The Black Box/Eye Candy

From Alien Skin Software comes another top-selling set of Photoshop plug-ins, The Black Box. Note that this package will soon double in size and change its name to Eye Candy.

DeBabelizer

Equilibrium sells an awesome image-conversion program called DeBabelizer. DeBabelizer is excellent for batch transformation of your pictures and is well known for its palette remapping capabilities. Many times, you will want to optimize or reduce the color scheme of a picture, and DeBabelizer is perhaps the best product available for this purpose. In addition, DeBabelizer is also widely used to collect a batch of files, which it analyzes for a common denominator palette, and then adjusts all files to use only the common palette. This is a sorely needed process for animation, game, and digital video developers.

xRes

xRes from Macromedia is a top-of-the-line imaging package and peer of both Photoshop and LivePicture.

THE TRICKS OF THE TRADE

Before we explain all your imaging options, we should provide you with a full understanding of how all these products and options work—because they really can work together.

Camera-Ready Package

The first image-processing package that you'll probably use is the one that is shipped with your camera. A half dozen or so of these packages are commonly included with digital cameras. They include Adobe PhotoDeluxe, Storm Technology's EZPhoto, Picturework's Photo Enhancer, and Agfa Fototune.

Depending on your expectations and the quality of the package, you might find this off-the-shelf software to be all you need for downloading and editing your photos. However, keep in mind that more powerful packages are available. Because these camera companies don't want to explode the price of their cameras, they usually don't package a top-of-the-line product like Photoshop. That means that what you get for free, while adequate, isn't as powerful as other professional packages.

Enter The Adobe Plug-In Architecture

Much of the material we explain in this chapter owes its existence to the creation of a special software technology that Adobe built for its Photoshop package—commonly called a *plug-in*. Adobe made plug-ins possible so that Photoshop could run mini-imaging programs from third-party vendors. This makes Photoshop continually expandable. If you find out about a new imaging process that interests you, it's likely you can obtain a plug-in so that you can use the process directly from within Photoshop.

Because Adobe opened up their Photoshop interface technology, there now are a host of imaging programs that support Photoshop-compatible plug-ins. In other words, you don't necessarily need to run Photoshop in order to use a Photoshop plug-in. You can buy a set of Adobe-compatible plug-ins that might run within the proprietary image-processing software that came with your camera—or even with shareware and freeware programs. For instance, there are lower-end programs like Paint Shop Pro that accept

Photoshop plug-ins. So, if you're on a budget, there's still a way to use great products like Kai's Power Tools.

Most of the software packages we cover in this chapter are imaging tools that are available in Photoshop, in a host of similar programs, or through a variety of Photoshop-compatible plug-in products like Kai's Power Tools or The Black Box.

SOME BASIC PHOTO IMAGING TIPS

If you're working with an image-processing package for the first time, you'll find the following advice useful. Even if you have some experience with image processing, you might find that the following advice offers you a tidbit or two that you haven't thought about.

Be Creative And Be Patient

If you don't consider yourself to be artistic, don't assume that means you can't be creative. You can. A digital camera and an image-processing package provide a way to let your mind go, and even run wild. The magic of computer imagery includes the ability to save or discard different versions of images that you process. So you can correct mistakes and then return to your original photo, or you can make a change that you don't quite like, and then alter the photo further—until you're happy. In other words, don't just crop a photo—brighten it and apply a filter, experiment, make collages, use different colors, morph objects into other forms, tell stories, add special effects. Whatever you do, make the most of the new power and ease of use that a digital camera has given you.

Take Small Steps

Whenever you adjust colors or apply filters, you'll find that the best results come not from making major changes, but instead from making minute change after minute change, especially when you deal with color changes. In other words, make incremental changes, not drastic ones. After you've made a change, take a close look at it. Is it too red? Too green? If you feel you need to make another change, go ahead, but do it gradually. Patience is important with image processing. The end result is just as important as the process you take to get there—perhaps more important.

Adjust Parts Of The Picture, Not The Whole Picture

A common mistake is to apply a filter to an entire image in order to solve a problem that occurs in only one section of an image. Don't do this. Instead, practice identifying the specific areas of a picture that are too red or green, and correct only those areas. If one area of your picture is too blurry, work on just that area. This takes skill and patience. The trick lies in learning to adjust one section of your image without disrupting the balance with other sections of the photo. Again, adjusting through a series of minute steps is the best route.

Calibrate Your System

If you're using Photoshop or another high-end image-processing product, you'll find that some built-in calibration tools are available. If you're not using such a product, you can best calibrate your system by first making sure your brightness and color settings are ideal. Also, if you use an ink-jet printer, you might do an initial printout of a range of colors, organized into large squares and perhaps a few gradients. Examine this printout and then run some other tests with different settings. You'll quickly learn how your printer handles color. You might find that it tends to favor certain types of colors more than others; you might also find, for instance, that certain flesh tones don't print well. Over time, you'll learn to adjust your pictures so that they print out ideally on your printer.

However, if you do not have these tools, do not attempt to do this unless you are a seasoned veteran. Color monitor calibration is a tricky business, and unless you know all the variables to take into consideration—such as the lighting around you—you could seriously disrupt your monitor and cause undesired effects. Adobe Photoshop's manual is very useful in this regard.

Even though you have calibrated your system, do not be alarmed if certain hues look different on your color printer than those on your screen. Even some of today's color printers have problems reproducing certain hues—especially flesh tones. The important point is that Uncle Sherman looks great on your printouts.

Save Often

This probably should go without saying, but we'll say it anyway: Save your work often—especially after you've made major changes that would require a lot of time to re-create. And always maintain a backup of the original until you are completely convinced it is no longer needed.

You should also keep raw imagery in a separate directory from altered imagery. Also, consider saving large projects in several instances—in other words, multiple versions of the same image—along the way to preserve backtracking ability. You can use a simple Pic1-1, Pic1-2, Pic1-3 file-naming method to help organize such save schemes.

Take Notes

This could be the most important tip we offer. Just imagine: You slave over a photo, making change after change, color correcting and recorrecting to get the perfect effect. For over an hour, you tweak colors, run filters, feather edges, add edge enhancements, and more. But later, after you feel satisfied with the end result, you can't remember what settings you used to get your image to its pristine state. You want to duplicate your work on other photos, but you don't remember what to duplicate! Use a simple pad of paper and pen, or type notes in your computer's word processor or text processor as you work. You'll have a complete history of the steps you've taken to create your work of art. If you need to reproduce your effort for another photo, you'll have detailed steps of what to do. Some image-processing packages even allow you to add comments to each photo. Make use of this feature.

Cutting Out Subjects From Your Photos

Some of the best digital photo work involves combining photos or simply cutting out objects from their background. Many beginners get frustrated with this step because, at first, it can be tough. With many image processing programs, instead of using the lasso tool to select a region, it can be easier to simply cut out the subject you want by first erasing the border and background. In addition, if you work at zoom levels, you'll find that it's easy to remove border pixels to preserve a perfect border around your image.

And don't get frustrated, Stick with it. Yes, some of the selection tools in various photo enhancement software packages can seem a bit awkward. But after you've mastered these tools, you'll come to enjoy editing your images, and you'll discover many innovative ways to combine a variety of images from different pictures to create fun and exciting collages and hybrid photos.

Each software package has its own set of tools. Most of the higher-end packages offer several types of ways to cut out photos. Two of the most used tools are the pen tool and the lasso tool. These two tools operate differently but provide similar results.

The pen tool operates by enabling the user to draw a path around the desired image to be selected, using bezier points. The path can be manipulated by using the arrow tool from the path pallette to select and manipulate bezier points that accompany the path around your image, as shown in Figure 7.1.

The lasso tool is more intuitive and straightforward than the pen tool. Using the lasso tool, just click and drag to select the desired area of an image.

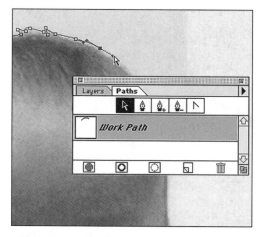

Figure 7.1
Bezier points on a path (created by the Adobe Photoshop pen tool) outlining a desired image selection.

However, a helpful tip in Adobe Photoshop is to hold down the option key (for Macintosh users) or Alt key (for PC users) while clicking with the mouse. This will enable you to manipulate your selection path and will give you greater control.

Learn To Zoom In

All the imaging products let you zoom in substantially on a picture. The best image-processing artists don't just learn to work with the zoom feature, they learn to *live* in zoom mode. The best adjustments to a picture will require handwork at very precise sections of your image. This is very time-consuming work, but the results you can achieve, with practice, are unbeatable.

Adjust Colors First, Then Apply Filters

Don't apply filters until you've color-corrected any problems that you detect. Once these problems are solved, you can apply filters. Filters do most of their work by analyzing the color differences between adjoining pixels—so the best results with filters will come only after the color scheme is ideal.

Read As Much As Possible—Build A Library Of Good Books

Image processing is like learning a musical instrument—you can never learn enough. To increase your base of knowledge—read, read, read. Fortunately, some excellent authors have written tutorials containing very thorough information for how to create specific types of effects for digital photos. At the end of this chapter, we'll list many of these books along with informational Web sites. In addition, we highly recommended that you invest a few dollars in a good book or two about Photoshop, LivePicture, or whatever is your main image-processing package.

Look For New Filters

Companies and individuals are continually developing new filters to help you create dazzling effects for your photos. By actively searching the Web and by searching through major graphics magazines like *Publish,* you can keep up to date on the latest and greatest filters. Every new filter expands your ability to create new images.

Explore, Explore, Explore

There are literally millions of tricks you can perform with your digital photos. Filters alone offer nearly an infinite amount of possibilities. The best transformations, though, usually come from passing a photo through several filters and color changes. So, take some time to just experiment with combinations of filters, color changes, and so on.

PROCESSING YOUR IMAGES

Regardless of what you want to do to improve, adjust, or manipulate a digital photo, the process always boils down to three distinct tasks:

- Handwork. This involves actually painting directly on an image or cutting and pasting objects within a photo.

- Color changes. There are so many ways to "enlighten" a photo simply by adjusting the color, contrast, and other color attributes of a picture.

- Applying Filters. Many filters, available with many different image-processing packages, can take a digital photo and drastically change its appearance or overall effect—often into something you'll like better than the original photo.

THE BASICS OF COLOR IMAGING

All digital cameras render graphics at 24 bits of color (or in terms of screen display—16.7 million colors). Display and video card manufacturers are fond of tossing out different pieces of information regarding their product, knowing full well that most users don't have a clue about the true meaning of this information. But it's important information to know, especially if you're going to be using a digital camera. In the following sections, we'll explain some features that are important to the way your monitor, video card, and digital camera combine to create images. However, do not feel overwhelmed. Although there is a lot that you can learn about color, the bottom line is this: If it looks good to you and you are happy with your image, that is all that matters. Art is very subjective. Just have fun. Start moving some pixels around and see what happens.

Color Concepts

Colors, of course, are actually transmitted via light waves. Our eyes are adept at dissecting that light and reassembling it into brainwaves that represent different colors. Essentially, the CCD in a camera is just like our eyes; it, too, reads light waves in such a way as to perceive color from them.

Digital cameras can then take this imagery from the outside world and translate it into pixels within our computer for storage and editing. Before digital photography, this could only be done via a scanner, and if you didn't own a scanner, you were at the mercy of the film developer. Now you're at the mercy of the CCD lens of your camera. You can, over time, learn to adjust for this. The best way, of course, is to use your camera a lot and pay attention to the way your particular camera tends to overinterpret or underinterpret the imagery you're photographing.

Interestingly enough, there are many different components of color. Most of these components deal with illuminated color, such as an image displayed on screen. Printed color is different, although we'll deal with that, too. Anyway, as a digital photographer and a person who will be processing digital images, you'll want to make sure you understand all of the various aspects of color. That's the purpose of the next few sections.

HSB

HSB is shorthand for Hue, Saturation, and Brightness. The HSB color scheme works by quantitatively representing these three basic descriptors of color. *Hue* determines the basic color that is representative of the wavelength of light reflected through an object. When an artist talks about hue, he or she basically means color.

Saturation, which is measured on a scale of 0 to 100, determines how gray the hue is. The less gray a color is, the richer it gets. A red with a saturation of 10 is a very dark and dull red. A red with a saturation of 90 is an extremely vivacious red—very bright. When photographers talk about saturation, they're referring to how dull or rich the hue is. Finally, *brightness* determines the overall darkness or lightness of a color, represented on a scale of 0 to 100, with 100 being white and 0 being black.

RGB

RGB is shorthand for Red, Green, and Blue. In grade school art class, we were taught that the three primary colors were red, yellow, and blue. That's true for print, which deals with *subtractive colors*, or what happens when light is removed from colors. With computer-displayed colors, we need to talk about *additive colors*, or what happens when different waves of light are added to existing colors. To understand this difference, think back to your first grade-school theatrical production. You'll remember that the stage lights were red, green, and blue. Yellow was nowhere in sight. Onstage colors were created by *adding* different combinations of red, green, and blue lights.

On your computer, the principle is the same, so forget everything about what your grade school teacher taught you about color mixing. RGB color schemes measure each single color in terms of how much red, green, and blue light spectrum it contains on a scale of 0 to 255. Zero is representative of black, and 255 is white. Over 16.7 million color combinations are possible in this scheme (256×256×256). For example, a bright blue in RGB might have red set to 0, green set to 0, and blue set to 246. Combining colors like red set to 237, green set to 138, and blue set to 46 provides a different color entirely—in this case, a bright orange. If all the colors are set to the same value, this creates various shades of gray.

CMYK

Now let's switch from displayed colors (light) to printed colors. With printed colors, we need to talk about CMYK, which is shorthand for Cyan, Magenta, Yellow, and Black. Cyan, magenta, and yellow are actually the three most ideal colors used for printing full-color images. CMYK images combine separate layers of an original image (called color separations) into a composite that has the ideal color combinations. Although cyan, magenta, and yellow are the primary print colors, they can't produce black. Black is actually the absence of all color—so no combination of colors can produce it. Consequently, black (the K in CMYK) is added to print images to create black sections of the image.

In general, the CMYK model is based on how different color inks are absorbed on paper to form different colors. That's what's meant by color *subtraction*. When one color is absorbed by another, it's said to be *subtracted* by the main color.

CMYK is the color model used by printers. Whenever you hear about the color separation process or four-color CYMK printing, realize this is all jargon used to describe a process by which you send an image to the printer in four parts, one sheet each for the four colors that are used to reproduce a full-color image. This seems counter-intuitive, because it seems like you're *adding* color on top of color. Just keep in mind that the camera that processes these four layers basically starts with black, and then uses the color separations to determine which colors to *remove* or subtract. By contrast, a printer has to combine the different layers of RGB colors to create a corresponding print view of the colors.

CIE L*a*b

In 1931, the Commission Internationale d'Eclairage (CIE) created an international standard for color representation. It was upgraded and refined in 1976, and is widely used. The idea was to create a system that eliminates the variability of color reproduction that exists between different color formats. In other words, CIE L*a*b is color independent. The color is composed of three elements:

- Luminance. This is the lightness of a color.

- The "a" color ranges. These range from green to red.

- The "b" color ranges. These range from blue to yellow.

A Few Words About Color Ranges, Color Monitors, And Color Limitations

Each of the systems just described use a varying total of colors that the human eye can see. CIE L*a*b is the most complete; it can create all the color possibilities capable with both the RGB and CMYK color schemes. Next is RGB, which can recreate the next-largest portion of the color spectrum.

Your monitor can also create output problems, because what you see on the screen isn't necessarily what you'll see on your printer. Your display often can't accurately display what will appear on your printer, for example, colors like cyan or magenta. In addition, not all monitors are alike; the same color on your screen might seem slightly more or less red, green, or blue on another monitor.

And, if you're wondering: Yes, all of this color information leads to headaches for photographers and digital graphics artists who want to ensure that the colors, as they see them, reproduce perfectly on other systems and in print.

If the ins and outs of color systems interest you, then check out this fantastic and very technical Web page called Poynton's Colour FAQ by Charles A. Poynton, located at www.inforamp.net/~poynton/notes/colour_and_gamma/ ColorFAQ.html. It's filled with all sorts of technical and mathematical information about the differences and intricacies of color.

WORKING WITH COLOR IMAGING

Most of the filters we've described so far actually rearrange pixels on screen and make a few color changes to existing pixels. Now we are going to talk solely about color changes. By simply changing the colors of existing pixels, you can do quite a bit with your photos.

The Histogram

Before you make any color adjustments, it's a good idea to first look at the *histogram* of your image. A histogram (like the one shown in Figure 7.2) is a bar chart that shows you how many pixels there are at different levels of brightness. By examining a histogram, you can determine key information about your image. If you have a lot of pixels at the same brightness level— either dark or bright—you might not have enough contrast in the photo to realize clear lines of detail. If the image is even at all brightness levels, you might have applied too many color changes and be "flattening" the image—that is, creating too much gray and washing out detail. In imaging, the brightness of a picture can be considered high, average, or low key. A high-key image contains mostly very bright pixels, while a low-key

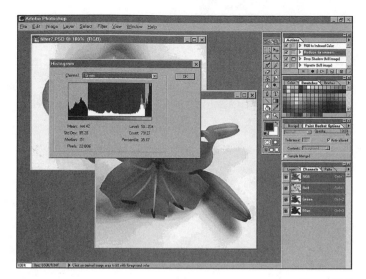

Figure 7.2
A histogram of an image shown in Photoshop.

contains a majority of dark pictures. An average key will have fewer dark and light pixels in favor of everything in between.

> The naked eye can certainly see the same basic information that a histogram initially provides. However, a histogram can provide details that are difficult to discern by even the most trained eye. If you're using a program that provides a histogram function, spend time with it to learn how it can show you a more defined view of how dark or how light your picture is. Experiment to determine how the changes you apply to your picture also change the histogram results.

Levels And Autolevels

Levels in Photoshop (see Figure 7.3) and other image programs refer to the ability to adjust an image's color base at the color composition level. For example, if you're using an RGB system to determine the colors of pixels, working with levels allows you to adjust brightness and darkness of the picture at the red level, green level, and blue level, which can give you very precise control over the tonal quality of an image. If a picture's reds are too dark, you might increase the brightness of the red pixels to compensate for this. *Autolevels* in Photoshop will actually analyze the contrast in the

Figure 7.3
Adjusting levels of an image in Photoshop.

image and adjust the levels automatically for a more proportionate range of colors. This is a nice, simple feature, especially if you don't have the patience or eye for fine adjustment. However, if you take the time to become experienced at setting levels yourself, and avoid the autolevels feature, you can gain some very precise control over a picture's tonal quality.

Curves

In Photoshop and other imaging programs, the *curve* tool provides an interesting way to adjust the tone and color scheme in your digital pictures (see Figure 7.4). Essentially, you are given a line that represents a 1:1 relationship across the brightness spectrum—dark pixels are still dark, and bright values are still bright. With the curve, though, you can stretch the line to remap brighter pixels specifically to become darker, or vice versa. As you remap the curve, the image will respond accordingly, showing the effects of changing the relationship that the curve originally represented. This is an excellent tool for isolating a specific range of dark or bright pixels and adjusting their level within the entire picture.

Color Balance

Is your picture too red or too blue? Color balancing is very important with digital cameras, which can play strange color tricks with light. Some

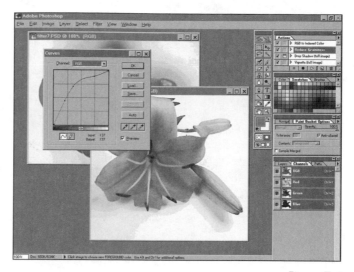

Figure 7.4

A curve adjustment shown in Photoshop.

lower-end cameras have problems with fluorescent light (which can make a photo too green). Some cameras with low-end CCD chips create red bleeding around the edges of images in low-light conditions. With color balancing, you can adjust the amount of each color component in your picture (for instance, if you're using RGB as your color composition system, you can affect the balance of red, green, and blue). Even most of the low-end packages that come bundled with these cameras offer this feature.

Color balancing can be tricky. The appearance of too much red might actually mean that the image doesn't have enough green and blue, which may sound the same, but isn't. When you adjust the color balance, experiment by lowering the one color that is overly apparent, as well as increasing the other colors. With the low-end cameras that we've tested, it seems that red tends to creep in when a lot of light is available, while green tends to wash out a little. Blue doesn't need as much color correction, except when a picture is taken in lower light conditions.

One easy way to adjust for color is to shoot against a white background. This way, you can immediately see whether the image has too much of a certain color. Also, consider buying some colored pieces of paper that show pure red, green, and blue. Then, when you shoot an object, place these sheets of paper in the picture to help later with image color calibration. After you're done, you can simply crop out the colored paper.

Brightness/Contrast

Digital cameras love light because they use the light to produce more contrast in images. By adjusting brightness and contrast, you can further enhance the lines in an image by widening the gap between dark pixels and brighter pixels, which will emphasize the lines and shapes in your image. Before you use a find-edges or sharpen-edges filter, it's a good idea to enhance the contrast first. Be careful, though, it's easy to overdo the contrast and brightness, which can wash out colors. Remember to adjust brightness and contrast incrementally, in several small steps, rather than trying to get them perfect at once.

Hue/Saturation

Hue and saturation effects allow you to broadly change the actual tint of an image as well as the depth or richness of the colors. Adding saturation to an image will deepen and brighten the color tones by not only brightening the specific color of a pixel but by making it less gray, and thus more pure.

One interesting effect available in Photoshop and similar products is the ability to colorize a grayscale image. First, open an image that you've already saved, sharpen it or make other changes as necessary, then convert it to a grayscale image. Next—and we're not kidding here—convert it *back* to an RGB image. Select Hue/Saturation and then choose colorize. Finally, select the actual tone and saturation of the imagery. The effect is best done by then selecting areas of your picture and changing the colorization in several spots.

Desaturate

Desaturation takes a color image and converts it to grayscale, but retains its color channels. Essentially, desaturation sucks out all the color by switching every pixel's color value to the equivalent gray value of the image.

Replace Color

Some programs allow you to click anywhere on an image and change the color of only the selected area. This can be useful for adjusting specific colors in your photos when they appear in isolated spots rather than huge, definable blocks.

Invert/Negative Image

Invert will change the color value of each pixel to its inverse value, on a scale of 0 to 255. So, if the red value for a part of an image is 213, then inverting it will change the value to 42. (All components of the color composition scheme will be changed at once.) The result is a negative image of your picture.

Equalize

Equalization first analyzes the brightness values in your picture. It then will treat the darkest color as black (even if it isn't truly black) and treat the lightest color as white (even if it's not fully white). Then, it will adjust every pixel value in the picture by redistributing the brightness in an equalized fashion—creating higher contrast and, most of the time, a lighter picture. This is a good color process to use for pictures that seem to be darker than normal.

Threshold

In Photoshop, threshold is an interesting color process. Simply choose a level setting, and Photoshop responds by changing all the pixels above that threshold to white and all pixels below the threshold to black.

Posterize

Posterization allows you to define the number of tonal levels in your image. A full, 24-bit image can have 256 possible tonal levels (0 to 255). By reducing this to, say, 20, the image will remap the colors in the image to 20 levels of tonal quality by shifting every pixel's value to its nearest allowable level. The lower you go, the fewer overall colors your picture will have. Using posterization effectively can help you create lower bandwidth pictures for use on the Web. Some programs don't offer a distinct function named posterize, but instead let you define exactly how many colors are allowed in an image. The program then posterizes the image based on that number of colors. The more posterized an image is, the fewer levels of tone it has, and consequently the fewer number of colors.

COLOR REDUCTION

When you create images for the Web, it's extremely important to optimize the size of each image (which we'll cover in Chapter 11). Color reduction is one of the best ways to accomplish this. As we've explained, there are several ways to reduce color, including posterization, dithering the image, or by using a product like Equilibrium's DeBabelizer, which provides some excellent color-reduction methods. Before you reduce the color of an image, adjust it so that it's as clear and sharp as possible. Then, you can go ahead and reduce colors and make final adjustments. If you'd like to find out more about color reduction, try the Bandwidth Conservation Society, which is on the Web at www.infohiway.com/faster/index.html. Here, you'll find several tutorials about color reduction as it pertains to image size optimization.

Another useful product for color reduction is HVS Color. This plug-in for Adobe Photoshop and Equilibrium DeBabelizer allows you to convert 24-bit images to 8-bit images with no visible loss in quality. It uses a proprietary algorithm that models the way the human visual system perceives and masks colors. HVS Color achieves its effect without dithering, which is very different from most other conventional reduction schemes.

OTHER FILTERS AND PROCESSES IN PHOTOSHOP

Photoshop 4.0 is the king of the hill when it comes to imaging filters. However, many of the effects that we'll describe in the following sections are also available in other image-processing packages, like Paint Shop Pro or the package that came with your camera.

Sharpen Filters

Sharpen filters increase the contrast of lines in your image, thus giving them more definition.

Sharpen And Sharpen More

Sharpen filters work by increasing the contrast of adjacent pixels. By changing the contrast between adjacent pixels—lightening one and darkening another—lines take a more robust form and thus increase in density, making an image appear sharper.

Sharpen Edges

Working in a similar contrast enhancement fashion as sharpen, a sharpen-edges filter only applies itself where major color changes take place, which is usually where different objects in a picture overlap. This provides a better definition of blurry imagery by working only at the edges, while leaving alone the heart of that object in your picture.

Unsharp Mask

This filter enhances the contrast of the defined edge of an object in a photo. The unsharp mask works great for blurry photos and can work well where there has been some blurring as a result of a camera's compression or color interpretation of an image. One line on the edge is lightened and the other edge is darkened again, providing for a more defined and robust line.

Before you use any sharpening filter, make sure you've tweaked the color scheme as much as possible, especially brightness and contrast. Also, consider zooming in and cleaning up some areas by hand before you run a sharpen filter. Then, when you run the filter, it will be able to better define the high areas of contrast to accentuate.

The Kai's plug-in called Sharpen Intensity greatly increases the control over an image's sharpness. This plug-in can be a great help in touching up an image that may seem irreparably blurry. Give this one a try. You'll quickly see what we mean.

Blur Filters

Blurring is the opposite of sharpening. Specifically, a blur filter softens an image's lines. This can be an effective filter for merging two objects from different photos.

Basic Blur

A basic blur filter looks for "noise" in an image and removes it. Noise refers to pockets of high contrast in a picture (such as a very light color next to darker colors). Blur removes these pockets by replacing the areas with pixels that are closer in color and hue to that of neighboring pixels and by averaging the pixels next to the edges and shaded areas in a picture.

Gaussian Blur

A Gaussian blur allows you to set a specific threshold for the amount of blurring that should be applied to an image. Essentially, a blur averages pixels and substitutes high contrast areas with them for smoother transitions. A Gaussian blur lets you affect how much that average should be.

Motion Blur

This special blur effect creates a "trail" of an image in a specific direction (that you set) and then blurs that trail to create a motion-like effect similar to what you would get if you took a picture of a rapidly moving object.

Radial Blur Filter

A radial blur is similar to a motion blur, except it has a radial blurry trail.

Smart Blur

This new blur filter, available in Adobe Photoshop 4.0, gives you more precise control over the standard blur filter. You can set the radius around each pixel that should be blurred and you can establish a threshold and quality setting as well.

Many times, you'll want to use blur to soften the edges of a photo, especially if you've worked by hand to remove a background or foreground object. Instead of running the filter and selecting the image area, use the painting tool to apply the filter results by hand for a much softer effect.

Noise Filters

As we've mentioned, an image is said to have noise when there are pixels that stand out against their surrounding pixels because of the contrast they create. Noise filters are used to remove these items (or introduce them) by changing the color levels of pixels to blend them away (or introduce them). Noise filters are excellent for removing specks from an image, some of which might be caused by dust or scratches. However, these filters rarely seem to work perfectly. You may have to go in by hand to solve the worst noise problems.

Add Noise

An add-noise filter introduces various pixels that are of high contrast to surrounding pixels in an image. In most cases, this is an automated process, but some products do allow you to set some attributes. Many people apply add noise to sections that have been touched up by hand to obscure any hard lines or obvious edges.

Despeckle

Despeckle is an anti-noise filter. It finds the edges of objects in an image and blurs the surrounding areas around the image to remove noise, without losing the line definition.

Dust And Scratches

This is sort of a super-despeckle filter. It looks for slightly larger lines or radial specs of high contrast and blends them away.

Median

A median filter helps blend pixels within a set radius that you determine. Once a radius is chosen, the filter goes to each pixel, then chooses the median value in all the surrounding pixels in the circle around it (as big as the radius defined it). Once that median value is determined, the filter will place that color in the original pixel's space. Since it discards pixels that are extremely different from surrounding pixels, this filter also reduces noise.

Adding noise is a great way to make a photo look old. First, adjust the photo so all areas are clear and correct. Then, add noise to the photo, and convert it to black and white or some other monochromatic tint. Feather the edges of the photo for a fun "old print" look.

Distort Filters

As the name suggests, all of these filters distort an image in some way—often by creating intriguing effects.

Displace

A displace filter modifies one image by using a second image to determine how to displace each pixel in the image. The filter reads in the displacement image and applies it to the first image. The displacement picture's pixel is analyzed for its gray value (the average of its RGB values on a scale of 0 to 255). If the value is below 128, the pixel on the first image is given a negative displacement, with 0 being maximum. If the value is above 128, then it is given a positive displacement, with 255 being maximum. A value of 128 produces no displacement.

Typically, you use this filter by first creating a custom displacement map, but you can actually use any other picture as a map—even another digital photo. However, expect less than desirable results when using another picture that hasn't been specifically prepared for the displacement filter.

Displacement takes time to master, but can be fantastic for creating distorted imagery. It's especially great once you learn how to create your own displacement maps. Displacement is a lot of fun with head shots.

Pinch

Based on the settings you give it, this filter will squeeze a picture inward or outward.

Polar Coordinates

To create a globe, cartographers take a rectangular map they've drawn and then crop it in such a way as to be able to wrap it around a sphere. If you look down from the top of one of these stitched-together spheres, the view is from one of the poles of the globe. This filter essentially tries to take a rectangular image and more or less create the same look to it.

Ripple

A ripple filter makes your photo appear as if it has a liquid form and has had a rock dropped in it or wind blowing over it.

Shear

This filter allows you to add bends or angles to a line. The filter distorts the image following the form of the shape you defined.

Spherize

This filter takes a photo and wraps it around a sphere shape. There are two forms you can choose—one that creates a ball-like sphere and one that creates a bowl-like sphere.

Twirl

Twirl takes an image and lets you twist it along the axis of a user-defined, windmill-like shape.

Wave

With this filter, you can essentially send a waveform through your image and distort it in a variety of ways. You choose the characteristics of the wave (such as frequency, amplitude, and wave type), and then your image is redrawn along that wave type with a ripple-like effect.

Zigzag

The zigzag filter distorts a selection radially, depending on the radius of the pixels in your selection.

Glass

Applying a glass filter to a picture makes the image appear to be on the other side of different types of glass, for example, a thick or watery glass. You describe the characteristics of the glass, and the filter does the rest.

Ocean Ripple

This is a more robust ripple filter available in Photoshop 4.0.

Diffuse Glow

Want to induce a spotlight look to a part of your photo? The diffuse-glow filter highlights light areas of your photograph around the edges of a selected area and, depending on the thresholds that you set, brightens the pixels to give a glowing look around the area.

Pixelate Filters

Pixelate-style filters can combine the pixels of an image into larger forms to create some interesting-looking transformations of your photos.

Color Halftone

A color halftone filter transforms your photo into a halftone screen with large circles in sizes that you specify. Each rectangular area is analyzed and turned into a circle with a brightness level equal to the pixels contained in the rectangle size.

Crystallize

The crystallize filter combines filters into single-color polygon shapes in widths that you define.

Facet

This is a great filter for digital photographers. Facet analyzes your image and locates the larger areas of a single color. Then, the filter adds more of that color to each area, resulting in a plainer style of imagery. Applying a facet filter repeatedly renders a painting-like effect to an image.

Fragment

The fragment filter creates a sort of double-vision effect by creating four copies of an image, averaging them in terms of color levels, and then off-setting them in all four major directions.

Mezzotint

The mezzotint filter transforms an image into a random pattern of highly saturated imagery with a specifically applied dot pattern. You select from a long list of dot and line patterns. Then, the filter applies your settings. The look is artistic in nature and can produce some interesting effects.

Mosaic

Several image packages have a mosaic filter. With some packages, this effect transforms your picture into a mosaic-like appearance. However, note that Photoshop's mosaic effect simply divides the picture into a set of square areas and then turns each of these areas into the same color after it determines the closest color that summarizes the pixels within the area. FDP's mosaic feature, on the other hand, creates true-looking mosaics.

Pointillize

This filter mimics a style of painting by the same name (mainly, Scurat's pointillism during the Impressionistic period). The image is broken into randomly placed dots with white space placed between them. The size of each dot is set by the user.

Render Filters

With a render filter, you actually introduce new visual elements into areas of your image.

The Clouds Filter

This filter will render a random generation of blue sky and white clouds—useful for generating interesting backgrounds for cut-out imagery.

Difference Clouds

The difference clouds filter randomly looks at sections of your image and replaces the current areas with new pixels that vary between the foreground and background color to produce a cloudy picture. In the process, the image's color scheme is actually inverted, so you will want to return the color scheme by running another iteration of the difference clouds filter or using the color invert option. If you continually filter an image by using this filter, it will eventually begin to turn the image into a marble-like texture pattern.

Lens Flare

Want to simulate a lens flare on your photo? This filter lets you place many different styles and intensities of lens flares onto your picture. They are uncannily realistic.

Lighting Effects

Lighting effects is a filter that offers many different options. You can apply up to 16 different light sources to your pictures, and you can choose from among several different lighting styles—the possibilities are endless. You can choose the texture of the image where the light hits, the intensity and positioning of lights, and how big the radius is. You can overexpose or underexpose the image, add shine effects, and more. This filter adds a lot of texture to an image.

Stylize Filters

The stylize filters produce a painted or impressionistic effect on a selection by displacing pixels, and by finding and heightening contrast in an image.

Diffuse

Diffuse gives your picture less focus by moving pixels at random. Adobe Photoshop offers you three options: The Normal option moves any pixel; the Darken option moves pixels, but only replaces light pixels with darker ones; and the Lighten option replaces darker pixels with lighter ones.

Emboss

An emboss filter creates a raised-looking image by first getting rid of the color, then going through high-contrast areas and tracing the image using dark and light lines. This process builds a 3D look into the image and creates an embossed effect.

Extrude

An extrude filter will draw out from each pixel in a certain depth range to give an object a 3D look.

Find Edges

The find edges filter moves through an image and looks for high-contrast areas that identify edges. Once it has found those areas, the filter draws a line around them and clears out the areas in-between, which results in a line drawing.

Trace Contour

Trace contour analyzes an image for the areas where colors go from dark to major brightness and draws a line around these areas. One line is drawn around each color channel. The end result is the creation of a borderline around major lines in your image.

Solarize

The solarize filter moves through an image and creates a picture that is between the negative and positive image of the picture. Use this to simulate the exposure of a photographic print to light during development.

Artistic Filters

With the release of Photoshop 4.0, Adobe added a number of filters that digital camera users will find both useful and fun, all of which existed previously as part of Adobe's Gallery Effects line. The artistic filter family in Photoshop allows you to transform your photos in ways that cause them to look as if they were constructed in a specific artistic style. You have 15 different artistic filters to choose from, and each contains a number of user settings that can provide a range of adjustments to that particular style.

The artistic filters are:

- Colored Pencil
- Cut Out
- Dry Brush
- Film Grain
- Fresco
- Neon Glow
- Paint Daubs
- Palette Knife
- Plastic Wrap
- Poster Edges
- Rough Pastels
- Smudge Stick
- Sponge
- Underpainting
- Water Color

> **Tip** Most of these filters are pretty much self explanatory, so we won't delve into them here. Experiment with them to see whether you like the effects.
>
> Paint Shop Pro, a lower-end photo imaging package for the PC that's available as shareware from JASC, Inc., has one artistic filter not found in Photoshop: The hot wax artistic filter. It makes your pictures look as if they were photos of a wax sculptures.

Sketch Filters

The sketch filters are cousins of the artistic filters in that they transform your images to look as if they were drawn or painted in a certain artistic fashion. The main difference is that these filters (with the exception of the water paper filter) render art that is monochromatic in nature. There are 14 different sketch filters—they too are fairly self explanatory.

The sketch filters are:

- Bas Relief
- Chalk/Charcoal
- Charcoal
- Chrome
- Conte Crayon
- Graphic Pen
- Halftone Patter
- Note Paper
- Photo Copy
- Plaster
- Reticulation
- Stamp
- Torn Edges
- Water Paper

Texture Filters

The texture filters are another great new addition to Photoshop 4.0. These filters allow you to define the type of surface that your picture should appear on. You can choose from a variety of film grain effects—mosaic tiles, stained glass, canvas, sandstone, and cracked surfaces. You can even use another picture as a texture. The edges of that picture will define the surface pattern created.

Photoshop's mosaic tiles and stained glass filters aren't a replacement for what's possible in Fractal Design Painter. And, even though they provide interesting effects, they don't offer the precision and rendering capabilities that are available in FDP's Make Mosaic and Make Tesslation products.

LivePicture And xRes: Photoshop Peers

LivePicture and xRes are two other excellent imaging packages that serve the professional level of the photo-imaging market. This chapter isn't complete without highlighting both of these packages.

LivePicture

LivePicture (see Figure 7.5) brings workstation-like functionality to PC users. The heart of LivePicture is its IVUE/FlashPIX imaging format. This technology allows you to work with extremely high-end files at very fast speeds. In fact, tests show that LivePicture is much faster at completing certain tasks than Photoshop. Thanks to these fast response times, Live-Picture is excellent for moving objects around in a photo. Text handling is also given high marks, and LivePicture excels at color correction and adjustment as well. LivePicture offers excellent tools for morphing im-agery, creating silhouettes, and for creating color separations used in high-end printing.

LivePicture, however, doesn't have all the features of Photoshop, and is considered a little harder to use (something that the makers of LivePicture are working hard to improve). LivePicture 2.5 does let you use Photoshop plug-ins and is seen by many as complementing (rather than replacing)

Figure 7.5
LivePicture's main advantage is its fast image-editing speed.

Photoshop. Many photographers use both products to take advantage of the different features they offer—for instance, they'll perform color correction and fast editing with LivePicture, and perform image manipulation and processing with Photoshop.

LivePicture has also released LivePicture Overdrive, which is essentially a "LivePicture Lite." Overdrive only works in RGB mode (no CMYK). With its lower price, LivePicture Overdrive is particularly aimed at Photoshop owners who want access to the quick editing features of LivePicture for such critical functions as cropping, moving, and rotating images.

xRes

While LivePicture is becoming a complementary product to Photoshop by providing specific aspects of photo imaging extraordinarily well, xRes is more of a complete Photoshop and Fractal Design Painter replacement.

xRes borrows a little of everything from the three most often used imaging products. First, it's mainly a Photoshop-like imaging package, and even allows you to use Photoshop plug-ins. xRes also works like LivePicture by introducing a special format mode that allows it to enhance the speed at which it can complete certain image manipulations. Finally, xRes also introduces natural media painting effects similar to Fractal Design Painter.

Overall, while the package is stellar, it also introduces a few new techniques—especially faster image editing. Still, while it seeks to replace all three of its competitors, xRes doesn't provide a 100-percent overlap of its competitor's features.

Comparing Photoshop, xRes, And LivePicture

So which package is best? This is an impossible question to answer simply because no package incorporates all the features of its competitors nor works identically to the others. All make use of Photoshop plug-ins, but that alone doesn't make a competitor equivalent to Photoshop. If you're truly a high-end user, all three might have a place in your tool chest. However, if your budget won't permit you to buy all three, check out the reviews (search for them on the Web) for each package to help you decide which packages you should choose first. These reviews cannot only provide you with up-to-date information on the latest versions, but they can help emphasize the differences, strengths, and weaknesses of all three packages. The truth is, none of these actually tries to displace the others. And in fact both LivePicture and xRes emphasize their co-existence with Photoshop. Want some general rules of thumb to use for deciding which packages to purchase? If you're going to be working with very large photos from a high-end camera, take a long look at adding LivePicture or xRes to your toolbox—they excel at large file manipulation. If you're a lower end camera user, Photoshop is a widely used and standard program that will handle just about all of your image-processing needs. If you feel compelled to have an exhaustive array of features, processes, and techniques available to you (and you have the budget to boot), you can't go wrong purchasing all of these products and exploiting their features.

Convolver Filters

MetaTools's Convolver is one of the leading Adobe Photoshop plug-ins. It offers a number of excellent features. Some of these overlap with similar filters offered in Photoshop itself—and in other applications—but the unique interface offered in Convolver makes it a useful substitute.

Take a look at what Convolver offers in the filter department:

- Darken/Lighten. Darkens or lightens an image.

- Blur and Sharpen. The blur filter blurs an image by softening the contrast between neighboring pixels. The sharpen filter does just the opposite—sharpens the image by increasing the contrast between neighboring pixels.

- Edges Amount and Edges Angle. Edges Amount is a variation of the edge enhance filter commonly found in many image-processing programs, except that this filter allows you to force the sharpening effect to be applied mostly along a specified angle.

- Relief Amount and Relief Angle. Convolver again takes a commonly found filter, emboss, and adds a twist. With the Relief Angle setting, you can adjust the angle of the embossing effect. Another difference is that this emboss effect doesn't gray out your colorizing options, which allows you to get a "color embossing" effect.

- Hue Rotate. By using Hue Rotate, you can cycle through different color tint effects, which simulates taking the photo with a camera using a color filter lens.

- Saturation. Adds or removes more color intensity from your photos.

- Brightness. With this filter, you can cycle through the results of a brighter or darker image.

- Tint. With the Tint filter, you can add a color tint to the photograph.

- Fade To Gray. This filter lets you cycle the colors in the photograph closer and closer to a flat gray.

- Color Contrast. This filter will intensify color contrast in an image. Bright areas are increased toward more white, while the darkest areas of the image are kept dark.

- Mutate. With the Mutate option, Convolver creates a series of mutated images by applying a random variety of Convolver's filters to the image. You can either select one or press the Mutate button again to see what other interesting looks this filter can create.

KAI'S POWER TOOLS

Probably no other Photoshop plug-in is as widely known or used as Kai's Power Tools (KPT). Again, this package of filters and accessories for Adobe Photoshop does have some overlap with Photoshop's built-in filters, but the package's unique interface makes it a worthwhile overlap. For instance, you may find it easier to apply the Gaussian filter with KPT than with the conventional Photoshop Gaussian blur method. Take a look at the range of effects that KPT offers you:

Edges

The Edges Lens filter helps you find edges, soften edges, and gives you directional edges that will sharpen edges along a specific angle.

Gaussian

The Gaussian Lens filter gives you four specific types of blur effects: Blur produces a standard blurring effect; Weave and Block blur an image, but also apply some extrusion effects to provide a texture-like look to the blurred image; and Diamond produces a diamond-shaped blurring effect.

Intensity

This filter increases the color saturation in an image.

Noise Lens

The KPT Noise Lens filter adds randomly placed pixels that create noise in an image. However, with this version, you can choose from dithered pixels, dark noise (Grime mode), colored noise (Special Color), and random noise but constrained to a specific color range (Hue Protection mode).

Pixel

The Pixel filter from KPT allows you to scatter the pixels in your photo in a variety of ways. You can diffuse them, randomly scatter them, or chose from two other modes: PixelWeather 1 or the more intense PixelWeather 2, which give you more control over the scatter manner of the pixels. You can also constrain the scattering in specific directions.

Smudge Lens

The Smudge Lens filter allows you to create either smudges or drip effects in a photo. The smudge effect, which affects all pixels within an image, creates a motion trail-like effect in an image and in any user-defined direction. The drip variant allows you to specify a color to smudge. You can affect the length of the smudge or drip by varying the intensity of the effect as well.

3D Stereo Noise

3D Stereo Noise lets you create a black-and-white 3D stereoscopic image from your photo. You've probably seen stereoscopic pictures; at first glance, they look like a meaningless jumble. You need to stare "through" them in a certain way until a 3D image begins to emerge.

Glass Lens

The Glass Lens filter in KPT is not, as the name seems to imply, a filter to create a glass window appearance; instead, it creates the impression that you're looking at your photo through a spherized glass object. The image can be distorted with a variety of such options as Soft, Normal, Bright, and Backlighting.

Page Curl

Page Curl is an interesting effect for photos. With this filter, you can simulate a corner of the photo actually curling away like a sticker from an object to reveal what's underneath. You can choose the corner, direction, and intensity of the curl, and you can specify how transparent the back part of the curl appears.

Planar Tiling

The Planar Tiling filter arranges your image like tiling on a floor. The image can be arranged as a simple tiling (a head-on view) or in perspective mode, with your choice of angle and slant of the perspective plane.

Seamless Welder

This filter helps you create seamless tiles. Seamless tiles are used often for 3D modeling of texture maps. Since the tiles are seamless when wrapped on a 3D object, the texture map doesn't break in any way.

Twirl

The Twirl filter works just like the twirl filter in Photoshop. You can set the intensity, direction, and radius of the twirl. One difference with KPT is the Kaleidoscope mode, which alters an image so that it appears as if it is being viewed with a kaleidoscope.

Video Feedback

Have you ever seen someone point a video camera at a TV that's showing the camera's own broadcast? Or have you ever held a mirror up to another mirror? This is the effect that the Video Feedback filter will apply to your image. You can set the positioning, angle, and size of the feedback window, which then trails off, getting smaller and smaller until it's gone. You can also choose from a rounded or square window.

Vortex Tiling

Even the manual for KPT admits that it's difficult to describe the Vortex Tiling filter. Essentially, it offers two modes: Normal and Pinch. Each mode twists and warps the photo, but uses tiling to keep the effect seamless. The normal filter is best described as making an image appear as if it was perfectly wrapped on the inside of a sphere, with your viewpoint being on the inside of the sphere. The pinch vortex takes an image and, according to the manual, "sucks your image into and through itself."

THE BLACK BOX/EYE CANDY

Alien Skin Software originally developed a set of plug-in filters called The Black Box. However, as this book was in development, Alien Skin announced that they were going to add 10 new filters to the product and change the name to Eye Candy. Unfortunately, other than being told the names of the 10 new filters, we didn't have access to the new product in time to fully explore them for this chapter. So, here are descriptions of the original 10 filters from The Black Box.

Carve

Carve uses shadowing and highlighting to create a beveled look to your image. The filter will also darken already dark areas. You can set the shadow depth, bevel width, darken intensity, and smoothness of the beveling. You can also choose a flat or curved shape to the bevel, add highlights, and adjust the light source.

Cutout

The Cutout filter removes a selection from an image, and then adds shadowing in the hole to give it a look of being cut out. You can select the size and positioning of the shadow, give it a blurry look, and choose a fill color for the cutout space.

Drop Shadow

Many Web images include a drop shadow to give a little extra depth to the images. With this filter, you can add a drop shadow to your selection. Choose the offset, blurriness, and opacity—and you're all set.

Glass

Here is yet another glass filter. This one lets you select the bevel width, color tint, opacity, and refraction of the glass. You can also control the number of flaws—such as hills and valleys—to the glass.

Glow

To use this filter, first outline the section of your image you wish to effect, then choose a width, opacity level, glow color, and a drop-off intensity. The filter will then render a glowing outline around the edges of the selection.

HSB Noise

HSB Noise lets you introduce noise to a photo. (Like other noise filters, it works by adding random high-contrast pixels to a photo.) The filter allows you to set the hue variation, saturation, and brightness of the noise.

Inner And Outer Bevels

You can give your imagery a variety of relief looks with either the Inner or Outer Bevel filters. Set the bevel width, type, shadow depth, smoothness, drop-off, and lighting elements. The filter does the rest.

Motion Trail

This effect is much like other motion-trail filters. You can set the length of the trail, opacity, and directional angle.

Swirl

Swirl is perhaps the best filter in Black Box/Eye Candy. It maintains the overall imagery of the picture, but renders it as if it where a picture of randomly placed whirlpools of color. You can choose the space and smear length of the pools, and the twist intensity, streak detail, and how warped the overall image should be. Smoothness can also be added to reduce graininess.

New Filters In Eye Candy

Eye Candy should be out by the time this book is released. It will include all the filters from Black Box—plus Fire, Fur, Chrome, Polygon, Antimatter, Vibrate, Warpo, Water Drops, and more.

FRACTAL DESIGN PAINTER

Fractal Design Painter combines image processing with an extensive computer paint package to create a unique product that many digital camera users might find extremely useful. By implementing image processing techniques, Fractal Design Painter actually allows you to mimic styles of painting, such as oil painting, charcoal, and impressionistic. With Fractal Design Painter's unique tracing paper method, you can use digital photos as the catalyst for the creation of unique computer art. Fractal Design Painter also supports Adobe Photoshop plug-ins, and contains many of the basic color imaging capabilities and basic filter capabilities of most photo imaging programs.

The following sections describe some of the basic and unique techniques available with Fractal Design Painter.

Basic Filters And Color Effects

FDP offers embossing, sharpening, motion blur, glass distortion, excellent lighting effects, and distortion effects that can morph part of a picture into weird shapes or growths. You can also apply unique textures to your image to give it a look as if the photo was printed on a distinct surface, such as canvas or grainy paper.

Mimic Many Art Styles

At the heart of Fractal Design Painter is the ability to create computer artwork that has the look of many traditional forms of artwork, such as pencil sketch, felt pen, or chalk. You can use Fractal's clone and tracing mode to literally paint over a picture, which transforms the photo into this art style.

Because you must do this by hand, you can control stroke directions and other nuances that give you more control than a blanket filter.

There are 11 specific cloning art styles:

- Felt Pen
- Pencil Sketch
- Hairy Brush
- Oil Brush
- Chalk
- Hard Oil
- Van Gogh
- Melt
- Driving Rain
- Soft Airbrush
- Impressionist

Hand-Made Tessellations And Mosaics

Two of the most powerful transformations you can accomplish with FDP are making mosaics and stain glassed (tessellation) paintings. The amount of control you can have over the size, shape, and direction of these geometric art forms is unreal.

Hand Detail

Fractal Design Painter is an excellent package to add to your imaging software library after you've already purchased a top-notch package, such as LivePicture or Photoshop. With FDP in your toolbox, you not only add some unique imaging effects but you also get some fine hand tools. The ability to use FDP to add a unique "by-hand" style to your digital photos and collages is unparalleled at this time.

If you want to stay up on all the latest and greatest options available with Fractal Design Painter, check out *Artistry Magazine*, which is published 10 times a year and is packed with information about FDP. A one-year subscription costs $49.95. To subscribe, send a check or money order in U.S. funds drawn on a U.S. bank, made payable to *Artistry, the news-letter*, to Karen Sperling, P.O. Box 8895, Calabasas, CA 91372-8895. The phone number for the magazine is 818-878-0853. Their fax number is 818-878-0856. You can mail, fax, or email (artistry@artnet.net) a credit card number to subscribe. Specify the type of card (Visa or Mastercard), card number, expiration date, name on the card, and the number of years you wish to subscribe.

KAI'S POWER GOO

We'll cover Kai's Power Goo in far more detail in Chapter 12. Although it's marketed (and for good reason) as a fun product, it does deserve serious status in your image-manipulation toolbox.

Kai's Power Goo is the best morphing tool available for growing, shrinking, moving, smearing, smudging, nudging, and smoothing a picture in realtime by hand. If you have an object that you're looking to ply into weird forms, Power Goo might be the tool for you.

IMAGE CONSULTANT IN A BOX: INTRODUCING INTELLIHANCE

Intellihance from Extensis is a unique Photoshop plug-in tool that you might want to try. Many of us who enjoy digital photography aren't Photoshop or imaging experts. Although we can spot and solve big problems and make a plethora of adjustments to a picture, getting an image "just right" can be time consuming and difficult. That's why Extensis created Intellihance. The product is sort of a built-in imaging consultant. Intellihance (as seen in Figures 7.6 and 7.7) lets you adjust a multitude of characteristics simultaneously, such as contrast, noise, color tone, and more. Then, when you're satisfied with the results, the product will analyze your current image and then, using the preferences you've set, it will apply a litany of Adobe filters to the image until the result is just like you've specified.

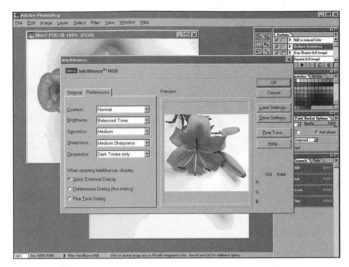

Figure 7.6

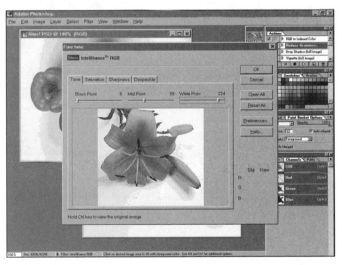

Figure 7.7

Intellihance from Extensis (Mac, above and IBM, below) allows
you to set many parameters at once, and then it analyzes the image and
uses the best approach possible to enhance the image based on those parameters.

Intellihance's interface makes it easy to preview the effects of adjusting a picture with a series of filters all at once, and the product speeds up the tweaking process considerably. After you've converted an image, you can always continue to apply single filters and color adjustments until you're completely satisfied.

SITES WORTH VISITING

Photoshop Techniques

http://the-tech.mit.edu/KPT/Techniques

Photoshop Techniques is a magazine published by Swanson Tech Support. At this site, you can find back issues in Adobe Acrobat format.

Photoshop Tips & Tricks Magazine

http://199.224.94.160/Photoshop

At this site, you can subscribe to the magazine, read sample articles, and sign up for a free first issue.

Ventana's Photoshop Page

http://www.vmedia.com/vvc/onlcomp/phshpfx/resource.htm

Ventana Communications has an extensive Web page of links to vital information, tips, and tricks about Photoshop.

Photoshop Sites

http://www.fns.net/~almateus/photos.htm

This site contains Photoshop news, and information about filters and plug-ins, as well as digital photography in general.

Fractal Design Painter

http://rezso.sote.hu/users/andras/Painter.htm

At this site, you'll find some good information about FDP, including an excellent article on how to make Mosaic paints with FDP.

Hot Photoshop Tips

http://www.publish.com/0895/tips/imageediting/index.html

Sponsored by *Publish Magazine,* this Web page is filled with tips on how to use Photoshop to enhance images and fix common problems in photos.

If You Want To Learn More…

There are dozens of great books about Photoshop and other imaging packages and image-processing techniques. Here is a selection of the ones we've looked at and like the most. I truly love the Wow! series from Peachpit Press; these books are especially useful for approaching various digital imaging tasks using helpful projects.

Professional Photoshop by Daniel Margulis (published by John Wiley & Sons, 1995, ISBN 0-4710-187-32)

Adobe Photoshop Handbook by Mark Siprut (published by Random House, 1995, ISBN 0-6797-532-57)

Photoshop F/X by Cathy Abes (published by Ventana Communications, 1994, ISBN 1-566041-79-1)

The Photoshop 4 Wow! Book by Linnea Dayton and Jack Davis (published by Peachpit Press, 1997, ISBN 02-01688-57-3 [Windows], ISBN 02-01688-56-5 [Mac])

The Painter Wow! Book by Cher Threinen-Pendarvis and Jim Benson (published by Peachpit Press, 1995, ISBN 1-566091-47-0)

Fractal Design Painter 4 Complete by Karen Sperling (published by MIS Press, 1996, ISBN 1-558284-82-6)

Fractal Design Painter: Advanced Tips, Tools & Techniques by Sherry London (published by Ventana Communications, 1997, ISBN 1-566045-03-7)

Live Picture Revealed by Josh Karson (published by Hayden Books, 1996, ISBN 1-568302-63-0)

Kai's Power Tools: Filters and Effects by Heinz Schuller (published by New Riders, 1995, ISBN 1-562054-80-5)

Kai's Power Tools 3: An Illustrated Guide by Nick Clarke (published by Peachpit Press, 1997, ISBN 0-201688-09-3)

Storing And Sending

Camera Images

8

A digital camera brings new meaning to

the phrase "hard drive" and the word

"email." The amount of space that digital

pictures require is immense by comparison

with other documents, like text files, spread-

sheets, or even database files; a few ses-

sions of downloaded photos can easily fill

an already crowded hard drive.

And the popularity of digital cameras has already transformed "email" into "photomail" for millions of people who are, or will soon be, emailing pictures to friends, relatives, and business associates around the globe. Some users simply load several pictures onto a disk and send them via regular mail. But the issue of space is still the same: How do you cram dozens of megabytes of images onto a disk that can be sent via the post office? (Hint: Don't use diskettes. Stay tuned....)

This chapter explains what you need to know about the electronic preservation of your pictures. Here's what we'll cover:

- How to efficiently store your photos on your hard drive, and how to back them up

- How to send your photos via email to other interested parties

- How to store your photos on removable media for mailing

- How to post your photos on various online forums and on the Usenet

- The best places to post your photos

- Software that helps you electronically organize your photos

Storing Photos

The primary destination for your downloaded photos is probably going to be your hard drive. But after you've downloaded a few sessions worth of photos, you'll probably realize that this approach is going to create storage problems. Your hard drive has to store files for other applications, not just your photos, and it doesn't take many photos to crowd out other applications and files on your hard drive. So, you'll probably want to invest in some form of extensive archiving device.

This approach isn't even very expensive. For most people, it means purchasing an iomega Zip or Jaz drive (costs are $200 or less for a Zip drive; $500 or less for the higher-capacity Jaz drives). These drives use removable disk cartridges that can store from 100 MB to over 1 GB of data per cartridge. Tape backup devices used to be popular for archiving massive quantities of electronic data, but they're rapidly going the way of the dinosaur. Tape drives aren't much cheaper than removable-cartridge drives, and they're much slower. Trust us, you don't want to purchase a tape drive for archiving your images. Instead look into the following products.

If you haven't already done so, it's a good idea to create a specific directory on your hard drive for storing your photos—at least until you purchase a removable-cartridge drive. Another piece of advice: Create separate subdirectories to keep separate the raw and processed copies of photos.

Zip Drive

iomega Corporation
1821 West Iomega Way
Roy, UT 84607
Phone: 1-800-MY-STUFF
Web address: www.iomega.com

Introduced in 1995, the Zip drive instantly became a hit product. It is a high-capacity storage or backup device that works just like a floppy drive. The unit cost is between $150 and $200, depending on your purchase location and rebates. Each cartridge holds 100 MB of data. Cartridges currently sell for between $14.95 and $19.95, depending on how many you buy.

Jaz Drive

iomega Corporation
1821 West Iomega Way
Roy, UT 84607
Phone: 1-800-MY-STUFF
Web address: www.iomega.com

If you're looking for a more extensive archiving system, you might consider the Zip drive's bigger brother—the Jaz drive. This product, also from iomega, sells for about $499 (plus around $100 for an interface), and each cartridge holds up to 1 GB of information (10 Zip disks). The cartridges for a Jaz drive sell for about $125 apiece (or less if you buy in packages of 5 cartridges or more). If you're going to be taking lots of high-resolution photos, or even many hundreds of lower-resolution photos, a Jaz drive might be more economical in the long run than a Zip drive.

SyQuest Cartridges

SyQuest Technology, Inc.
47071 Bayside Parkway
Fremont, CA 94538
Phone: 510-226-4000
Fax: 510-226-4102
Web address: www.syquest.com

For some of the fastest mass storage available on removable cartridges for both the Mac and PC, check out SyQuest's new EZFlyer 230 drive, which sells for about $400. Cartridges, which can store from 135 MB to 230 MB of data, cost from $20 to $30. The major advantage of the EZFlyer: A Zip drive can transfer up to 1.44 MB of data per second, whereas the EZFlyer can transfer up to 2.4 MB per second. The downside of the EZFlyer is that the Zip drive is becoming more popular and widely used, so if you want to exchange photos with other users or give them to service bureaus for professional output, you'll find it easier to locate users who have Zip drives than SyQuest drives.

MCD Drive

Nomai
4301 Oak Circle, #20
Boca Raton, FL 33431
Phone: 1-800-55-NOMAI
Fax: 407-391-8675

If you want to combine speed with mass storage, you'll certainly want to consider the MCD drive from Nomai. This drive, which retails for about $580, stores 540 MB of data on each cartridge. Although that's less storage than a Jaz drive, consider this: The MCD drive has a blazingly fast transfer rate of 8.5 MB of data per second (compared with 5.53 MB per second for a Jaz drive). Another advantage of the MCD drive is that you can make the cartridges SyQuest compatible (44 MB, 88 MB, and 270 MB) in order to exchange data with SyQuest users. The MCD drive comes in SCSI or parallel connection flavors.

Vertex Drive

Pinnacle Micro, Inc.
19 Technology
Irvine, CA 92718
Phone: 800-553-7070
Phone: 714-789-3000 (international)
Fax: 714-789-3150
Web address: www.pinnacle-micro.com

Now we're talking *mass* storage. In our opinion, most 650 MB rewritable optical drives offer little advantage over a Jaz drive. They typically cost more and store less. However, the Vertex optical hard drive from Pinnacle Micro has raised the competitive bar a bit. The Vertex drive stores 2.6 GB on each removable optical disk cartridge, and at $1,500, the Vertex drive isn't cheap. But if you want virtually unlimited storage space for your images, this is the drive to have. Each rewritable optical cartridge costs about $190.

To ensure the safety of your most precious photos, consider doing a large backup every so often and placing the cartridges in a safe deposit or fire-safe box. According to some of our research, the one thing people fear losing most during a catastrophe is their collection of family photos. There's no reason to delay these backups because you can make as many electronic copies of a digital photo as you want, at no extra cost (unlike film photos).

PHOTO ORGANIZING

One thing you quickly learn with a digital camera is that, before you know it, you've got hundreds of photo files scattered across your hard drive, and you can't figure out what's where. After you've got cartridge after cartridge of archived material, and you can't figure out which cartridge contains that favorite photo you took on your Yosemite trip last fall, you're going to become annoyed. To prevent these problems, you'll want to consider purchasing some special organizing software and consider some simple tips for organizing your photos.

Organizing Programs

A software organizing program is a browsing package that displays your graphics files as a thumbnail (a small, low-resolution image). This way, you don't need to open each image to determine its content—a big timesaver when deciding where to store or archive photos. Instead, by reviewing thumbnails, you can easily swap photos between directories, delete un-wanted photos, copy photos, and so on. An organizer is basically a multimedia file manager. A good PC program that fits this bill is JASC's Media Center, shown in Figure 8.1. Extensis's Fetch (formerly Adobe Fetch), shown in Figure 8.2, will do the same for Macintosh users.

Media Center

JASC, Inc.
P.O. Box 44997
Eden Prairie, MN 55344

Phone: 612-930-9171
Fax: 612-930-9172
Web address: www.jasc.com

Figure 8.1
JASC's Media Center.

Figure 8.2
Extensis's Fetch.

Media Center is an excellent organizing package for your Windows PC. It understands most graphics file formats, plus it supports MIDI and WAV files as well as other media file types that you may find on the Internet or from other graphics sources. Media Center displays a thumbnail of each image in a giant window, and you can organize materials into albums and topics to easily track photos on your hard drive or archived cartridges. Media Center is available as a shareware download from the JASC Web site. Upgrading to the registered commercial version costs $39.

Fetch

Extensis, Inc.
55 South West Yamhill St., Fourth Floor
Portland, OR 97204
Phone: 503-274-2020
Fax: 503-274-0530
Web address: www.extensis.com

This product was known as Adobe Fetch before Extensis bought the program and lowered its price to $99.95. Extensis is in the process of upgrading the product and staffing up to support it. Fetch is an excellent tool for organizing all your digital photos on the Mac. (By the way, don't confuse this product with Dartmouth University's Fetch program, which is an FTP tool.)

Organizing Tips

There are many things you can do to better organize the many photos you've taken and downloaded:

- Back up regularly: Constantly remind yourself to back up your photos. If you have only one copy of an important photo, that's one copy too few.

- Archive constantly: Store only the most useful and current photos on your hard drive, and archive the rest. Don't wait for files to build up on your hard drive over time; instead, immediately archive images that you don't intend to use. Why? If you do this immediately, the memory of each picture's characteristics is fresh in your mind. Then, you can add explicit notes to each photo file when you archive. These notes will help you quickly find and retrieve photos that you want to use later (sometimes years later).

- Add notes about photos whenever possible: This is an extension of the previous tip: You may want to keep a separate database, using a program like Access or Filemaker Pro, that contains the name of each photo, and a series of comment fields to search by. By adding notes such as lighting conditions and where and when you took your photos, you can pinpoint favorable conditions under which to take digital photos, and you can more easily locate photos that you want to recall.

- Give your photos descriptive file names: One fundamental rule for organizing many similar files on a computer: Devise a file-naming system that describes your files accurately, then stick with this system. For instance, you might save each file with a name that describes the date on which the picture was taken (for instance, P12-2-96), or name files according to subject—animal1.tif, landscape2.tif, and so on. Creating descriptive file names with Windows 95 is especially easy, because you're not limited to the 11-character file names enforced by DOS. This luxury, however, brings one hazard: Long file names encourage some users to ramble rather than to be concise. "I took this one at dawn at Yosemite" is not a good file name.

A Gallery Of Possibilities

The following color pages illustrate the heart and soul of digital camera photo-editing possibilities. We've run some typical low-end photos through the type of popular image-editing and transforming packages available, and came up with some out-of-the-ordinary results.

This section should serve as a menu for you to view what's out there for your photos. Most of the lower end cameras come with a simple processing package, however, you'll see that there a host of other packages that may be bought separately, with features that can give you hours of fun with your digital photos.

Artistic Filters

Some of the best filters to use are "artistic" filters, which render your photos in different art forms. All of these were done with Adobe Photoshop filters, except the Hotwax picture, done with JASC's Paint Shop Pro.

Watercolor

Original photo
taken with Kodak DC50

Sponge

Dry Brush

Fresco

Film Grain

Smudge Stick

Rough Pastels

Underpainting

Poster Edges

Cutout

Plastic Wrap

Paint Daubs

Neon Glow

Hotwax

Palette Knife

Brush Strokes

Adobe Photoshop's Brush Stroke filters simulate painted effects that are a result of various brush strokes and techniques that printers commonly use.

Original photo
taken with Olympus 200L

Accented Edges

Angles Strokes

Crosshatch

Dark Strokes

Ink Outlines

Spatter

Sprayed Strokes

Sumi-e

Some additional effects capable with Photoshop, Eye Candy, and Fractal Design Painter are shown here.

Original photo

taken with Kodak DC50

Adobe Photoshop's Glowing Edges filter

Eye Candy's Swirl filter

Felt Pen Brush, Fractal Design Painter

Stylize

Stylize filters produce effects that use a combination of pixel movement and high contrast color schemes to create interesting effects, such as emboss and solarize.

Original photo
taken with Kodak DC40
Photo courtesy Nicole Colon

Colorize

Adjust Curves

Emboss

Solarize

Pixelate

Adobe's Pixelate filters let you adjust the image to create pixelated photos—imagery that is composed of large areas of equivalent color.

Original photo
taken with Kodak DC40
Photo courtesy Nicole Colon

Pointillize

Facet

Mosaic

Fragment

Pixel Wind

Crystallize

KPT & Alien Skin Filters

Two of the most well known filter packages are Alien Skin Software's Eye Candy and Kai's Power Tools. Shown here are some of the more interesting filters from each package.

Original photo taken with Olympus 300L

KPT Pixel

KPT Page Turner

KPT Vortex

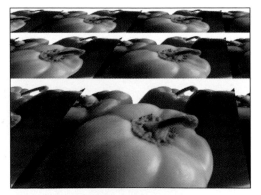

KPT Planar Tiling

KPT Twirl

Special Effects

Fractal Design Painter allows you to mimic a number of art styles. Using a digital photograph as a base, you can create many different styles. All of the Fractal Design effects shown—Mosaic, Stained Glass, and Impressionist—are hand painted. After setting a style, you use the brush to paint over the photograph, and your strokes are converted into the style you choose. Fractal Design Painter also has distortion filters, and it can work with any Adobe Photoshop-compatible filter, too. With the Adobe Photoshop effects below—Convedges, Convreli, and Chrome—you can produce some unique images. Paint Shop Pro's Hotwax filter is another simple effect with a big impact.

Original photo taken with Olympus 300L

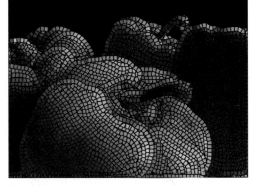

Mosaic

Convreli

Convedges

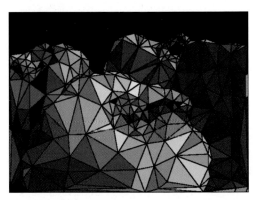

Stained Glass

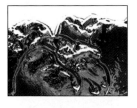

Chrome

Hotwax

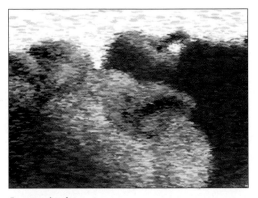

Impressionist

Sketch Filters

Adobe's Sketch filters allow you to render your photos in various monochromatic art styles.

*Original
photo
taken with
Kodak DC50*

Bas Relief

Chalk & Charcoal

Conte Crayon

Graphic Pen

Chrome

Photocopy

Reticulation

Plaster

Stamp

Torn Edges

Water Paper

Note Paper

Halftone

Image Adjustment

You can achieve a number of effects without filters by manipulating the color of an image. Under the "Image" menu option in Photoshop, go to "Adjust" to alter hues, saturation levels, contrast, and color balance.

Original photo
taken with Kodak DC50

Brightness/Contrast

Color Balance

Colorize

Curves

Kai's Power Goo

By far the funkiest program for creating new works from your digital camera pictures is Kai's Power Goo, which lets you twist, smudge, twirl, grow, and shrink your pictures, all in realtime.

Original photo taken with Casio QV10A

Goo in action.

Squeeze down for a fat-head effect.

Grow it.

Twirl it.

Bulge it in.

Bulge it out.

Squeeze up for a big-brain effect.

Gallery

The previous pages showed you the purist form of filter application, but the fun part is applying multiple color changes and filters to your photographs for truly wild effects.

Kai's Power Tools offers a cool effect called Vortex. This flower shot was cropped, sharpened, and saturated using Photoshop. This picture was shot with an Olympus 200L camera.

Here we've created a very dramatic image. In Photoshop the original was inverted and then a KPT filter called "scatter horizontal" was applied to give the object fuzzy edges. The original photo was taken with a Kodak DC50.

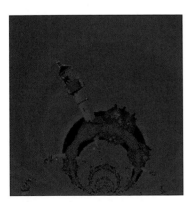

Believe it or not, this used to be a landscape photo of a light house. First, we applied the KPT Vortex Tiling filter, then "adjust curves" to enhance the color, and finally cropped the image to simplify it and give it a focal point. The original photo was taken with a Kodak DC50.

Above: *Using Photoshop, clouds were rendered, two photos were sharpened and merged, and then a canvas texture was added for further effect. Lastly we drew in the "string" to connect the hand to the air balloon.* ***Left:*** *Again using Photoshop, the balloon was stylized with the extrude option and then "adjust curves" was applied. Both original shots were taken with a Kodak DC50.*

To texturize this photo, we sharpened it initially in Photoshop, and increased the effect by running it through the sharpen edges and edge angle filters provided by MetaTools Convolver. Then we applied the Hot Wax filter, using Paint Shop Pro. Finally, we cropped the photo to increase its impact. This picture was shot with a Kodak DC50.

This picture was created by pixelating the skyline of a sunset photo in successively smaller squares for a digital look. Then, from Kai's Power Tools, Planar Tiling and Page Curl were added. This picture was shot with a Kodak DC50.

Creating an antique look isn't too hard. First, convert your photo to black and white, then give it a yellow tint. Pass it through a noise filter, and once through a film grain filter for your final rendering. This picture was shot with a Kodak DC50.

This photo was enhanced by using KPT Gradient Designer in Photoshop. The applied gradient is a combination of a transluscent radial sweep and a pattern called "Jade Sector with Waves." The original photo was taken with an Olympus 300L.

Kai's Convolver has a Mutate option that applies a random set of filter effects. The result is an Andy Warhol-style picture. This picture was shot with a Casio QV10A.

Screen Shots Of The Programs In Action

This section was brought to you by…

Eye Candy from Alien Skin Software

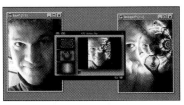

Kai's Power Tools from MetaTools

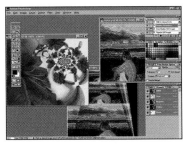

Photoshop by Adobe

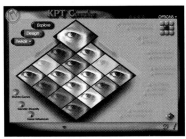

Kai's Convolver from MetaTools

Intellihance from Extensis

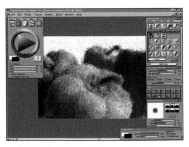

Fractal Design Painter from Fractal Design

Paint Shop Pro from JASC, Inc.

Comparing The Cameras

The images in this section represent the full spectrum of cameras and

photo capabilities that are available to create digital photography.

We've taken great care to prevent this from being a showcase of work

by professional photographers (although some professional photogra-

phy is included). Instead, we want to show what is possible at a range

of levels, from amateur to photography buff to consummate profes-

sional. For most images, we've included the resolution at which the

image was captured, along with the image's storage requirements.

Keep in mind that most digital images are in a compressed format.

That means the amount of hard disk storage will be different from the

amount of memory space required to load and open the image. Where

possible, we provide you with both the hard disk and memory storage

requirements for the photos in this color section.

Low-Resolution Images

"Low resolution" generally refers to any image that is smaller than 640×480 in resolution.

This photo was taken at one of the lowest resolutions available with a digital camera—320×240 with the Epson PhotoPC. This low-cost camera is currently one of the most popular cameras available to consumers. Amateur photographers from 8 to 80 can all achieve outstanding results with this camera. In fact, this photo was taken by a budding photographer who at this writing is still waiting for her ninth birthday. Even at such a low resolution, the lighting contrast that she achieved between the mountains and the sky is excellent. (File size: 16 K on disk, 225 K in memory.)

Desert, low resolution
Photo courtesy Brittney Hafeli

Here's another photo taken at low resolution (320×240) with the Epson PhotoPC. Although the facial detail of the subject is weak, the colors of the sky, mountains, trees, and earth are true. (File size: 23 K on disk, 225 K in memory.)

Ghost Mountain, low resolution

Medium-Resolution Images

Medium-resolution images typically range from 640×480 to 800×600 resolution.

This outdoor photo was taken with the Epson PhotoPC at its 640×480 resolution setting. Notice the shift in contrast as your eye moves from the left side of the photo to the right side, indicating the different manner in which the camera handles outdoor and indoor (or shaded) light. (File size: 49 K on disk, 900 K in memory.)

Fruit, medium resolution
Photo courtesy Epson Corporation

Flowers, medium resolution
and low resolution

These nearly identical photos were taken at different resolutions with the same camera—the Epson PhotoPC. The photo at the bottom right shows the result of taking the photo at the camera's lowest resolution. The larger image shows what can be achieved by setting the camera at the higher (680×480) resolution.

Leaves, medium resolution
Photo courtesy Epson Corporation

The Epson PhotoPC also does a good job at focusing on images at close-up range, as this photo shows. The composition of this photo is interesting, too, because it seems to move from summer to fall to winter. Notice that the tree in the background, left, still has all its green color. The close-up of the leaves in the center of the image is in full fall foliage, while the tree in the background, right, has shed all of its leaves. (File size: 63 K on disk, 900 K in memory.)

This photo, even though it was taken under minimal lighting situations, shows some very nice gradations in color in both the sky and the water. The dark tree line, with intermittent house lights shining through, makes a nice separator between the sky and the water. There are actually houses in the foreground; however, because the camera emphasizes objects that are lighted, they are almost impossible to see and help the viewer to focus on the reflected light in the bay. The digital camera's thirst for light also gives the urban lighting a glowing effect, which helps to punctuate the muted tones of the photo. This photo was taken with a Kodak DC50 camera at 756×504 resolution. (File size: 990 K on disk, 1.9 MB in memory.)

Sunset, medium resolution

Imagine how this image would look without the presence of the lobster boat, which turns an otherwise nice sunrise into an exciting and well-balanced composition. Amateur photographers are often surprised to discover that a natural scene that looks beautiful to the eye can appear mundane when it's photographed. To avoid these disappointments when you shoot scenic photography with your digital camera, look for objects that will stand out and give the eye something unique to focus on. We also cheated a bit on this one by adding some Photoshop effects to give the photo a more surreal, painting-like effect—but that's one of the tremendous advantages of digital photography. The image-editing effects we used also increased the size and resolution of the image slightly. The image was taken with a Kodak DC50 camera and the final resolution of the image was 1019×461. (File size: 985 K on disk, 1.3 MB in memory.)

Morning, medium resolution

High-Resolution Images

High-resolution images typically refer to anything at or above 800×600, and currently include images in resolutions as high as 4096×4096.

Playground, high resolution
Photo courtesy Polaroid Corporation

This image illustrates the color clarity, contrast, and subtle hues that can be achieved with the high-resolution Polaroid PDC 2000. This shot was taken at 800×600 resolution, so technically, it barely qualifies as a high-resolution image. However, the results in this photo are striking. The focus is on the light reflected on the metal bar in the foreground; but, many of the other bars and objects in the photo appear to be amazingly sharp. (File size: 1.1 MB on disk, 1.3 MB in memory.)

Sunflower, high resolution
Photo courtesy Polaroid Corporation

The detail that can be achieved with the Polaroid PDC 2000 is truly remarkable. This image demonstrates how well this camera can reproduce a close-up image, at 1600×1200 resolution. However, expect your hard disk to pay dearly for storing images of such high resolution. (File size: 3.3 MB on disk, 5.5 MB in memory.)

Carousel, high resolution

Photo courtesy Polaroid Corporation

This image contains some subtle contrast that most digital cameras can't achieve. Notice the objects that appear next to the horses' legs at the bottom right of the photo. This image was taken at 1600 ×1200 resolution on the Polaroid PDC 2000. (File size: 5.5 MB on disk, 5.5 MB in memory.)

This photo was taken with the Dicomed Big Shot 4000 camera, a professional, extremely high-resolution camera that is popular among photographers who shoot images for full-color print advertisements. Notice how well this image shows differences in flesh tones. The inset image of the model's left eye shows the detail that can be achieved with this camera.

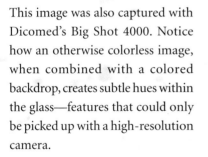

Model, high resolution
Photo courtesy Dicomed

This image was also captured with Dicomed's Big Shot 4000. Notice how an otherwise colorless image, when combined with a colored backdrop, creates subtle hues within the glass—features that could only be picked up with a high-resolution camera.

Lemon with Cherry, high resolution
Photo courtesy Dicomed

Business Ideas

These three images show how two photos—one a full shot of a bouquet and the other a close-up of the bouquet—can be combined to create a more interesting advertising composition. Both images were shot using a Kodak DC50. (File size of combined photos: 128 K on disk, 312 K in memory.)

1.

2.

3.

Photos courtesy Eastman Kodak

Shoes, medium resolution
Photo courtesy Eastman Kodak Company

This shot provides an interesting way to combine a product shot with other objects to show both perspective and color quality, and to enhance the attractiveness of the product itself. This image was taken with a Kodak DCS 460 professional-level camera. To fit within a small, product frame, this product shot has been sampled down to a 200×300 pixel dimension from an original, high-resolution image of 2036×3060 (original file size, 18 MB). (Final file size: 24 K on disk, 175 K in memory.)

This image, shot with the Epson PhotoPC, demonstrates how you can show off your corporate headquarters, storefront, or other place of business using a digital camera. Such images can be used in advertisements, professional business reports, on letterhead, in slide shows, and much more. This image was shot at 640×480 resolution. (File size: 53 K on disk, 900 K in memory.)

Corporate building
Photo courtesy Epson Corporation

The shots below, also shot with the Epson PhotoPC, illustrate the way realtors and apartment owners can use digital photos to show off their properties—or how you can use a digital camera to help sell your own home. Ideally, outdoor shots of property should be taken on a clear day when the sun is fairly high in the sky and behind you. Of course, it isn't always possible to have such optimal conditions when you need to take photos. However, that's one of the advantages of digital photography—you can easily adjust lighting conditions through the use of image-editing techniques. The images here were taken under a cloudy sky, when lighting was not ideal. To correct this problem, an image-editing program was used to boost both the brightness and contrast of the images. These two sets of images show both the before and after results of editing for lighting. (File sizes: 69 K on disk, 900 K in memory.)

Apartment, dim lighting   *Apartment*, bright lighting

House, dim lighting   *House*, bright lighting

Scientific Photos

The photos on the following two pages use homemade "Cookbook" cameras that can be attached to telescopes, microscopes, and other viewing devices to take color, digital photos. The Cookbook camera is actually two CCD cameras described in a book titled *The CCD Camera Cookbook* by Viekko Kanto, John Munger, and Richard Berry. One camera uses the inexpensive TC211 CCD chip, so it is called the Cookbook 211. The other camera uses the larger and more sensitive Texas Instruments TC245 CCD chip and is called the Cookbook 245. Both CCDs are made by Texas Instruments. The book contains step-by-step instructions and computer software for building and using both CCD cameras.

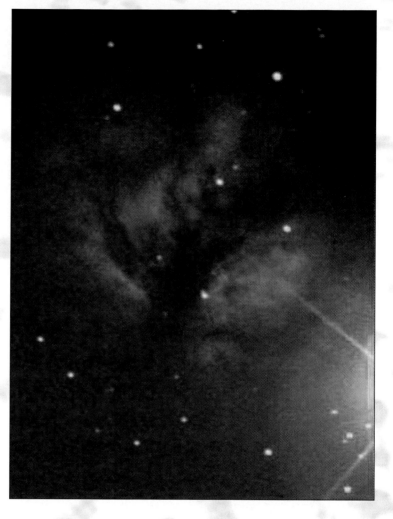

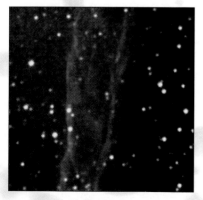

This page shows various photos taken by astronomers using a Cookbook camera attached to personal or observatory telescopes. The typical cost to build a Cookbook astronomy camera is as little as $250. The cameras run software programs that specially process the pictures. Many people who use the Cookbook camera run the software on notebook or laptop computers so that they can cart the camera and their telescope to a remote place away from city lights. Cookbook cameras can produce exceedingly amazing imagery. However, imagery is usually captured not in split seconds as with regular cameras, but over the course of 30 seconds to several minutes while the CCD array intensely scans the scene. (File sizes vary, but most are at low resolutions—under 640×480.)

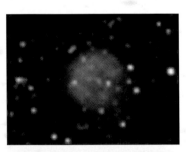

All Cookbook photos courtesy Richard Berry

Make sure each name will help you remember what the image is when searching for it years later.

- Constantly delete poor photos and duplicates: It's important to spend time culling and deleting poor or unneeded photos from your overall collection. Not every picture is a "keeper." Even if you have unlimited storage space (yeah, right), review your photos from time to time and delete those that you don't have any use for. This not only frees up storage space, but it also makes it easier to find the photos you do look at frequently.

- Print thumbnails and place them in a binder: Purchase a large, three-ring binder and, from time to time, print your thumbnails. Then, organize them in the binder. Because a printout of each thumbnail includes the file name, the image is easy to retrieve.

- Name each storage medium: If you archive your images to Zip or Jaz cartridges, make sure you electronically include a volume name for each cartridge. This volume name can be included with your thumbnails or in your database of photo names. Then, physically write the volume name on a label affixed to the cartridge. This procedure will make it easier to find a cartridge that you want, especially after your archive library has grown to a dozen cartridges or more.

WinZip And StuffIt: The Art Of Collection And Compression

If you're already an email expert, you're no doubt familiar with Zip files (most prevalent on the PC/Windows platform) or StuffIt files (most prevalent on the Mac platform). If you aren't familiar with these archiving programs, you need to learn about them as soon as possible. They're essential tools for sending photos via email or for storing a lot of photos on a disk or cartridge.

WinZip and StuffIt solve two problems: You can use WinZip or StuffIt to collect a number of photos into one file so that you don't have to attach photos to a number of separate emails. Second, these programs compress the information to make the file as small as possible so that you spend less time sending the file. Several compressed large images can also fit on one diskette.

After your images are sent, the recipient can download or copy the file and unZip or unStuff them, at which point they're separated into individual files and expanded back to full size. This method of sending files is so common that some online programs, such as America Online, actually unZip or unStuff a file automatically after it has been downloaded.

In other cases, though, your recipient will have to use the WinZip or StuffIt Expander. It is also possible to create a file, called a Self-Expanding Archive, that will automatically extract itself. For more information on the way WinZip and StuffIt work, see Chapter 6.

Where To Get WinZip And StuffIt

Here's where to find compression and uncompression software online—for both PC and Mac users.

WinZip

Nico Mak Computing, Inc.
P.O. Box 919
Bristol, CT 06011
Web address: www.winzip.com

WinZip is free to download; however, if you use it frequently, Nico Mak requests that you send a shareware fee.

StuffIt

Aladdin Systems, Inc.
165 Westridge Drive
Watsonville, CA 95076
Phone: 408-761-6200
Fax: 408-761-6206
Web address: www.aladdinsys.com

Several versions of StuffIt are available. At Aladdin's Web site, you can download the StuffIt Expander programs for free, in both Mac and PC versions. The other commercial versions of StuffIt must be ordered from Aladdin by phone.

RUNNING WINZIP TO CREATE A ZIP FILE

Step
1
Determine the files you want to send
Save the files in the format you or your recipient wishes them to be in.

Step
2
Launch WinZip and begin a new archive
Click on the New button in WinZip and type a name for the Zip file. In this example, we'll name our file Example.Zip. Click on OK when you're done. The WinZip title bar should display the name of this new Zip file.

Step
3
Add the names of the photos you want to send
For each file, click on the Add button and then choose from the dialog box the name of the file you wish to add. You'll notice at the bottom of the File Add dialog that you can choose a compression style. Normal compression is fine in most cases, but sometimes you might want to choose Maximum for particularly large files. Repeat this for each file you want to add.

Step
4
Close the archive
When you've completed your archive, choose Close Archive from the File menu. Your Zip file is now ready to be sent.

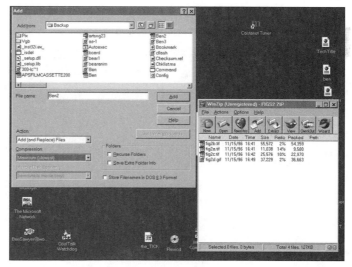

Figure 8.3
WinZip in action.

Running WinZip To UnZip A Zip File

Step
1

Receive or download the Zipped file and run WinZip

Once you've either received the file from email, downloaded it from the Web or online service, or copied it to a disk, start WinZip.

Step
2

Open the Zip file you want to unZip

Choose Open from the Zip file toolbar and select the file you want to unZip from the File dialog. After you've selected the Zip file you want, a list of the files that are in the Zip file will appear in the WinZip window.

Step
3

Select file and choose Extract

With WinZip, you can choose the file you want to extract, and either extract it (by clicking the Extract icon) or simply load it directly from the Zip file into your editing program.

Using StuffIt (For Mac Users) To Compress Files

Note: To perform this project, you must have a version of StuffIt (such as StuffIt Deluxe) that allows you to compress files.

Step
1

Locate the files

Use the Finder to click on a directory that contains the files you want to Stuff.

Step
2

Start StuffIt

Locate the StuffIt program on your hard disk, then double click to launch it.

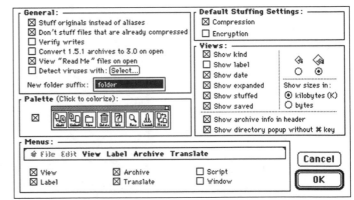

Figure 8.4

StuffIt's options dialog box.

Step 3 *Identify the files that you want to compress*

Click on File|Open, then locate the directory that contains the files you want to compress. Click on the New button to indicate that you want to create a new archive. Give the new archive a name.

Step 4 *Compress the files*

When the StuffIt button bar appears, click on Stuff. In the left side of the dialog box, use the drop-down list box to click on files that you want to Stuff. After you click on each file, click the Add button to indicate that you want to add it to the archive. After you are done, click the Stuff button to Stuff all files into a single SIT archive.

Translate
Change Password...
Convert 1.5.1 Archive

AppleSingle ▶
BinHex4 ▶
btoa/atob ▶
CPT Expand...
DeArc...
MacBinary ▶
PKG Expand...
Segmenting ▶
tar ▶
Text Convert ▶
Unix Compress ▶
UnPack...
UnZip...
UUCode ▶

Figure 8.5
StuffIt's compression choices menu.

UNCOMPRESSING A SIT FILE ON A MAC

Uncompressing a Stuffed file on a Mac is practically child's play, as long as you have some version of unStuffIt on your hard drive.

Step 1 *Open the SIT file that you want to uncompress*

Double click on the SIT file that you want to expand. Your Mac should recognize this as a Stuffed file and automatically launch your version of StuffIt.

Step 2 *Select the files to uncompress*

Hold down the Shift key and click on each file that you want to uncompress within the archive (probably all of them). If you know that you want to uncompress all files, select Edit|Select all from the menu.

Step 3 *Uncompress the files*

After you've selected all files, click on the UnStuff button. StuffIt will uncompress the files. If the program finds any duplicate file names in the directory that you've selected, it will prompt you for permission to overwrite the existing files.

SENDING PICTURES VIA EMAIL

Emailing photos can be tricky. Some email programs don't offer this feature; and some email systems don't support file attachments, while others convert attachments in such a way as to render them virtually unreadable. However, email programs are increasingly being designed to support graphics file attachments.

Step
1
Collect and archive your pictures

If you're only sending one photo, you can send it without Zipping or Stuffing it (as long as it is no larger than 2 MB). If you're sending more than one picture, you should certainly consider Zipping or Stuffing them.

Step
2
Launch your email program

After you've decided which files you want to send and have archived them using WinZip or StuffIt, launch your email package. For this example, we're using Microsoft's Internet Explorer's built-in mail program. After your email package is up and running, sending the file is easy. Simply fill out the To and Subject lines, and then type the body of the message.

Place some data about the picture in the Subject line so that your recipient will know what he or she has when the email arrives. In the message body area, type whatever additional information you want to include with the picture.

Step
3
Attach the file

Almost every email program provides a way to attach a file to an email message. Look for the Attach file menu item in your email program. With Internet Explorer, this option is in the Insert menu item and is available by clicking on the paper clip icon. Doing so will bring up a File dialog box, where you choose or type the name of the file you want to attach. After you've selected the file, click on OK.

Step
4
Send the file and check for errors

When you're satisfied that your note is complete and the correct file is attached, you can send your email. It's a good idea to request that the recipient send a message back to you stating whether the attachment was received successfully. Some email systems include an option that tells you automatically when a recipient has received an email message.

If you're new to the process of attaching and sending files, test this first by sending yourself a file or two.

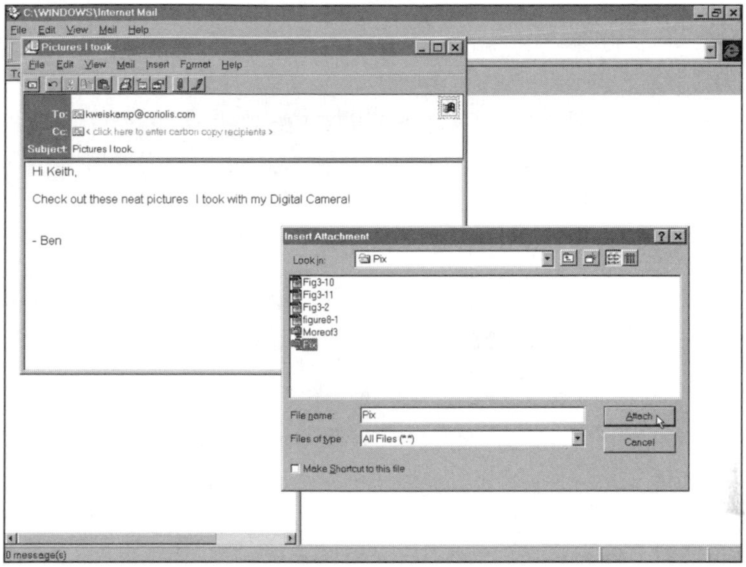

Figure 8.6

Attaching a file in email with Internet Explorer.

Pictures And The Usenet

The Usenet is a collection of Internet newsgroups that work like bulletin boards. Each newsgroup serves a special interest (such as rec.games for game enthusiasts or alt.binaries.animals for people who want to exchange information about pets and other animals). Sometimes, people post pictures to a specific newsgroup. In some cases, a newsgroup (such as alt.binaries.pictures.vehicles) exists solely to trade and post pictures.

Where To Post Pictures

We recommend that you spend some time reading various newsgroups with your online service or Web browser. When posting images to a newsgroup, make sure your pictures fit the specific interest area of the group. When posting to a group that doesn't have an interest in your images, they'll not only be neglected, but you might also get "flamed" with messages from newsgroup users telling you to go elsewhere. (The Internet can be a cruel world.) If a newsgroup includes an FAQ (Frequently Asked Questions) message, make sure the newsgroup's interest area matches the content of your images. After you've found a group that interests you and lets you post pictures (again look for the FAQ first), use the following instructions to post your pictures.

If you want to post an image, select the newsgroups you want to post it to, then add a subject and message note. Then, attach the file. With newsgroups, you'll want to post graphics in either GIF or JPEG form, which can easily be read by many basic newsreaders. See Chapter 6 for more information on file formats.

With many newsgroups, you need to post your pictures as part of a large text message. This requires you to encode the file before you post the message.

Stored, Organized, And Sent

In only a few pages, we've explained the software and hardware you can use to keep all of your digital photos organized and stored properly, and how to email pictures or post them to a newsgroup. A digital camera and digital photos ensure that pictures will never grow old or get damaged, and you can send your images easily anywhere in the world. Although computers and computer communications enable us to work and live farther apart, they can also bring us together in some fascinating ways.

ENCODING PICTURE FILES FOR EMAIL AND NEWSGROUPS

Many email and news servers automatically encode your attachment before it's sent over the Net, and then decodes the message at the other end. However, not all email clients or Usenet news readers are created equal. If you find that the systems you're using don't allow for attachments or seem to mangle them, you might have to do the encoding yourself.

Step
1
Get a good UUEncoding program

UUEncoding is the major way to send image files over the Web through email or to a newsgroup. Good UUEncoding programs are available for both the Mac and PC. On the PC, the most popular Windows program is called Wincode. On the Mac, the most popular program is called UULite.

WinCode is available on the Web at www.membersglobal2000.net/snappy/index.html.

UULite is available on the Web at www.macworld.com/cgi-bin/software.pl/TelecomInternet/Software.518.html.

Step
2
Start your email program

Launch your email application and then type an address, subject, and body text for the message. If you use Eudora mail, make sure you turn off Guess Paragraphs (you can change this feature by clicking the Switch button). If Guess Paragraphs is left on, Eudora will change the carriage returns at the end of all UUEncoded lines to spaces. This will cause most decoders to fail.

Step
3
Run Wincode or UULite

Now you're ready to encode the image that you want to include in your email. We'll use Wincode for this example. After you've launched your encoding application, choose Encode from the File menu.

Step
4
Choose and process the file

One great feature of Wincode is that you can copy the image to be sent directly to your clipboard. The file will be processed and the computer will beep when it's done. The encoded text is now in your computer's memory waiting to be pasted into your email message.

Step *Paste the encoded file into*
5 *your email message*

After you've encoded the image properly, go to the bottom of your message and paste it there. Now click the Send button.

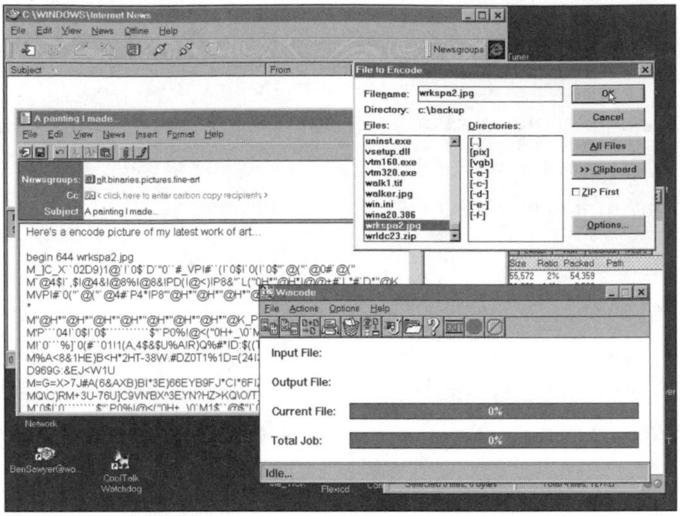

Figure 8.7
Wincode in action.

Digital Camera Projects

9

We've tried to include as much detail in this chapter as possible. However, this is a "what to do" chapter, rather than a "how to do" chapter. For each project, we've outlined a sample idea of how you can use your digital camera to do fun or useful things. In doing so, we offer a few tips, along with the basic information and knowledge we learned by working through each project a few times ourselves.

ABOUT THE PROJECTS

The projects we present in this chapter are not limited to the methods that we used—they just present one means to an end, and there are many ways you can use your digital camera. By reading through these projects, we think you'll begin to realize how versatile your camera really is, and you can dream up entirely new projects to do on your own.

There are many available programs that can be used to work through these projects. We'll showcase several popular packages in this chapter, but with the exception of the very inexpensive Goo program, none of these projects is limited to a specific software package. If you have a decent image-editing package—even one as inexpensive as Paint Shop Pro, PhotoDeluxe, or LivePix—you can do the majority of these projects.

CREATING A PHOTO COLLAGE

My friend's favorite pastime is to take a collection of photos she has taken throughout the year and, with some glue and a large piece of poster board, create a collage of photos. This is a great project to do online with your digital images.

A quick art lesson, first. *Collage* is French for "pasting," and was first initiated by Picasso in 1912, when he pasted printed oilcloth to his "Still Life with Chair Caning." (This piece is on display at the Museum of Modern Art in New York.) Technically speaking, some people reserve the term "collage" to describe a mixture of paintings and pasted objects, where the term *assemblage* is used to describe a final piece of work created entirely from pasted objects. Whatever you choose to call it, what we're about to describe is a lot of fun to do.

Photographing For A Collage

When you're taking pictures for a collage, consider these key points:

- *Shoot to cut*. Make sure the subject of the photo you might be cropping is as big as you can make it.

- *At an event, get many different shots.* Many significant events are temporary, so the more photos you take, the better you'll remember the event and be able to illustrate it for others. Plan ahead for big events and bring a laptop, if possible, or extra PCMCIA cards if your camera accepts them.

- *Shoot for memories.* Take photos that help you remember an event; look for that special photo that really defines the time and place of the event. Capture event-specific imagery, like event posters, or other scenes that could have occurred only at the event.

- *Shoot natural scenes.* It should go without saying that the best shots at family events and other fun gatherings occur when people are *not* posing for pictures.

WORKING WITH PHOTO CLIP ART

Your digital camera need not be your only resource for artwork when you do image-editing projects. In many cases, you'll find that photo clip art can help you out immensely. In fact, merging your digital camera photos with photo-quality artwork can be a fun project in and of itself. For example, order a surface-of-the moon picture from PhotoDisc and then place your kids on it—add in a space ship or two to create a funny greeting card to Grandma.

Whether you're creating a greeting card, calendar, or just a fun image, the best place to order clip art is from the Seattle-based company called PhotoDisc. They'll sell you an individual image or one of their many well done CD collections. You can order via phone or directly from their Web site.

PhotoDisc is located on the Web at www.photodisc.com.

PUTTING YOUR COLLAGE TOGETHER

Before we continue, let's cover some general tips:

- Make sure you've got plenty of memory, at least 16 MB, in your computer. You'll have a lot of large graphical windows open, which eat memory.

- Archive the original photos before working with them. It's easy to make a mistake and, after altering a photo to paste it into a collage, unwittingly overwrite the original.

- Learn to be an expert at cutting out objects from digital photos; remember what we discussed in previous chapters—erase away unwanted stuff from images, magnify to do the detail work, and take your time.

Step *Start with a desired canvas size*

1 A photo collage is destined for one of two places—either to be output as a high-quality print, or posted to a Web page. In either case, you'll have a standard size to design for. First, create a new canvas; if you're designing a collage for the Web, pick a size in pixels. If you're planning to print your collage, choose a size based on inches. If you plan to create a poster, create an image size that will scale well to the poster size.

Figure 9.1
A sample collage.

Step *After creating your canvas, start working*

2 When creating a collage, begin at one corner and move out. It doesn't matter which corner—just pick one. Open your first picture and decide how you want to position it. Here are some tips for placing pictures into a photo-collage:

- Go for variety. Cut your photos into different shapes.

- Place pictures at unusual angles.

- If you have Photoshop, place pictures on different layers to help make the collage easier to edit.

- Edit or image-enhance your photos *before* pasting them onto your collage canvas.

- Consider your enhancement options. Think about wild color schemes or tinting photos. Try using filters to create neat effects and then combine the results of different techniques.

- Don't blend the seams of each photo together until you're finished with the overall composition.

- Try to use all the white space in a picture. Don't let specks of background be noticeable.

Step *Crop, blend, process, save, and print*

3 After you've added all your images to the collage, crop the entire collage so that no background is visible around the edges. Also, spend some time blending the seams of images together. If there is a large area of white space in the photos, think about placing the entire collage on an interesting-colored or patterned background.

When printing your collage, you could work with a local print shop or service bureau to create a large-size print, or you can cut your piece into square overlapping sections and print them out separately, and then paste them together with rubber cement and poster board.

Step *One step further...*

4 Another approach is to individually print each photo, then cut and paste those photos directly onto a poster board or some other surface. What's cool here is that you can experiment with large collages. After all, printing poster-sized imagery from your computer isn't cheap. So, if you want to create a large, but less expensive poster, consider this route. The only downside is that each work will be one of a kind—not reproduceable.

Combine your computer artwork with other art forms for a true collage experience. For example, one contemporary artist creates paintings with pieces of art pasted over ink-jet-printed photos.

BUILDING COOL FONT EFFECTS

In this project, we show how to exploit one of the best features of a digital camera—the ability to photograph text (or some interesting object) from any surface and then use the text (object) within other images. You can use this technique to create unique fonts or drop caps (a capital letter that typically starts a page and is larger or more stylized than other text characters) for use on Web pages, newsletters, and other publishing media. The following project describes how to cut out and organize objects from larger pictures and reuse them.

We can create two basic types of font effects with a little help from a digital camera. The first effect uses a picture (or series of pictures) of letters of the alphabet to create new fonts. The second effect is to mask an existing font over a specific image or series of images to create a unique-looking texture to an existing font. Let's dive in and discuss both techniques step by step.

Step
1
Take cool pictures of interesting letters

First and foremost, think about the types of places where you might find cool letters. Don't think so much about what letter you specifically need at any given moment—just concentrate on collecting, over time, a large and diverse collection of letters. Above all, be concerned about copyright laws. Not all signs, logos, and typefaces you encounter can be photographed and used freely. To protect yourself from copyright infringement, concentrate on things like road signs, manhole covers, graffiti, old signs, and painted ads on sides of buildings. Letters on cornerstones of buildings can work well, so can license plates (although you might want to be careful here, because some people might react negatively to someone taking a picture of their license plate). The bottom line: This project works well when you construct words from letters that are obtained from familiar things. The words end up looking like a puzzle—it invites viewers to try to guess where each letter was obtained.

Step
2
Evaluate, crop and archive

Once you've taken the photos, download them and open them in your favorite image-editing program. Review each image and discard the ones that don't appear to be worthwhile. Then, for each image that you keep, crop it down to a decent size and save it in a non-lossy format (use a TIFF or PICT format). It's a good idea to create an easy-to-understand file-naming scheme. Consider defining each name based on the letter type the image contains, its relative size, whether the image contains uppercase or lowercase characters, and which letter of the alphabet it contains. Here's the format we use:

[**Font Style Category**]-[**FontSize s/m/l/x**]-[**LC or UC for case + letter**]

Thus, a graffiti uppercase B, which we captured very close up for good size, would **be grafxucb.tif** or if our operating system supports long file names **graf-x-uc-b.tif.**

The reason this type of file naming scheme is important? Some programs don't offer a way to preview your images. So, sometimes a well defined file name is the only way to identify an image quickly.

Tip   Include the surrounding area of the letters you shoot. The more texture you have beyond the font, the more options you have in terms of how you shape the cutout of the font when you actually use it.

Once this is done, archive the batch of letters onto a Zip drive or other removable media. It's a good idea to have a single removable drive that contains all of your photo fonts.

Step
3   *Cut out the font*

Many times, you'll want to cut the font completely out of the background. Let's look at some cutting techniques closely.

In the following series of shots, we've suggested different ways to cut out a font:

- Trim around the letter, as in Figure 9.2

- Create a rough trim, as in Figure 9.3

- Cut out a square, as in Figure 9.4

- Do a wild trim job, as in Figure 9.5

With the last two, you're trying to make as much use of the surrounding texture as you are of the letter itself. Both font texture and background texture make a photo-based font look unique.

Of course, the most important thing at this point is to have a decent collection of photos. This means capturing at least two (if not several) instances of every word in the alphabet and at least one set of uppercase and lowercase letters. Over time, you'll want to add to these sets to increase your options.

Step 4 *Build a word*

In building a word, there are a few things to consider before you start manipulating the photos.

Figure 9.2

How should the photo fonts be cut out and sized?

There are several ways of cutting out a font. First, you can cut out the font and square it (or cut out some other shape around it), allowing the background texture to be part of the word. Or you can cut out each letter specifically. You can also cut out the font in the shape of the letter—but not perfectly, which is what we did for our example.

Figure 9.3

What style do you want?

For example, the words "hot" and "cold" could be styled differently with different sets of photos and effects. Sometimes this necessitates that you do some investigation to locate and photograph very specific images for specific, desired effects.

Figure 9.4

Where will your photo font be used?

The Web can attractively display low resolution images that you couldn't get away with in most print or desktop publishing situations. In addition, if your desktop publishing project is going to be in black and white, then the shape of the font is far more important than the texture or color of it.

Figure 9.5

UNUSUAL TEXTURES

One of the most common graphical font techniques is to take a typical font from your computer and use it as a mask. By placing text over an interesting photo, you can create a really neat headline. This is a fun and interesting approach for Web pages, slide shows, and especially desktop publishing projects.

Shooting For A Font Texture

When you photograph a background for fonts, you'll want to shoot with an eye for texture. To find the most interesting texture possible, keep these points in mind during your photo sessions:

- Look for photos that have high contrast and rich colors.

- Try to find photos that have a good horizontal aspect.

- Focus on the middle one-third of the picture. Often, this is the "sweet spot" that you can use for a font texture.

Creating The Word

We've created words using two different programs and have discovered that both programs handle this task quite differently. We're going to show how it's done with Paint Shop Pro, but if you have Fractal Design Painter (especially for Mac fans), you can find an excellent tutorial of this task on page 45 of your *Painter 4 Tutorial Manual*.

For our example, we chose a specific sunset picture taken in August on a hill in Portland, Maine, with a Kodak DC50 camera. The rich middle of the shot and the hues brought out in it really look great.

CREATING ORIGINAL TEXTURES FOR NON-ORIGINAL FONTS

Step **1** *Open your background photo*

Open the background photo and apply any filters that you wish until you arrive at the desired background effect.

Step **2** *Create the text mask*

The text mask is created on a new canvas in Paint Shop Pro. We simply created a large word, in all uppercase, using a thick font (in this case, it's Impact), and then simply converted it to a negative image so that the letters are now drawn with the transparent color. The word is then selected and copied.

Step **3** *Apply the mask*

After the text mask is copied to the clipboard, switch to the background photo and select Paste as Transparent Selection from the Paint Shop Pro's Edit menu. You will then be able to place the text over the most appropriate part of the background photo and, with a little blurring of the edges and perhaps a drop shadow, you've got a wonderful text effect.

Figure 9.6
The photo mask completed.

CREATING FUN CALENDARS

Many people create calendars using their computers and various desktop publishing programs. But with a digital camera, you can take calendar creation a few steps further because you can add photos and special photographic effects.

Shooting For A Digital Photo Calendar

Snap pictures of family members at holidays and during visits. One of our friends takes photos of family members during special occasions, then creates calendar photos that are momentos of birthdays, holidays, anniversaries, graduations, and so on.

Show off family trips as "pictures of the month." Or, during the year, look for a great photo taken each month for showing off in next year's calendar. One idea is to take photos of family members using backgrounds that reflect the time of year—autumn leaves in the background for October, snow in the background for January, and so on. You can also create shots of the family in exotic settings, such as "on the moon" or other fantasy surroundings.

Finding Your Software

There are several excellent programs that offer you the ability to quickly set up your own calendar—Broderbund's Print Shop, Adobe's PhotoDeluxe, Microsoft's PictureIt!, and LivePicture's LivePix (shown in Figure 9.7). All have templates and wizards that can help you create your own calendar. You can even create simple photo calendars in Microsoft Word (as shown in Figure 9.8). If you don't have any of these programs, LivePix is on the companion CD-ROM. (For Windows users only, the project below outlines how to create a calendar, regardless of the software package that you use.)

Figure 9.7

Using LivePix to make a calendar.

Figure 9.8

You can even use Microsoft Word.

CREATING THE CALENDAR

Step **1** Collect your photos and create a plan

You'll want to gather all your photos first, of course. At this time, determine whether you want to use one photo per month or several for each month. Additionally, decide now what sort of calendar you're going to create. If you plan on making something really fancy, you might want to consult with your local printer to make sure they can handle the file formats and calendar size that you plan to use.

Our idea was to make a really simple calendar printed on a color laser at a local Kinko's, fading a nice shot behind the days of the month and then framing each month.

Step **2** Create the calendar

Here's where you'll really come to appreciate the value of a nicely automated template. Creating the text for your calendar means knowing exactly how many days are in each month, what day of the week starts the month, and then format all this information in a calendar form. Yuk! How can we do this more easily? Well, we cheated by using Word for Windows to create the text part of the calendar. We copied the numbers and other text to the clipboard while they were in full-screen, print preview mode and pasted them into our image-editing program. You can use any desktop publishing package to do the same thing.

Your calendar can produce any of a number of formats. Here are a few formatting suggestions:

- Make a traditional calendar with a two-page spread—the top page being a fantastic photo and the bottom page being the days of the month. This means you'll have to give your files to a full-scale printer if you want good size and quality.

- Create a simple one-sheet design. By sticking with one sheet, you can do all the work yourself, and printing isn't nearly as expensive or time consuming.

- Fade the picture behind the text.

When you're done, you can bind the calendar and use it. One idea is to buy some cheap plastic frames from Pier 1 Imports (or any photo or art store), and then place the calendars in frames for hanging on walls.

CREATING GREETING CARDS

Creating a greeting card with your digital photos is easy. But that doesn't mean you can't do a little added work to make your cards that much better!

You can create some great cards with just your camera and your own layout software or decent imaging package. Beyond that, though, simple products like LivePix, PictureIt!, Broderbund's Print Shop, and Microsoft's new Greetings Workshop can lead you step by step through dozens of greeting-card ideas for all sorts of occasions.

Step

1 *Consult with your printer*

If you're going to make a greeting card, make it a really nice one. Take your completed file to a good print shop and have the contents of your card printed on good card stock rather than bond or book paper. Even if you own a good color printer, a print shop is a better bet if you want professional-looking holiday greeting cards. Before you create your card, be sure to call your print shop and discuss with them how to get the best output. Ask them what file format they prefer, what card stock you should use, and ask them for any preferred sizes. And don't forget about the envelopes. Your print shop probably works with several stock sizes, so you'll want to discuss the dimensions to ensure that your cards will fit in an envelope.

Step

2 *Photograph your card images*

Some family cards simply contain a nice shot of the family gathered together. But if you're single or you want to send the card to people other than family and friends, you might want to opt for the non-family picture route. The goal of creating a holiday card is to come up with something that represents you as much as it does that particular holiday or greeting.

A friend of mine in Portland, Maine, ventured outside on a snowy day in early November, and took a picture of a well-known (at least in Maine) statue near his house of a lobster man. The statue provided a personal connection (proximity to my friend's house and representative of his city and its history), and the snow symbolized the time of year (Christmas). See Figure 9.9.

Figure 9.9
Digital cameras are great for creating cards.

Step 3 *Work on your composition—accentuate the greeting and give the photo a personal touch*

In creating a greeting card, if you simply paste a photo on the front of a card, you're defeating the purpose and capabilities of your camera. You want to adjust and enhance the image so that you emphasize the connection between your photo and the greeting. A little effort goes a long way here and really helps to personalize your card. My friend added his own touch of a drawn-in Santa hat to accentuate the holiday greeting of his card.

Step 4 *Typeset some text and head to the printer*

Once you're satisfied with the image on the front of your card, open up your word processor or favorite page layout program and typeset a nice greeting. Then, take the completed file to take to your print shop for printing. If you're making a holiday card rather than a card to a specific person, be sure to have the print shop make some extra copies. We guarantee that you'll think of people you want to send the card to at the last minute, so it's best to have some spare copies handy.

If you want, you can certainly print your card on your home or office printer. Let's look at some options and ideas here. First, you'll want to get the best paper you can afford for your printer. In Chapter 10, we showed you some places to get some great paper (such as Paper Direct), and we talked specifically about photo inks and photograph-quality paper for ink-jet printers. Once you've got the proper paper, you have a couple of additional layout and print options to consider. For instance, you can create the card with your favorite imaging program; or you might opt for a professional page layout program, like PageMaker or Quark XPress; or you might want to use a simpler program designed for home use, like Print Shop or Picture It!

In any case, the most important issue to deal with is dual-side printing. Dual-side printing is not good for the health of many desktop printers; make sure to wait for the ink to dry before printing the second side of a sheet, and don't print hundreds of cards this way. In fact, if you're going to print more than 20, we recommend that you use a professional print shop instead of your personal printer. Also, print the side with the least imagery first.

CREATING STITCHED PHOTOS

Here's a cool project you can do with your digital camera: Create a "stitched photo" that's composed of several consecutive shots that are pasted together to create one long panoramic-style photo. There are, as we've mentioned, special panoramic cameras (see Chapter 2), but they can be expensive and, unlike other cameras, they're useful *only* for photographing panoramas. So, to keep things inexpensive, we're going to show how to do some tricks and tips with your garden-variety digital camera to create cool, panoramic photos.

This project is easy to grasp, but difficult to master. Still, with a little effort, you can expect pretty good results. The standard way to produce a panoramic image is by using landscape-style photos (photos that are longer than they are high), but we'll explore other variations after we've worked through a standard stitching example.

The best way to get you excited about creating a stitched photo is by showing you how neat it can look. Figure 9.10 shows a stitched photo of Two Lights Park on the coast of Cape Elizabeth, Maine. We did a few image processing tricks, which you'll learn about a little later on. This isn't a "perfect" picture; we wanted you to see what essentially was our first attempt at this project.

Every time you do a stitch, you'll get better at it. Most of the improvement comes from learning more about the various imaging options and learning how to take the raw photos better. With practice, you can expect to create some really cool stitches.

Stitching Is As Practical As It Is Fun

Although we can always say we do stitching and other image-editing for fun (because we do), we also can legitimately say we're doing these projects to accomplish something useful, and we can point to stitching as proof:

Figure 9.10
Our first attempt.

- Stitches can make cool banners for Web pages and newsletters.

- Stitches also make excellent image maps on Web pages (like the room shown in Figure 9.11).

- Use long stitches as backgrounds in multimedia programs, or scroll the image through a smaller window (you might even do this with Shockwave and put the result on a Web site).

- Stitches can also make nice desktop backgrounds.

Shooting Photos For Stitching

There are several ways to shoot pictures for stitching:

- Do it freehand, by standing still and keeping your hands and arms steady. Then, just pick a spot and pivot a few degrees for each shot.

- Use a tripod or some other object to hold the camera steady. For our very first stitch, we took the pictures freehand, keeping the camera as steady as possible and pivoting around the scene. The results weren't too bad, and while the finished image had some major misalignments, the final image does capture the look of this scene better than any single photograph might have (see Figure 9.11).

- Some tripods are really designed to help you create panoramic photos. One is the Kaidan QuickPan, which retails for between $200 to $300 and does wonders in terms of helping you line up a series of panoramic photos.

- If your scene doesn't curve and can be done as a series of horizontal shots, you might just use a level surface and slide the camera across.

Figure 9.11

A stitched photo of a true "home" page for use as an image map.

Here's the bottom line: The key to creating a good stitched photo is to take the time to line up your shots correctly. You want to minimize the effect of misalignments so that, in the end, you have a set of images that can be combined as seamlessly as possible. Also, if you're going to take the time to stitch photos, you want to make sure you're creating an image that will interest or excite other viewers. So let's explore some additional tips for creating a well aligned, interesting set of photos that can be stitched together into a panorama.

Lining Up The Shot

As with all photography, it is crucial to find an interesting subject. Landscapes work great—not only for their attractiveness, but also because you can use more effects blending the photos without making the misalignments obvious.

Here are two tips:

- Pick a subject that provides good visual cues from photo to photo (in other words, you can see where one photo continues from another photo).

- Pick a subject that also has a strong middle or clear horizon line in it.

As we've already mentioned, because you're taking several photos that are intended to be stitched into a panorama, you will need to overlap the photos as seamlessly as possible. To do so, you will need, at the seams of each photo, some good "landmark points" that you can easily use to overlap the photos later when you download them to your computer. Figures 9.12 through 9.17 show the individual photos we took for our landscape stitch. For each photo, we picked a visual cue, such as an island in the background or a table in the foreground, to use to determine how far to move the camera to make sure we had overlaps that would allow us to line up the photos later during the stitching process.

With a stitch, the most glaring errors usually are in the foreground or bottom third of the picture. Even after cropping and blending photos, that's still where the naked eye picks up misalignments. If we can make the heart of the stitch look nearly perfect, and if we take a photo that draws the viewers toward the middle (in the case of our coast shot, that's the ocean line and the tree line), then viewers won't notice minor misalignments as much, and their overall impression of the photo will be strong.

Figure 9.12

Figure 9.13

Figure 9.14

Figure 9.15

Figure 9.16

Figure 9.17

*A look at the raw photos we took
for our stitch.*

Taking The Pictures

The best stitches are usually four or five pictures wide. They also don't have to be very long, so the higher the resolution of your camera, the wider you can go in terms of overlap to keep your ultimate pixel size down. For our second stitch (Figure 9.11), we used an Epson PhotoPC, which has a decent resolution of 400+ pixels wide. We kept the overlap narrow. So, a four-picture stitch ended up being about 1300 pixels wide. Always keep the size of the stitch in mind, because a photo (and especially multiple photos) eats memory resources. Unless you've got a ton of RAM, don't try a 15-picture stitch—especially if you want others to view the photo on their computers.

After you've selected a subject, line up each individual shot before taking the photos. Keep in mind the location of the visual cues that you'll use to stitch the photos, later and, with these cues in mind, pay careful attention to how far you should turn or move the camera. After finding the desired photos, click away, always trying to keep the camera steady and being especially mindful to keep the vertical height of the camera consistent.

As a final tip, be sure you take each picture with the same shutter, light, and flash conditions. One problem you can see in our scenic stitch (and in the individual pictures) is that the light varies through the length of the photo because we didn't keep these settings constant (the camera would default to a different light setting if we turned it off between photos) and also because the lighting changed over such a large distance (something you can't always control). You can always clean up these discrepancies with your image-editing software later, but remember, it is always best to take the best raw image possible.

So now it's time to take some photos and bring 'em back to the computer.

STARTING THE STITCH

Step *Gather your photos*

1 Download all the photos so that you can work with them in your favorite image-editing program (in this case, we used Paint Shop Pro, version 4). Make sure that each photo will overlap with another.

Step *Begin with a new canvas*

2 Create a blank canvas to work from and cut and paste the first photo on to that new picture. We always work from right to left—that's the way we took the photos. This canvas will be large, so make sure you have enough real RAM memory to work with it without your system having to use virtual memory (hard disk space), which will slow down the editing process considerably.

Step *Enhance the photo to create the desired image*

3 Take some time with your image-editing software to improve the appearance of the *first* pasted picture in the larger document. We've found that the most significant problems with digital images are lighting oriented—and when you're trying to stitch multiple photos together, these problems are compounded. So, expect to spend some time matching up the brightness and contrast of the photos. Sometimes, you might have to play with two or more pictures, looking for a common ground in lighting. Don't always try to change one photo to match the other; instead, work on changing both so that they appear to match their counterpart better. By doing this, you'll more quickly arrive at a good match. In the case of our example, we've improved the brightness and contrast of the picture and applied an edge-enhance filter. When you're satisfied with the quality of each photo, save it to a file.

Step *Create the physical matchup*

4 Now we're ready to attach another photo to create our first true stitch. Cut the second photo in the series and paste it into the first stitch scene. As you can see from our example back in Figure 9.9, we used a distant island and the natural line of the horizon of the ocean to align the photo. Even so, there were some vertical differences between the photos once they were pasted. Still, the overall alignment is quite clean.

Now we've got some photo enhancing to do to match up the brightness and other picture qualities to make sure the entire stitch scene genuinely looks like one picture. This can take some time. The more familiar you become with tweaking a photo to a desired brightness, contrast, and other qualities, the faster will be the stitching process. For the most part, this is a trial-and-error process—you will become quite familiar with the Undo feature of your image-editing program when you're creating stitches. So, save often as a precaution against making changes you don't want to keep.

Step 5 Enhance the matchup

As you can see in Figure 9.18, after about 10 minutes of light work, we were able to considerably improve the contrast between the first and second pasted pictures in the stitch scene. A fine-tuning approach that may help at this point is to use a painting product and do hand blending at various zoom levels. This is a painstakingly slow process, but the results can be rewarding and downright awesome. For now, let's move through the rest of the pictures, repeating steps 3 and 4 until the entire scene is complete.

Step 6 Isolate the best portion of your panoramic image

To create our final stitched photo, we used only the first four of the original six photos we took. So far, not too bad a job—there are some visible foreground misalignment problems in the bottom-middle of the image, but the center line (the ocean horizon) is very accurate.

There are also visible seams due to the brightness and contrast differences between each photo, so we still have more work to do. Before we make these corrections, though, we're going to cut out the portion of the stitch that we want to keep. Notice how, in the example, our cut removes the bottom portion of the picture, because that is where it had a serious alignment problem. By making the cut, we end up with a markedly better photo.

Figure 9.18
The final raw scene after stitching.

After you've cut out unwanted content, play with your software's imaging options to create a consistent brightness, contrast, and color level across the final image. In performing these image-editing techniques, we've found that it's best to first get a consistent brightness and contrast, then begin playing with the red, green, and blue settings to get a consistent color. Finally, touch up the seams directly by either zooming in and painting them by hand (a tedious process, but offers the best results) or cut and paste a few nearby pixels over the seam.

Step 7 *Final cleanup and presentation*

For our final photo, we decided to shrink it and add some blur effects to mesh the various images further. The result is a nice scene that we placed on a Web page to accompany a description of Maine. We applied a "hot wax" filter, which created a nice painting-like effect but also distorted the image enough to reduce some of the inconsistencies that can occur when different photos are stitched together. See Figure 9.19 for an example of this.

Figure 9.19
Our stitched photo, using a "'hot wax" blurring effect to reduce the misalignments.

Some Fine-Tuning Tips

Together, we've stepped through an actual stitch. The resulting imagery looks good, but there are still a lot of steps we can take to improve the design. So, let's step through some other ideas for improving stitched photos.

Use Various Blur Effects Or Other Imaging Options To Distort the Image

It's a great idea to take a product like Adobe Photoshop or Photopaint and experiment with different effects—like hot wax or line drawing—to create such a soft look on your panoramic image that some of the seams tend to disappear. Blurring options working well, and resizing down to a much smaller picture size can also make the image appear more like a continuous image.

Switch Between Portrait And Landscape Orientation

One other neat idea—although it's one that requires a bit of photographic talent—is to mix, across the scene, a series of photos in both portrait and landscape mode. This is a great idea for scenes that include several tall objects, such as buildings or trees. The trick here lies in lining up the shots, because in switching the camera back and forth between landscape (holding the camera horizontally) and portrait (holding the camera vertically) orientation, it can be difficult to keep all the shots aligned correctly.

Switch To A Panoramic Camera

In Chapter 11, we discuss two exciting new technologies, QuickTime VR and Surround Video. These two technologies, one developed by Apple and the other developed by Microsoft (respectively), were created specifically for displaying panoramic imagery. If you use either of these technologies, part of the development process includes using a special panoramic camera, which can take one huge, seamless shot. Panoramic cameras can cost over $2,000. For many digital photo enthusiasts, these cameras aren't an option. A more realistic approach is to practice at stitching multiple photos until you get really good at it.

CREATIVE COLORING BOOKS AND PUZZLES

If you're a parent or teacher, you know that isn't easy to keep kids enter-tained. However, you don't need to spend a lot of money entertaining your kids if you have a digital camera. With only a little effort, you can create at least two fun projects for kids to have fun with—coloring books and puzzles. Let's explain the best way to create each of these projects.

Creating A Coloring Book

At first glance, you might think it would be easy to create a coloring book—just snap a photo and then run a "find edges" filter on it to remove the color. Try it, though, and you'll probably discover what we've already no-ticed—the results are not great. First, the "find edges" filter creates too much detail, and the image doesn't look anything like a typical children's coloring book image. So, let's take a few paragraphs to provide a few tips on generating coloring book imagery from your digital camera photos.

You can create two types of coloring books for children—one for on-screen coloring in your favorite graphics package and one for coloring or painting on paper.

Shooting For Coloring Book Imagery

Let's first consider some pointers for creating the printed form of a color-ing book:

- Detailed imagery doesn't work. You want imagery that contains clear lines—in other words, distinct shapes that can be distilled into very simple line imagery.

- Find objects that kids would enjoy coloring. Look for neat-looking cars or planes, nature scenes, boats, and cool buildings. Close-up faces can work well, too.

- Shoot for high contrast. With a digital camera image, you will need to look for the best possible contrast, so shoot object art in front of a white background, and shoot outside imagery on sunny days.

CONVERTING A PHOTO TO QUALITY COLORING BOOK LINE ART

First, load an image into your image-editing package. We'll use JASC's Paint Shop Pro for this example.

Step 1 *Trace over key lines with a thick black brush*

After you load the image and before you continue any further, make sure that black is truly black—black portions of the image should be 0 values. With many packages (as is true with Photoshop or Fractal Design Painter), you can simply use a layer (Photoshop) or tracing paper option (Fractal Design Painter) to do this really easily.

In Paint Shop Pro, it's not too much more difficult to convert your image to a plain, line art look. After you draw out the lines, go to the menu bar and choose Masks|New. When the dialog box appears, choose "Any non-zero value" as the mask choice, and click on OK. Then, choose a white brush or an eraser, and simply paint out all the color of your image. The line art should be all that remains. See Figure 9.20 for an example of this.

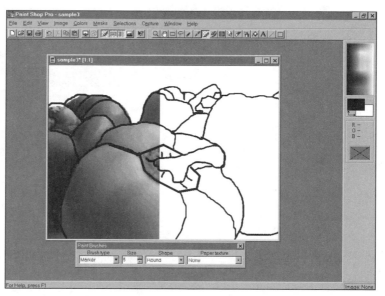

Figure 9.20
Creating a coloring book.

Step 2 *Enhance the line art*

After you delete the picture layer or erase the imagery with a mask, you'll see a decent line image. But unless you're highly experienced in image editing, you'll probably find it necessary to improve the image. For instance, you can vary the thickness of lines, improve the shape of a line, and so on. You might also run a few blur filters on the image to soften the lines.

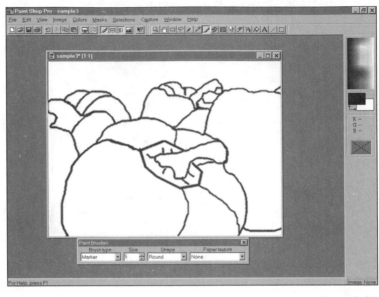

Figure 9.21
The final image.

Step 3 *Convert the image to pure black and white*

Now take the final image and convert it to a one-color image, which sharpens the lines for printing (especially if you've run a blur or two to soften their shape).

Step 4 *Color it on screen or off*

Don't hesitate to print out the image for off-screen coloring. We recommend using a heavier paper stock.

CREATING A PICTURE PUZZLE

Puzzles aren't just for kids. Many adults have fond memories of piecing together picture puzzles. And many adults continue to enjoy working on picture puzzles. But kids love them, too. Picture puzzles are one of the purest forms of "edutainment." They teach kids the patience to work through a difficult problem one step at a time, as well as how to associate similar images. With a digital camera and a little bit of time, you can create your own puzzles.

Step 1 *Shooting for a puzzle*

All kinds of imagery work here. But, essentially, you want to provide a photo that has lots of variety from left to right, top to bottom. Because digital cameras bring out an image's detail best when plenty of light is available, this means it's best to shoot a puzzle image on a bright sunny day.

Step 2 *Creating the puzzle*

There are two ways to create a puzzle from your digital photo. One way way is to order blank puzzles from Pro-Distributors (http://www.prodistributors.com), which work with thermal transfer paper to create puzzles. This company offers simple 30-piece puzzles (great for young kids), in lots of 10, for around $30. Another company, Joslin Photo Puzzle Co., offers a 110-piece puzzle, a 75-piece puzzle, and some heart-shaped ones. Contact the company at:

Josline Photo Puzzle Co.
P.O. Box 914
Southampton, PA 18966
Phone: 215-357-8346
Fax: 215-357-0307
Web address: www.jigsawpuzzle.com

The second approach, of course, is to create your own puzzles by pasting a nice print onto a solid piece of form board. Then, using a razor knife and a straight edge, begin cutting the image into simple triangles, rectangles, and other polygonal shapes. True, this approach won't produce the same traditional shapes as common puzzles do, but the results will still provide a lot of fun. In fact, these can be more challenging to put together than traditional picture puzzles.

Be sure to use a razor knife and cut straight edges to create puzzle pieces. If you use scissors and no straight edge, the result will be less-than-perfect shapes.

Multimedia Screen Savers, Slide Shows, And Outputting To Videotape

Thanks to your new digital camera, you now have hundreds of photos and thus lots of memories. But, hey, what good are they unless you take the time to view them or, especially, share them with others. One way to do this is to create slide shows or screen savers of your photos—either for your own enjoyment or for the enjoyment of others. By combining your digital photos with other computer-generated effects, you can transform a screen saver or slide show into a complete multimedia story.

Think about it for a moment. What other system allows you to easily add text, sound effects, music, and pictures to create a composite, multimedia presentation? Multimedia effects are something only a computer (with the help of your digital camera and the images you've capture) can bring to life with ease.

SHOOTING FOR YOUR SLIDE SHOW OR SCREEN SAVER

Step 1

Tell a story—use interrelated photos

Random slide shows depicting unrelated memories are not nearly as compelling as a set of photos that have been organized into a common thread describing a special event, a specific group of friends, or a special interest.

Step 2

Add sounds and descriptions to enhance the memories

Some digital cameras let you capture sound, too. If your camera doesn't include this feature, you can still capture sound with a microcassette recorder (which is typically less than a $50 purchase). Let's say you meet an interesting couple while you're on vacation, and you decide to take their photo so that you'll have a way to remember them. Why not ask them to record a greeting? Or, if you're on a hike, record the sounds when you snap a photo of a nice view. Even a scene that seems silent at the time you take the photo can reveal many subtle sounds (the sound of wind rustling the leaves, bird calls, the distant sound of a flowing brook) when you play back the tape.

Although the idea of recording sound with your photos might sound strange at first, it's really an ideal concept. Your computer is a multimedia machine. With the right hardware and software, you can download and display images, record and play back sounds, and much more. The sounds that you record can later be digitized using a sound digitization package, and then played back automatically when you view the related photos. You might also want to jot down some notes when you take photos, because most image-editing programs allow you to add comments to your photos. The bottom line: A picture might be worth a thousand words, but words and sounds can add a thousand memories to a single picture.

Step 3

Put your slide show together

To create a slide show, of course, you will need a good slide show program. If you want to be ultra fancy, you could use a major multimedia authoring program like Macromedia's Shockwave or Strata's Mediaforge. An easier route is to use the PowerPoint program that comes with Microsoft Office. If you don't own Office and don't plan to purchase it, you might want to consider one of several good shareware programs that are designed to help you create and edit slide shows. Here are a couple of recommendations:

VideoFun

Applied Insights
100 Oriole Parkway, #310
Toronto, Ontario, Canada M5P 2G8
Web address: www.rose.com/~lgozum/

VideoFun works with several different graphics file and sound file formats, and offers some interesting image improvement features, audio capabilities, and many options (fade, dissolve, and so on) for transitioning from one photo to another. A slide show that you create with VideoFun can also be used as a screen saver.

Quickshow Lite

Alchemy Mindworks, Inc.
P.O. Box 500
Beeton, Ontario, Canada L0G 1A0
Phone: 905-936-9501
Web address: www.mindworks.com

Outputting To Videotape

Computers seem to be everywhere today, yet it's amazing that so many people still don't own one—or at least not a multimedia-compliant computer. On the other hand, almost every home has a VCR. So, for relatives and friends who don't own a computer, you can make it easy for them to see your shots by placing your images on videotape. When your computer displays graphics, it does so in a format that's compatible with VGA or SVGA monitors. However, videotape output needs to be in a format that televisions use. In North America, this format is called NTSC video (the acronym stands for National Television Standards Committee). But don't let this minor technical glitch get in the way. There are plenty of graphics adapters and other specialized hardware, probably available at your local computer store, that will allow you to record your graphics and sound output in the NTSC format. In layman's terms, this means that, with a simple and inexpensive hardware purchase, you can record your digital photos from your PC directly to videotape.

 If your sound card is advanced enough to support a mixer and if you have a mixer available, by all means use it. Turn down the CD audio output to about 1/3 of the MIDI and audio channels before outputting your slide show. This will ensure that MIDI music and audio annotations to photos can be heard over any CD tracks you might output.

Basically, you need to purchase a good PC-to-TV display device. This device lets you display your computer on a standard TV or through any VCR. One of the leading manufacturers of such devices is AITech International:

AITech International
47971 Fremont Blvd.
Fremont, CA 94538
Phone: 510-226-8960
Fax: 510-226-8996
Email: Info@AITech.com
Web address: www.aitech.com

AITech's main product line is the ProPC series of display converters. The company offers several models, each with a different price, feature set, and overall quality. Their current top-of-the-line product is the ProPC/TV I, which can display an image of 640×480 with up to 16.7 million colors.

They also offer a pocket version for laptop road warriors and the ProPC/TV Plus, an earlier (and cheaper) model of the ProPC/TV I.

Some Output Ideas

After you've set up your PC-to-TV device and have compiled your slide show, you should hook up both the display and your computer's sound card to your VCR. VideoFun lets you mix CD audio as well as MIDI and WAV audio to your audio output. So, don't skimp when it comes to creating high-quality audio for your videotape.

When traveling to foreign countries, purchase CDs of local music to add some flavor to slide shows of your trips.

FUNKY MASKS

Creating a cool mask is another great project you can work on with your digital images. There are several ways to do this. For instance, you can:

- Take a picture of yourself, and then distort it in all sorts of ways.

- Create a black-and-white mask of line art and then color it in to create a different look.

- Merge your face with other artwork, like a monster's face or an animal.

When you shoot photos with the intent to create a mask, you need to make sure you get plenty of diverse and interesting head shots. Position your subject's face to fill as much of the viewfinder as possible.

CREATING YOUR MASK

Creating a mask is as easy as working through a summer-camp arts-and-crafts project: You'll need some string, scissors, a few pieces of gory or otherwise exciting clip art, your camera, and some imagination. For this project, you'll create a mask from an image of yourself that you've already downloaded to your computer.

Step 1 *Load your face*

First, you need to make sure the image size is appropriate. This isn't too difficult to do. Simply load the image of your face into your image processing program (for this project we used LivePix), crop it, and resize it so that it fills as much of the page as you want. Cut out any excess picture so that only your face is visible. Then optimize the image for color, sharpness, and contrast.

 If you use Goo from MetaTools, be aware that Goo does not work well with high-resolution images. You will lose some detail in terms of resolution if you use Goo to morph an image. Still the masking possibilities with this product are quite cool. (For more information on Goo, see Chapter 12.)

Step 2 *Make changes*

Now that you have a starting point (your own digitized face), you can begin to warp and distort the image.

 With a group of kids, take photos of each child in the group. Later, create masks that are composites of each other's faces. This will give the kids something to enjoy and to share with each other.

One of the most interesting type of change is to merge your face with other elements. Start with your correctly sized picture, and then, via some nice photo-quality clip art, cut and paste different elements onto your face. Then, use some blending tools to mold the elements together to create a seamless image. This process is a lot of fun, especially for kids.

 When you're grafting imagery onto your face to create a digital photo mask, try to keep some identifiable aspect of your face visible in the mask. A mask is a lot more fun if viewers know who's face is behind the mask.

Step 3 *Printing the mask*

Before printing your mask, first make sure that the mask's colors are what you want. In creating color masks, it's worthwhile to spend time playing with the saturation to see what alien color schemes you can produce—a simple, undistorted face with a wild color scheme can be an interesting mask.

> Heavy paper stock works great for masks. If your printer won't allow you to feed heavy card stock, take the images to a good copy shop.

If you plan to print your mask on a black-and-white printer, make sure you convert the image to grayscale first, and sharpen the image as necessary to make it look good in black and white. We were able to get some good printouts by converting our masks to just two-color black and white, with dithering. Figure 9.22 shows a sample mask being made with LivePicture's LivePix. Finally, make sure that the mask is sized properly for the page before printing.

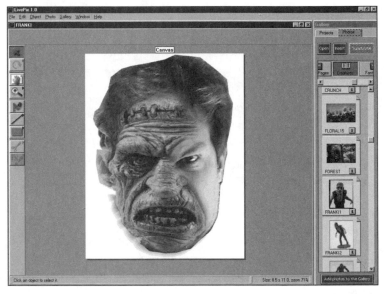

Figure 9.22
A mask made with LivePix.

Consider printing masks in a distorted form. For example, instead of printing a mask to fit a face perfectly, make the mask really obtuse by printing it very wide in landscape mode, as shown in Figure 9.23.

Figure 9.23
A mask shaped for landscape printing.

THERMAL TRANSFER MADNESS

Perhaps the most intriguing project is to output your images to a non-standard surface, such as a T-shirt or a coffee mug. Typically, these kinds of prints are achieved by using a thermal, or heat, process. Thermal transfer is achieved by first printing out an image onto special thermal transfer paper. Then, that paper is placed on a T-shirt or coffee mug. Next, heat (either in an oven or through the use of a hot iron) is applied until the paper transfers the imagery onto the cloth or coffee mug.

In Chapter 10, we provide the names of a few companies that specialize in thermal transfer paper. You'll want to consider these options if your printer's manufacturer doesn't offer thermal transfer paper. Also, thermal transfer works best when you use an ink-jet printer. If you have a color laser or other printing device, you'll need to first print the image, and then take the printout to a service that provides a color copier and have them use Pro Distributor's color copier thermal transfer paper. Don't use thermal transfer paper in a non-ink-jet printer!

Creating A T-Shirt

T-shirt transfers are easy to do: Simply create a mirror image of your photo in your image-editing program, and then print it onto transfer paper. Buy or find a good T-shirt that has nothing on it. Then, using an iron, gently press the paper onto the shirt. Use the largest iron you can find. If you have an interest in doing this commercially, you might even consider purchasing a heat press (the cheapest we found costs about $500).

You can order T-shirts and other basic clothing on the Internet by using Hanes2U, a service of the Hanes company. You can visit this site at www.hanes2u.com/. The company even sells a line of clothing specifically designed for heat transfer, called Hanes Printables.

Hanes also sells specialized T-shirt creation software for $39.95. Find out more at their site!

How To Iron On A T-Shirt

First, cut away the excess paper from the printed image. Don't use an ironing board; instead, use a flat formica or glass surface—dents or impressions can destroy the desired results of a transfer. In fact, it's a good idea to place a smooth pillowcase over the surface and smooth it out so there are no wrinkles. Next, place the main transfer area of the shirt onto the pillowcase and place the paper onto it, making sure that the paper is over the pillowcase.

Press the iron down on the paper firmly; don't use steam, and make sure you set the iron to the highest heat setting. It takes only a few seconds to melt each area of the image to the shirt. Also, cotton fabrics work best; with other fabrics, you'll have to experiment to see what results you get.

Most importantly, be careful not to move the paper—take your time and be steady. Mistakes can be costly. Without waiting for the paper to cool down, pull the paper away like you would a bandage—firm, quick, and steady. If the paper resists, place it back down and iron it for a few more seconds.

Photo Coffee Mugs

To print an image on a coffee mug or other drinking mug, you first need to print a mirror-image of the artwork to a specially coated piece of paper, which is then taped to a ceramic mug and heated in an oven. If you want to do this commercially or as a regular hobby, you can purchase a specialized mug-heat press for about $950.

You'll also need specially coated mugs. You can find a list of suppliers for these mugs on the Web at apparelex.com/blanks/subl50c.htm Most of these companies deal with commercial vendors, so they'll probably expect you to buy in bulk.

Go thermal-transfer crazy! Geo Knight & Co., Inc. makes a huge line of professional-quality, heat-transfer presses. These are expensive items, but if you want to pump out digital photo-based art on just about any surface, they're the company to consider. Here's their contact and Web site information:

Geo Knight & Co.
54 Lincoln Street
Brockton, MA 02403 USA
Phone: 508-588-0186
Fax: 508-587-5108
Web address: www.geoknight.com

Printing Your Photos

10

So you've figured out how to download your images, save them to your computer's hard disk, and even how to edit them. Now what? If your main reason for capturing digital photos is to display them on your Web site, you're all set. But if you have other uses in mind for your images, you'll want to read this chapter. We think you'll be surprised at the number of printing options that are available to you.

There are literally dozens of reasons why you might want to print your digital photos. And for each reason, there are several possible ways to output your images. Perhaps you've created a business logo that is a composite of the name of your company in stylized type and a photo of your main product or your service "in action." The logo is stored in your computer and displayed on your Web page, but you can go a lot farther by thinking more creatively. Why not have the logo printed on a T-shirt that you can give to selected customers? Or you could have the logo printed on a coffee mug that you distribute to customers. The logo could also be printed on a brochure that describes what your company has to offer.

If your images are more personal in nature, your printing interests might be different. You might want to have a digital family portrait printed on a personalized Christmas card, or you might want to capture images for use in a newsletter that you distribute to friends or others who share a particular hobby of yours.

The options for printing digital images are almost unlimited. Let's say you own a wood cabinetry business. Do you realize that there are devices that can print a digital photo onto almost any surface—including a block of wood or even a sheet of sandpaper? It's true, and that's just a quick example. Regardless of your business or personal needs, you can do some very creative things with your digital images if you know what options are available to you. That's what this chapter is all about.

WHAT TO PRINT?

It's useful to survey the array of equipment and services that you can use to output your photographs—and this chapter is mostly devoted to explaining these technologies and products. However, let's quickly consider the specific things you actually can create once you're ready to output your photos. These ideas might give you some additional ideas for using your digital camera.

Greeting cards. Why give your money directly to Hallmark when you can be your own greeting card creator? Using card stock quality paper, or by going to a print shop, you can create cool photographic greeting cards or Christmas postcards. LivePix, Picture It!, or Broderbund's Print Shop all have easy-to-use templates that allow you to create awesome cards for any occasion.

Posters. Send your photo to a print shop that offers poster-sized printing. Posters can be as small as 11×17 or as large as 36×144 or larger. If you decide to purchase a poster print, spring for the extra money to get a good lamination because you'll be able to preserve the print for dozens of years or more.

T-shirts and coffee mugs. Using thermal transfer paper, you can print your creations and then transfer them to T-shirts and other items, like coffee mugs. To create these products, check with the home page of the manufacturer of the printer you bought. HP and other printer manufacturers sell specialty paper kits. If you can't find such offerings from your printer manufacturer, here are two places to order thermal transfer paper:

Pro Distributors
2811 74th St., Suite B
Lubbock, TX 79423
Phone: 806-745-3692
Web address: www.prodistributors.com/

This company offers both laser and ink-jet thermal transfer products.

Nu-Jet
9918 Spruce Ridge Drive
Converse, TX 78109
Phone: 210-599-7045
Fax   210-650-4318
Web address: www.nujet.com

This company specializes in ink-jet thermal transfer, and specialty papers and inks.

Business cards, brochures, and other desktop publishing staples. Digital photos are, of course, well used in desktop publishing circles. One of the best resources here is a desktop publishing supply house called PaperDirect. They offer a huge range of card stock, business cards, brochure paper, visor kits (great for trade shows), and much more. You can get the Paper Direct catalog by contacting them at:

PaperDirect
100 Plaza Drive
Secaucas, NJ 07094
Phone: 800-A-PAPERS
Fax: 800-44-FAXPD
Web address: www.paperdirect.com

Other ideas. Let your imagination go wild. Create masks for children (using Goo!) create puzzles by gluing a photo print to card stock and then cutting it out. Create key chains or ID badges or commemorative credentials for events.

> **Tip** Don't try to cut a puzzle by using scissors or by creating typical "puzzle-like" shapes. Instead, use an exacto knife to cut out typical geometric forms, like triangles, rectangles, and squares.
>
> Laminating machines can be found at any Kinkos print shop, however, these machines are relatively inexpensive to purchase. Staples sells machines for as little as $40, and the laminant costs about $20 for a package of 50. You'll also need a good paper cutter, which will run you from $25 to $50.

All in all, we've got a pretty simple rule to follow: The more you expand the types of things you create, and the more you emphasize the role of your digital camera in creating them, the more you'll enjoy and justify the costs and special features of your digital camera.

PERSONAL PRINTING MADE EASY

There are several software packages that make it easy for you to create some interesting custom printing. Two popular packages are Broderbund's Print Shop and Microsoft's Picture It! Both packages contain templates that you can customize to create greeting cards, business cards, brochures, certificates, and other common printed formats. Picture It! also allows you to do some basic image editing, such as cropping out unwanted objects and correcting red eye, as shown in Figure 10.1.

Both packages are specifically designed to meet the printing needs of home and small business users. Their underlying concept is simple: Create a software package that lets people who aren't professional designers create professional-looking designs. However, because both packages are so easy to use, they're limited in what they can do. If your design needs are more sophisticated or if you're willing to take the time to learn some sophisticated commands and techniques, you'll want a more robust package, like PageMaker or Quark XPress.

LEARNING THE ROPES

There are three basic routes you can take to print your images: You can print them to a printer that's connected to your computer (output quality is usually poor to average); you can take them to a local print shop that accepts digital images (output quality is average to good); or you can take them to a *pre-press service bureau* (output quality is usually excellent). Of course, there are cost/quality tradeoffs with all three. We'll provide detailed

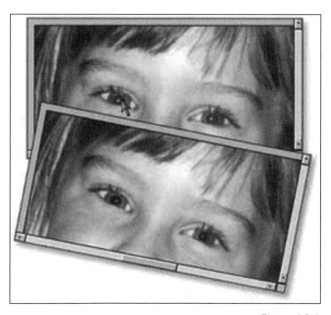

Figure 10.1
These photos show the before and after effect of using Picture It! to remove red eye from a photo.

discussions of all three types of output later in the chapter. For now, we just want to make sure you're aware of some concepts and terms that are integral to digital printing.

DPI, RGB, And Other Suspicious Acronyms

When you were in grade school, remember how you drew? You used an implement—such as a brush, a pencil, a crayon, or even your fingers (with finger painting) to make sweeping strokes to create houses, jet fighters, a portrait of your mother, or whatever. Such sweeping strokes are called *continuous tones*. In other words, a color continues uninterrupted from one part of the paper to another. And because people learn this type of imaging at such an early age, they have difficulty understanding why digital output is so different. And it is *very* different.

A digital image never contains continuous tones. A traditional film-based camera can produce a continuous tone image, due to the way sensitized film records light waves. But a digital camera works differently—and the key word here is *digital*. A digital camera stores a binary representation of an image—a series of 0 and 1 *digits* (get it?) that can be represented in a computer. A photograph stored in your computer is nothing more than a series of 0 and 1 digits carefully arranged so that the electron guns in your monitor can convert them to pixels on screen. But a printer doesn't use pixels (picture elements). Instead, it operates in terms of *dots per inch (DPI)*. *All* printers work this way, from the lowliest desktop color printer to the largest web offset printer. We'll come back to DPI in a moment. For now, we need to digress.

The distinction between screen displayed photos and printed photos doesn't just have to do with computers and digital data, although that's important. It also has to do with the nature of ink. On your computer's monitor, there are actually three layers of phosphor pixels: one layer for red, one layer for green, and one layer for blue. The electron guns fire each pixel within each layer at a different intensity to create different hues. When these combinations of hues blend together, they can create literally millions of different colors. For this reason, monitors are said to display RGB (red-green-blue) colors. Obviously, a printer can't work that way because it deals with ink, not light.

Keep in mind that we're talking about color printers here. Black-and-white printers operate a little differently from the technique we're about to describe. Color printers use either an ink-jet, thermal, laser, or image offsetting technique to print images. That distinction, though, isn't important right now. What's important is the different ways colors are represented in print versus on screen.

Elsewhere in the book, we explained the difference between additive and subtractive colors. Screen colors are *additive*—that is, you add more red, green, or blue in combinations to create a desired color. The more you add of one primary color, the lighter the shade of the resulting color. When all three colors are combined at their maximum hues, it creates white light. This can be a difficult concept to grasp because we don't view the world as light, except on our television and computer screens. We actually view objects based on *the colors of light that they absorb*. That's called *subtractive* color, because whatever colors are not absorbed, or subtracted, by an object are visible to the naked eye. And that's how color printing works.

As you might guess, because printed color is the reverse process of color produced by light, the ink colors are also reversed—well, sort of. The primary colors for printing are cyan (a pale blue that is the opposite shade of red), magenta (a reddish-pink color that's the opposite shade of green), and yellow (which is the opposite shade of blue). How do we know this? Well, when you combine cyan and magenta in print, you get blue. When you combine cyan and yellow in print, you get green. When you combine magenta and yellow, you get, what? You guessed it—red.

But there's a glitch here. On monitors, the combination of red, green, and blue creates pure white light—the spectrum of all colors. In theory, then, the combination of cyan, magenta, and yellow should create black, the absence of all colors. However, unlike light, ink tends to be impure—just a bit less divine. So, when you combine cyan, magenta, and yellow, it actually yields a kind of muddy dark brown, not black. So, true black ink needs to be added to create black. So printing ink actually comes in four colors— cyan, magenta, yellow, and black. You might think, then, that the acronym for this color scheme would be CMYB. But you'd be wrong. Printers long ago realized that the B in black could be confused to mean blue. Instead, they used the last letter in the word "black" to represent it. So, printed color is said to be composed of CMYK.

And now back to dots per inch (DPI). Film photographs from a traditional camera can produce continuous tones, because light is directly converted into a printed image (after a bit of film-bath processing, of course). So the issue of RGB versus CMYK doesn't enter the picture (pardon the pun). But digitally produced photographs can never produce continuous tones. That's both due to the way computers work and the way printers work.

You already know about the binary (digital) nature of computers, so we won't rehash that here. Except you do need to know that all printers have to convert each binary digit in an image into a printed dot, of a specific color. But not all printers are created equal. Some printers can print more dots than others. And how do we measure that? You guessed it—in dots per inch. If only life were that simple.

In printing, an inch is not measured the way you would use a ruler—from one end to another. In printing, an inch refers to a *square inch*. So, when we talk about dots per inch, we're talking about the number of dots that can be squeezed into a box that's one inch on all sides. That's where printing terminology gets fuzzy. People in the printing industry also talk *about lines per inch (LPI)* resolution, because all printers—ink-jet, laser, and imagesetters—print from left to right, across one line at a time. (That's actually the same way electron guns scan a computer monitor, but apparently the print industry is more fussy than the computer industry.) But for the most part, printing outlets and service bureaus vary their prices based on DPI rather than LPI.

Printing At Home

If you want to print your images at home or at your place of business, you'll want to consider choosing from among three types of printers:

- Color ink-jet printers

- Color laser printers

- Dye-sublimation printers

In the following sections, we'll explain the advantages and disadvantages of all three types of printers. One point that we want to stress, though: All of the printing technology we're about to discuss deals with *color* printers. You don't really want to output your images to a black-and-white printer, do you? Also, for each printer category, we'll give one or two examples of popular printers. Keep in mind that these aren't endorsements—they're basically arbitrary examples that we've selected due to their current popularity. There are hundreds of printer manufacturers, most of who make some excellent printers. At the end of this chapter, we'll provide a list of Web sites of major printer manufacturers. You'll want to visit these sites before you select a printer.

Color Ink-jet Printers

Although you may want to print your digital photos in a high-quality format that only a service bureau can provide (which we'll discuss later), for instant gratification you'll certainly want to consider purchasing a color printer. That way, you can get a quick glimpse of how your photos look in print. Ink-jet printers are the most affordable route for home printing of color images. Basic ink-jet color printers can be purchased for as low as $350.

However, the low-end models, as you might expect, offer lower DPI resolutions than laser color printers. Don't be fooled though, ink-jet printers can be pretty sophisticated, mainly in terms of the number of pages they can output per minute. High-end models can cost more than a new car and are really designed for printing companies for use in printing customer jobs. For instance, the HP Design Jet 755CM retails for $12,000, and LaserMaster's DisplayMaker Express printer retails for a whopping $90,000.

Ink-jet printers work by using a cartridge that contains separate columns of cyan, magenta, yellow, and black ink. The printer creates output by thrusting dots of ink, one at a time, onto paper from the cartridge and through the printhead's nozzles. To create true color, the printhead needs to pass up to four times across every print line, so output of a single page can often take several minutes.

Although the resolution of most ink-jet printers pales by comparison to what laser color printers can produce, many ink-jet printers can create reasonably high-quality outputs—but typically at less than 360 DPI.

Tip If you own an ink-jet printer, at some point in its life the printhead is going to become clogged with dried ink. When this happens, the software program that you use to print your images is probably going to tell you that the printer is un-available, out of paper, or some other obtuse message when you try to print. If you repeatedly receive this kind of message, it's probably time to open the printer and, with a needle and some rubbing alcohol, clean out the printhead nozzles.

One of the best and most affordable ink-jet printers on the market today is the Epson Stylus Color 500. The printhead has 60 nozzles, which allows it to output images at up to 720 DPI. The suggested retail price for the Stylus Color 500 is $329—so this is one of the best bargains in town. By comparison with color laser jet printers, though, the Stylus Color 500 is a bit slow. It can print 1 page per minute at 360 DPI resolution, and requires about 2 minutes to print an image at 720 DPI. If you have a few spare minutes for printing and want high-quality output at a very affordable price, this is one product that you'll want to check out. Here's how to contact Epson:

Epson America, Inc.
20770 Madrona Ave., D1-04A
Torrance, CA 90509-2843
Phone: 800-289-3776
Web address: www.epson.com/graphicarts/

Hewlett-Packard is another major manufacturer of quality ink-jet printers. They're continually improving versions of their popular DeskJet line of ink-jet printers. You can contact HP and find out about their printers at:

Hewlett-Packard, Inc.
3000 Hanover St.
Palo Alto, CA 94304
Phone: 415-857-1501
Fax: 415-857-7299
Web address: www.dmo.hp.com/peripherals/printers/main.html

PHOTO QUALITY INK-JET PRINTS

The big movement in ink-jet printing across all the major brands is for re-creating photographic quality prints. By utilizing high-quality ink-jet technology, and paper akin to photography paper, you can create print outs that (except at close inspection) look like real photo prints.

Color Laser Printers

Color laser printers cost more than ink-jet printers, but you pay for the quality of a laser. Color laser printers can print pages faster (typically from one to three pages per minute) and usually at higher resolutions than ink-jet printers. Color laser printers use laser and drum-scanning technology, coupled with the use of different colored primary toner bottles, and they can achieve resolutions of 1200 DPI and higher.

One of the most popular color laser printers is the Hewlett-Packard Color LaserJet 5, which can output 3 color pages per minute at a resolution of 1200 DPI. The color blending scheme that the printer uses is so sophisticated that, when images are printed on coated paper, they're virtually indistinguishable from true photos. In other words, they virtually look like continuous-tone images. The printer comes with a whopping 20 MB of on-board memory and a 250-sheet feeder.

So, will you pay for all this power? The Color LaserJet 5 retails for about $6,000. In truth, this printer is positioned for businesses that do a lot of color output; it's not really geared for home use. If you don't have that kind of cash on hand, but you want this kind of color printer firepower, you might want to call your local printer/photocopy shops. This printer is becoming quite popular at these establishments. They'll typically charge you up to $10 per color print. This may seem steep, but remember: You would have to have them print about 600 images in order to justify the cost of purchasing the printer for yourself. If you purchase a color ink-jet or dye-sub printer (see the next section), and then only want a few superior-quality photos printed for special occasions, then you might want to investigate whether a local print shop in your area uses the LaserJet 5 or a comparable color printer.

Hewlett-Packard does not sell their printers directly. If you want to order one, you'll have to do so through an authorized distributor (virtually any reputable computer store). However, if you want more information on the HP Color LaserJet 5, you should visit Hewlett-Packard's Web site at www.dmo.hp.com/peripherals/printers/ljcolor5.html.

Several other major manufacturers and models also exist. Be sure to check out the following printers, which may have specific features you seek:

- Tektronix Phaser 550 at www.tektronix.com/Color_Printers/products/550.html

- QMS magicolor LX laser printer at www.qms.com/www/products/lx.html

- Apple's Color LaserWriter at product.info.apple.com/printers/colorlaser/

 The human eye can't perceive differences beyond 150 DPI. So, if you don't plan on sending an image to a higher-resolution press, you can save your imagery at 150 DPI and cut down the file size dramatically. Most digital cameras on the low end will produce imagery at 72 DPI, but if you use a camera that produces higher-resolution imagery, this can be a useful tip.

Dye-Sublimation Printers

Dye-sublimation is a hot process, literally. A dye-sublimation printer (usually just called a dye-sub printer) uses a thermal, heat-treating technique to output images to paper. Thermal techniques for printing have been around for decades, but dye-sublimation is a relatively new process. In dye-sublimation, colored dyes on a printer ribbon are converted from a solid state to vapors and then pressed onto a surface (such as paper), where the vapors cool back into solid colors.

Dye-sub printers typically have resolutions of about 300 DPI. That doesn't *sound* impressive, but when you see the results that a dye-sub printer can produce, we're pretty sure you *will* be impressed. The dye-sublimation process allows the four CYMK colors to blend more precisely than what you would find from the output of a color ink-jet printer. With an ink-jet printer, the primary colors tend to overlap just a bit, giving the printed image a grainy appearance. A photograph output from a dye-sub printer, however, truly looks like a continuous-tone print—like one you would get from traditional film.

Dye-sub printing is not an exact science, though. An image printed on a dye-sub printer can look a bit blurry. Usually, you can correct this problem in Photoshop (or a comparable image-editing program) by applying the Unsharp Mask filter (see Chapter 7) before you print your images. Also, the heating-and-cooling process used by a dye-sub printer takes time. You'll typically have to wait three to five minutes for a single image to be output. But that's a lot better than the one-hour photo service you get from the store up the street, right?

Most dye-sub printers are designed for use by pre-press service bureaus (which we'll discuss later in the chapter) to provide test prints for publishing companies, advertising agencies, and other graphics professionals. However, a few manufacturers make dye-sub printers targeted for the home and small business market. One of the coolest of these is the FARGO FotoFUN! printer, which is specifically designed to output digital photos. Prints are output on specially-coated paper in formats as large as 4×6 inches. The printer can even laminate the photos. (*Lamination* is the process of applying an extremely thin film over the surface of an image to protect it from wear and damage. Traditional film-processed photos are almost always laminated. Calendars, too, are usually laminated.) The FotoFUN! printer retails for $500. For 36 sheets of the specially coated photograph paper, you'll need to spend an additional $35.

Here's how to contact FARGO:

FARGO Electronics, Incorporated
7901 Flying Cloud Drive
Eden Prairie, MN 55344
Phone: 800-327-4622
Fax: 612-941-7836
Web address: www.fargo.com/fotofun.html

A lot of color printer manufacturers try to fool you by expressing resolution with two numbers—for instance, 600×300. The implication is that their printer can print 600 dots vertically and 300 dots horizontally—in normal portrait mode on 8 1/2×11 paper. If you multiply this, you come up with a resolution of 180,000 DPI. Pretty awesome, right? Wrong—they're not really talking about dots per inch. These numbers just mean that the printer can create an entire image on an 8 1/2×11 sheet using 180,000 pixels. If you convert that to true DPI, it comes out to about 300 dots per square inch. The point is, when you see a printer advertised as having a resolution of 600×300, or some other 2 numbers, you need to ignore this and ask or determine what the true DPI is. Normally, when a manufacturer gives you these numbers instead of a true DPI, it's because they're not exactly proud of their printers' DPI numbers. So, be suspicious.

SUBMITTING YOUR PHOTOS TO A SERVICE BUREAU

First, we need to explain that the term *service bureau* is a bit misleading. Traditionally, graphics service bureaus have existed to serve the *pre-press* needs of the publishing industry. This included creating four-color separations, match prints, and other color work that a publishing company needs before sending a book to press. Today, more and more service bureaus are recognizing the importance of digital photography consumers, and are willing to work with consumers to help them get their photos into print in as high a quality format as possible.

But there's another reason why the term "service bureau" is borderline meaningless: Many printing companies today have the equipment required to do what used to be exclusively the domain of service bureaus. So, when you consider sending your digital images to a third-party company for output, consider both traditional print shops and companies that consider themselves to be service bureaus. The bottom line is that you need to ask questions to find out what services a particular company offers, and whether their prices are within your budget. In the next few sections, we'll detail the services available, both from print shops and from service bureaus.

There Are Print Shops, And Then There Are Print Shops

The biggest problem you'll have in dealing with print shops lies in determining the levels of service they can provide. We recently walked into one print shop that couldn't print our digital images, not because the shop didn't have the appropriate software, but because they didn't even have a computer! Other print shops (including the chains, like AlphaGraphics and Kwik Kopy) are tuning into the times, and offer excellent digital processing and printing services. When you deal with print shops, you need to ask a lot of questions to make sure they can provide the services you need. The first question you need to ask is whether they can read and work with your digital images. If they can't, walk away, and find a print shop that can work with you and your images. Also, make sure the shop can output images in color. Here's an example of some other questions to ask:

- Can you print color digital images directly from disk to paper or film?

- What compression schemes and/or file formats do you support?

- What system do you use to output color digital images?

- What is the highest DPI resolution your color output system can support?

- What are my output options? Can I print to film, or do I have to print to paper? What kinds of paper do you offer?

- What delivery systems do you offer? Can you work effectively with email or via FTP sites? Do you have a Zip drive or other mass archiving system for large amounts of photos or large-sized photos?

These questions all involve issues regarding the hardware, software, and paper that the company uses (we'll have more on paper choices later in this chapter). But you'll also want to ask questions about pricing and how long it will take to complete a particular job. It's also a good idea to ask how much color digital imaging the shop does on a regular basis. Increasingly, print shops are beginning to specialize in outputting digital images, and have invested considerable costs in purchasing thermal or laser printers to support high-quality digital output. These shops are the ones most likely to advertise their ability to output directly from disk. Again, though, the watchword is "color." Even if a shop advertises its ability to output directly from disk, make sure they can output in *color.*

However, if you want to print brochures or forms that contain digital images that you've captured, you might want to consider printing in black and white (also called one-color printing). You'll save quite a bit of money by printing in one color, especially if you print in volume. If you elect to print your images in black and white, the color services available from a print shop might not be important.

If you do want to print brochures, catalogs, advertisements, or other documents in full color (called four-color printing), *and* in volume, you'll probably want to make sure the print shop can output pages as *four-color separations.* A four-color separation is comprised of four layers of film—one layer each for the cyan, magenta, yellow, and black content of the page. Each layer of film is then made into a flexible metal plate that can be used by a printing press. A page is then run through all four plates to create the full-color printed page.

Most consumers won't need color separations. However, if you use your digital camera and your digital images for business purposes, color separation output might be important to you. It's probably true to say that a majority of print shops cannot create four-color separations—usually because they are not equipped to output to film. For this task, you might need to turn to a pre-press service bureau (which we'll discuss shortly).

Here are some of the digital-photography tasks that a traditional printing company should be able to provide. For these tasks, we're assuming that you want to include a photo as part of your composition:

- Print brochures from a PageMaker or other page-layout file

- Print business cards, envelopes, and letterhead

- Print newsletters and announcements

- Print carbonless forms

- Perform embossing and laminating

- Create posters and other oversized documents

Costs vary tremendously from shop to shop and for type of job, region in which you live, type of paper you want, how quickly you want the job done, and many other factors—so we won't try to provide a detailed list of costs for you. In general, though, it has been our experience that print shops using the most up-to-date equipment tend to charge less than shops that offer less sophisticated equipment. That's probably because state-of-the-art automation allows a shop to print more jobs in less time, resulting in higher profit margins. So, always ask about the equipment that a shop uses. Of course, in order to understand the answer that you get, you'll need to make sure you're somewhat knowledgeable of output equipment. The hardware information provided earlier in this chapter should help you acquire this knowledge.

Many print shops have Web sites and provide online services. If you would like a good list of online print shops, organized by city, visit the following Web site:

www.abcdprint.com/p-link/citiestxt.htm

The Service Bureau Edge

Most pre-press service bureaus specialize in processing color images, and most service bureaus today are well equipped to handle digital images provided on disk. As we mentioned earlier, one advantage of using service bureaus is their ability to output images as four-color film separations. But there are many other advantages to using a service bureau.

Chiefly, a service bureau will be better equipped than most print shops to provide you with diverse color printing options—output to a dye-sub printer or to film, output available in a number of different resolutions, and, perhaps most important, output that can be *color corrected*. Most service bureaus have people on staff who are highly skilled at identifying and correcting color, sharpness, and other problems within images. You will need to pay extra for the services of these experts, but it can be worth it—especially for images that have important meaning to you. Of course, if an image specialist identifies problems in an image, you can correct the problem yourself and then have the image reprinted. Or, you can allow the service bureau to correct the problem (which will cost you more, of course).

If you do a lot of digital image processing, it can be very useful to develop a good working relationship with a service bureau. And the service bureau does not have to be local. Many service bureaus provide online services that allow you to send images via email or to an FTP site. However, even if a service bureau provides these online services, it can sometimes be more expeditious to send images on disk via regular mail or overnight delivery. Why? High-resolution images can be 20 MB or larger. Online transfer times for these images can be excessive. In these situations, it's usually easier to send images on a SyQuest, Zip, or other removable cartridge.

Online Service Bureaus

To help you understand service bureaus better, we'll provide you with a brief survey of some service bureaus available throughout the U.S. All of the service bureaus we'll mention have Web sites and provide online services to some extent. However, not all of these bureaus accept images via online email or FTP. In any case, you'll probably find it helpful to visit these vendors' Web sites to find out more about the services they provide.

The Graphics Gallery

4443 Cox Road
Glen Allen, VA 23060
Phone: 804-270-5300
Email: gallery@richmond.infi.net
Web address: www.infi.net/~gallery/about.html

The Graphics Gallery caters to both consumers and business customers. They accept files online via email, and they can read and work with files produced by popular image-processing and desktop publishing programs.

The Graphics Gallery can output images to film, slides, overhead transparencies, prints, and more. They also specialize in manipulating and color-correcting digital images, and they can help you lay out and design brochures, ads, and other documents that contain both text and images. Another important service: The Graphics Gallery can help you create your Web pages—or if you have the money to spend, they'll create your entire Web site for you.

Digital Color Graphics

Fayetteville, NC

Phone:	910-486-6262
Email:	dcg@dcgraphics.com
Web address:	www.dcgraphics.com

Digital Color Graphics provides a wide variety of output through their extensive collection of equipment. You can output to paper (a number of options), slides, film, and more, plus you can elect to print using ink-jet, dye-sub, or laser printer technology (up to 1200 DPI). DCG also can create complete Web pages for you. Their Web site includes an interesting section on tips for submitting files and working with color images.

TCS Graphics

547 Tarncit Road

Hoppers Crossing, Victoria, Australia 3029

Phone:	(03) 9741-1702
Email:	TcsGraphics@access.net.au
Web address:	www.tcsgfx.com.au/

Not in the U.S.? Here's an Australian company that specializes in providing graphics design services for consumers and small businesses, including designing brochures, newsletters, business cards, and more. TCS also offers extensive pre-press and color services, including the ability to output to film at up to 3000 DPI or to paper (at up to 1200 DPI). Even if you don't want to send your files down under, this site contains some excellent tips for creating PostScript files in preparation for printing. Go to TCS's home page and then click on the Do's and Don'ts button.

Alliance PrePress

246 Harbor Circle
New Orleans, LA 70126
Phone   504-243-2334
Fax   504-246-8895
Web address: www.pre-press.com

Alliance PrePress specializes in four-color separations. If you're interested in color separations for business purposes, this is a good company to consider. They accept files online from anywhere in the world via their FTP site.

Digital Pond

250 Fourth St.
San Francisco, CA 94103
Phone   415-495-7663
Fax   415-495-3109
Web address: www.dpond.com

Digital Pond offers a wide range of pre-press and printing options, including poster printing, a variety of color outputs, and much more.

Sonic

1227 Liberty St.
Allentown, PA 18102
Phone: 610-437-1000
Fax: 610-437-4568
Web address: www.fastcolor.com

You can submit and order a variety of output options from Sonic—a large printing company. They have an especially interesting set of options in poster-size printing, offering sizes of up to three feet wide by any length, with a variety of finishes.

Printing costs can vary widely from shop to shop, especially on larger-size output and in ordering in quantity. Be sure to shop around—we've provided a few print shop examples here to give you a sample of what's available, but most areas have regional shops that will offer a similar array of

features. As more companies compete nationally via the
Web, expect pressure to increase and prices and services
to improve.

Using Substrates

In printing, the term *substrate* refers to the type of surface on which an
image is printed. When you consider how you want to print your images,
you'll want to consider the surface on which they're printed. Why don't
print shops and service bureaus just use the term "paper"? Actually, images
can be printed on a variety of surfaces, from film to wood to sandpaper
to... well, the options are virtually unlimited. Choosing a substrate involves
two factors: print quality and desired effect.

Print Quality

The quality of your final printed images is highly dependent on the type of
surface to which you output your images. In general, you need to consider
the extent a surface allows ink or toner to *bleed*, or absorb, into the surface.
For instance, paper is porous. That is, it contains microscopic spaces, or
"holes," that cause the ink to sink beneath the surface of the paper. Some
porousness is good, because it allows the ink to "bind" to the surface, so
that it won't smudge and will remain relatively permanent. However, too
much porousness can reduce the quality of printed images. With text,
porousness isn't all that important because a slight diffusion of type characters is not very distinctive. But with photographic images, porousness
can seriously reduce the quality of an image—especially with ink-jet printers—because a percentage of the ink used to create the image seeps into
the paper, instead of becoming part of the image.

To reduce porousness in your images, you should use a *coated* paper, one
that is covered with an extremely thin film of plastic. Coated paper is still
porous, but much less so than regular bond paper. Regardless of whether
you print to your own personal printer or you have a print shop or service
bureau output your images, you should always make use of coated paper.
You'll pay more, but when you see the results, you'll probably agree that
the coated paper is worth the added cost.

In reducing porousness, you can take a good thing too far. For instance, many color printers accept transparency film, which is almost totally non-porous. When you print an image on transparency film, you'll notice that the resolution is exceptionally sharp. However, if you don't handle the image *extremely* carefully, you'll also notice that the output image is highly susceptible to smudging. Some printer manufactures make specially treated transparency film that is slightly porous, enough to allow the image to bind to the film. You might be able to find these special transparency films at your local office-products store. However, these films are very specialized and are typically designed to work with specific printers. If you want to create transparencies with your color printer, you might need to order the transparency film directly from your printer manufacturer. If you request transparencies from a print shop or service bureau, you're probably in good shape—they'll almost certainly have transparency film specially designed for their color printer. Some companies also manufacture paper that is specially designed to print photographs.

Desired Effects

Most printers can output to a substrate that is in a sheet form. This includes paper, film, transparencies, and any other surface that is very thin, flat, and flexible.

We've already explained that paper can be coated to reduce its porousness. But another factor in choosing paper involves its *weight* or *thickness*. Both terms are actually synonymous, but different printing companies and paper manufacturers use different terms. In the U.S., paper thickness is actually (and strangely) defined in terms of its weight. Paper weight is based upon the total weight of 500 sheets, in which each sheet is 25×38 inches. Yes, that's weird. Really, though, all you need to know is that paper from 40 to 60 pounds is typical for single sheet output. Most books that you read use paper within this weight range. Paper over 60 pounds is considered to be *card stock* or *cover stock*—that is, it is too inflexible for book pages and is more suitable for book covers, greeting cards, or other single-sheet uses.

Many print shops, service bureaus, and even paper companies prefer to measure paper based on the width of the paper in thousandths of an inch (mils). Book paper typically measures between .02 to 1 mil. Paper beyond this thickness is generally considered to be card or cover stock paper.

Other Surfaces

The world of printing has extended far beyond paper. Machines are available that allow you to print your images to virtually any flat surface. For instance, the Professional ColorPoint 2 PSF printer, by Seiko Instruments, allows you to print images to T-shirts or any other polyester or rubber surface—even to rugs! The ColorPoint, like most printers that provide similar capabilities, uses a heat transfer process to melt and bind a paper copy of an image onto a fabric surface. Surprisingly, these printers are not that expensive—they range from about $500 to $1,500. But, unless you plan to do a lot of this kind of printing, you probably won't be motivated to buy one of these printers. If you do want to print to a T-shirt or other polyester or rubber surfaces, you'll most likely find an equipped printer at a local T-shirt retail outlet rather than at a print shop. In any case, you can contact Seiko Instruments at 408-922-5949 (in California) or 800-888-0817.

A few companies manufacture printers that can print to just about any large surface that is flat enough to accept a print—including sandpaper, wood, and sheet metal. Alpha Merics manufactures two printers that service these needs. However, these printers are not cheap (between $50,000 and $75,000), so they're really intended for specialized businesses, not consumers. However, if you want your images output to a unique service, you can contact Alpha Merics at 805-520-3664 for a list of vendors that offer this service.

In this chapter, we've attempted to provide you with all of the information you need to print quality images—both at home and through print shops and service bureaus. But keep in mind that every printer operates differently, and every print shop and service bureau provides different services. Before you purchase a printer or use a particular print shop or service bureau, you need to ask questions to make sure you'll get what you expect in terms of performance. This chapter helps you become a better-informed consumer of printer products and services available for digital imagery.

Digital Cameras And

The Web

11

Digital camera manufacturers should give

a hearty thanks to the Web and the popu-

larity of Web publishing, because the Web

is perhaps the biggest reason why digital

cameras have become so popular.

In Web publishing, pixel resolution—not overall resolution—is most important. For desktop publishing, a camera with 640×480 resolution pales in comparison to high-resolution cameras. But for Web publishing projects, a 640×480 graphic may even be too big. And with 1024×768 cameras starting to move into the price range of current low-end cameras, it's even more important for Web developers to understand which cameras work well for shooting photos that will appear on the Web. So, it's obvious that we need to cover as much about digital photos and cameras on the Web as we possibly can.

DIGITAL PHOTOS ON THE WEB: THE BASICS

In Chapter 6, we covered all the major file formats that digital camera owners might encounter. As you might recall, many of these formats, such as progressive JPEG and GIF89A, have become important due to their ideal suitability for Web publishing.

With Web graphics, you're typically going to use one or more of these graphical file formats, plus you'll want to try to get the best graphics quality for the least size. At first glance, this might seem easy—take a picture, download it, then upload it to a Web page. But that's the lazy way. You can take a lot of additional steps to get the most out of your image on a Web page. Additionally, if you want your image to be part of an animated or transparent GIF, you'll have to convert it from a 24-bit image to an 8-bit GIF image, which means you'll want to get the best image with far fewer colors than the original image contained. Even then, you may want to reduce the colors and size of the file, while at the same time trying to maintain a good image. The tradeoff is simple: Smaller files load fast, a critical factor in keeping viewers at your Web site, but small files are less attractive than larger, higher-resolution files. Creating Web graphics at an ideal size and resolution requires a balancing act between these two factors. Let's take some time to talk about the tools and techniques for creating good Web graphics from your photos.

Optimizing Your Web Images

When we discuss Web graphics with others, the word optimization comes up repeatedly. Since modems aren't very fast (by comparison with hard disks and other local storage media), the goal is to keep imagery as small as possible so they can load quickly. There are many ways to do this, so let's review each approach.

First, we're assuming that you've downloaded and saved your camera images. We save our camera images as uncompressed TIFs to avoid any image loss. Saving images as JPEGs certainly reduces image size, but the JPEG format also reduces image quality, so we won't save anything in JPEG until we're finally ready to output the images to a Web page. (Keep in mind, though, that some low-end cameras only allow you to save images in JPEG format.)

Optimize For Quality

The first task is to edit your image until it is as good as you expect it to be in terms of brightness, contrast, color, and so on. Only then should you evaluate and process the image for size optimization. Once you are satisfied with the image's quality, save it.

Optimize Image Size And Crop

With Web graphics, the easiest way to reduce the file size is to reduce the size of the photo itself. First, you'll want to crop the photo to remove any unnecessary imagery. Then, experiment by resizing the image.

> **Tip** Some programs, such as Paint Shop Pro, offer a resize and resample option. For many purposes, both options yield the same results. However, resampling tends to offer better quality at the expense of speed.

Determine Bit Depth

After you've determined the optimum size for your photo, the next step is to decide how many colors will be used in the image and, if necessary, what sort of scheme will be used to determine the best colors. Let's cover this color-depth decision-making process now.

Essentially, making a decision on color depth begins with a simple question: Do you want to be above 256 colors or below? JPEG is used for graphics at or above 256 colors, while GIF is used for images that contain fewer than 256 colors. However, in some low bit-depth situations, you might opt for JPEG simply because it can load images faster than GIF. In the near future, if PNG and FlashPIX become popular, the format choices for high-color pictures will be even more numerous. For now, though, let's just talk about GIF and JPEG, and bit depth in general.

When you consider bit depth, you need to experiment to see how far down you can reduce an image while maintaining an acceptable picture resolution. You also want to watch the file size—sometimes, a file will be larger when saved as a JPEG than if it were saved as a GIF. This, of course, is only a factor with pictures that have fewer than 256 colors. As FlashPIX and PNG grow in popularity, you'll want to watch your Web file sizes carefully to determine if these new formats are more appropriate.

Let's start our color-depth examination by taking a picture and then looking at it under a variety of formats and sizes.

The color depth that can be deemed acceptable is really up to you and the purposes for which you want to use an image. For example, if you want to display photographic images as realistically as possible, then you'll want to avoid reducing the color depth of the image in any way. However, if you simply want to create a nice logo or a textured background on a Web page, a very reduced color scheme would be adequate. In some cases, a very low-resolution, low-color image can be used as a thumbnail. Then, when the user clicks on the thumbnail to see more, the full-scale, full-color image will be opened.

Posterization

Posterization is one way to reduce the number of colors in an image. But a posterized image usually has large areas of flat color. Posterization can be a nice effect, but it won't allow you to maintain any photorealism.

Desaturating

One way to reduce the size of your bit depth is to switch to a tonal color scheme, or even to black and white. Sure, you're giving up the impact of color, but in some cases this can be a nice effect.

Optimize The Palette

The number one way to adjust the size of your image without losing resolution is to optimize the palette, mostly through reduction. Using advance palette math, several programs provide advanced palette features that can help you reduce the number of colors in your image. The fewer the number of colors and the larger the area of repetitive patterns or flat color, the smaller your image will be when the file is compressed and saved.

Paint Shop Pro and DeBabelizer both have various color reduction schemes. Paint Shop Pro can optimize an image for a variety of color levels, including any number of colors between 1 and 256. PSP's palette reduction capability isn't bad, but other programs can do better. (See the section "Palette Optimization Programs," later in this chapter.)

Add A Watermark

As digital photography and the Web continue to grow in popularity, photographers of all levels have the option to copyright and protect their work. If you're an amateur photographer and don't expect to make any money from your images, then copyrighting your work might not be much of an issue. However, you don't want to get burned. If your Web site contains an image that others might find useful on their Web sites—especially on commercial Web sites—then you might want to consider copyrighting your images. If you fail to copyright your work and it turns up on a commercial Web site or in a commercial publication, you're going to be pretty darned irritated.

To deal with this situation, Web developers have created a new technology that makes use of *digital watermarks*. With this approach, you can place an almost imperceptible watermark in your graphic, which makes it almost impossible to use the photo in newsletters and in almost every other printed format, but doesn't really detract from the image when it is displayed on the Web.

KAIDAN VR RIGS

When it comes to Video VR, the company to visit is Kaidan, a major manufacturer of digital camera and Video VR accessories. They make a huge selection of specialized camera rigs, which can help considerably with your Video VR exploits.

Note: Prices are current as of January 1997. Check out Kaidan's Web site for sales and price changes.

QuickPan Panoramic Tripod Heads And Accessories

Kaidan currently makes three major VR panoramic heads. The QuickPan QP-4 is their top-of-the-line tripod head. It consists of a base unit and a universal camera bracket. The QP-4 will work with most standard 35 mm SLR and rangefinder cameras, as well as digital cameras and camcorders. This rig runs around $600.

The next step down is the QuickPan QP-5, which drops some features available with the QP-4, and sells for just under $400. Finally, there is the QuickPan QP-6, which sells for under $500 and contains a mix of features available with the other two panoramic heads.

Kaidan also sells various components of the QuickPan series separately, so you can upgrade to more complex parts whenever you wish. The company also sells other accessories, such as stereo camera rig accessories and specialized holders for certain types of cameras.

Kaidan

703 East Pennsylvania Blvd.
Feasterville Business Campus
Feasterville, PA 19053
Phone: 215-364-1778
Fax: 215-322-4186
Web address: www.kaidan.com

Magellan Object Rigs

Creating an object movie can be tricky, but with Kaidan's Magellan object rigs, it gets a lot easier. These rigs make it easy to position an object and then strap a camera onto a movable boom to shoot the object with excellent precision. Several versions of the rigs are available:

- **The Magellan QC** is the smallest and least expensive of this line and can handle objects as large as eight inches in diameter and seven pounds in weight. This rig has been designed for use with many different cameras, but works especially well with the Connectix Color QuickCam digital camera—a very affordable camera if you're on a tight budget. This rig sells for about $400.

- **The Magellan 1000** is a mid-sized, manually operated rig capable of handling objects as large as 3 feet in diameter and 100 pounds in weight. The swing arm will accommodate 35 mm cameras, digital cameras, and camcorders (five-pound maximum weight, 1/4" or 3/8" tripod mounting socket). This rig sells for around $2,000.

- **The Magellan 1500** object rig is a motorized version of the Magellan 1000. Kaidan will offer an upgrade kit to existing 1000 owners when this product ships.

Meridian Object Rigs

- **The Meridian C60** series will be the next generation of large rigs from Kaidan. However, at this writing, there is no specific information about this product line, which is expected to debut for shipment in the spring of 1997. The Meridian C60 series is expected to support even larger objects than the Magellan 1000.

And even though a watermark doesn't detract from the presentation of an image on your Web site, if someone tries to steal the image for use on his or her own site, you'd be able to prove the image is yours because, when the image is magnified, the watermark will clearly appear. This technology offers all of us protection against unauthorized use of our work in this digital age.

Adding a watermark to your Web images is, of course, optional. Photoshop's version 4.0 is the first major program we've seen that incorporates a watermark filter.

Choose Your File-Format Details

After you have determined the optimum resolution and bit depth for your Web image, along with the most appropriate graphics storage and display format, you'll want to decide on a few important details that GIF and JPEG offer. As you might recall from Chapter 6, there are several variants of both GIF and JPEG. Interlaced GIF images resolve gradually into a Web display, growing progressively more detailed as more of the image is displayed. Progressive JPEG offers a similar feature to JPEG imagery—allowing progressive JPEGs to unfold gradually as a Web page is being displayed. In addition, you might also want to consider the transparent GIF format, which allows natural display of irregularly shaped objects by denoting a transparent background when your image is loaded into a Web page.

Tip Watch for two new formats to increase in popularity on the Web, and experiment with optimization for these new formats. FlashPix, the new format from LivePicture, and PNG a new format from a consortium of top graphics programmers, are quickly gaining popularity. The PNG format can usually create smaller file sizes than GIF and offers much of the same functionality. FlashPix promises to revolutionize the photorealistic category of Web graphics now ruled by JPEG, by displaying and saving an image so that it can be viewed or opened at different resolutions.

PALETTE OPTIMIZATION PROGRAMS

Several new programs are specifically designed to help you optimize graphics for the Web. Here's a collection of some of the better optimization packages.

ProJPEG And PhotoGIF

BoxTop Software, Inc.
One Research Blvd., Suite 201
Starkville, MS 39759
Phone: 601-323-6436
Fax: 601-324-7352

These two sets of Photoshop-compatible plug-ins are designed to help Web enthusiasts optimize graphics for their Web pages.

PhotoGIF can perform palette optimization and compression, and can output files using custom or fixed palettes (much like the specialized Netscape palette). PhotoGIF can also help with animated GIFs. This is the best tool for creating animated GIFs directly in Photoshop. PhotoGIF also makes it easy to create transparent GIFs.

ProJPEG helps you edit and manipulate your JPEGs for optimal display. You can preview various image qualities to avoid trial-and-error frustrations, and you can use various palette optimizations to produce JPEGs that can be as much as two to five times smaller than typical Photoshop JPEG output.

At this writing, ProJPEG and PhotoGIF are only available for the Mac version of Photoshop, but hang on! BoxTop is hard at work developing a Windows version of these packages. Expect them soon—probably by the time you read this.

DeBabelizer

Equilibrium
3 Harbor Drive, Suite 111
Sausalito, CA 94965
Phone: 415-332-4343
Fax: 415-332-4433
Web address: www.equilibrium.com

Now available for both Mac and Windows 95/NT, DeBabelizer is the king of the hill when it comes to palette tools and batch processing. Its most signature feature is called SuperPalette, in which the program takes a batch of photos and creates a single optimized palette from them, and then remaps each picture perfectly to that palette—a feature that has to be seen to be truly appreciated. This is a great feature if you're planning to create a GIF animation slide show of a group of dissimilar photos, or if you want to display a group of photos as GIFs on the same page.

DeBabelizer doesn't stop there. This package can read and write over 90 different image, animation, and digital video file types. It can extract all the graphics from an HTML file or Web site and then remap and optimize all the palettes for them. (This is an awesome capability, especially if you already have a Web site replete with unoptimized pictures.) DeBabelizer can import images directly from your camera if it's a TWAIN-compliant device (which most digital cameras are). The program also has full Photoshop plug-in, import, and export support (great for batch processing using Photoshop's filters) and supports extensive scripting and wizards for automation and ease of use.

DeBabelizer Pro is available for Windows and for Mac. In addition, you can also order DeBabelizer Lite for the Mac, which is a scaled-down version of the Pro package—among other limitations, it lacks scripts and some of the advance palette tools of the Pro package.

DIGITAL WATERMARKING

The leading company for digital-photo watermarking is Digimarc. Adobe uses their filter technology in Photoshop 4.0. If you don't have Photoshop, but you use a program that supports Adobe Photoshop plug-ins, you can order the plug-in directly from Digimarc. After you've acquired the plug-in, you must register with Digimarc as a subscriber. The most current price we've seen for a plug-in subscription is about $150 per year. Digimarc keeps all your information in a database online. When your watermark is encountered, an interested party can search the database to find out how to contact you. This helps make watermarking not only a protection tool, but also a sales tool.

Digimarc

Digimarc Corporation
521 SW 11th Ave., Suite 200
Portland, OR 97205

Phone: 503-223-0118
Fax: 503-223-6015
Web address: www.digimarc.com.

You might never need digital watermarking. But if you decide that this is an essential safeguard for your images, it's important to also recognize that watermarking is an easy process. When you're ready to output your image, run the Digimarc plug-in. It lets you set various information, including how visible or durable an image's watermark is. (We've successfully removed a watermark, but the resulting image was so unusable it wasn't worth the effort.) After the watermark has been embedded, you can save the image. The watermark stays with the image in some form and can be read by a Digimarc plug-in.

Digimarc certainly has the early lead in bringing this technology to consumers, but look for other watermarking technologies from other large companies, including Kodak and IBM.

CREATING AN ANIMATED GIF

Animated GIFs provide one of the easiest ways to spruce up a Web page. They're simple to make, they add action to a page, and, if done properly, they won't take up much bandwidth. The only way to get a similar effect is to create a Java applet or to use a plug-in like Macromedia's Shockwave— both of these solutions, while offering other attributes (such as sound), can be a bit of overkill.

When it comes to creating an animated GIF with a digital camera, you can take two routes. First, you can simply take a group of pictures and hand-animate them, or you can create a successive series of frames using still-frame animation similar to that used in Claymation schemes. In fact, Dreamworks Developer used this method to shoot all the animation for their video game, The Neverhood. They built elaborate clay sets and models and then, using a Minolta RD-175 camera (a high-end digital camera), they shot thousands of frames of animation.

While an animated GIF doesn't take nearly as much effort as this, we certainly want to experiment with some basics of camera-based animation. Consider a few examples.

A Simple Slide Show

The easiest approach is to display many different photos by simply showing a series of successive slides. Animated GIFs can have delay times set
between each frame, so it's easy to set this up.

Still-Frame Animation

We can do quite a bit with still-frame animations. First, we could simply
take an object or figure and shoot successive shots of this object in different positions. Or we could create other types of camera animations. For
example, we could simply take a continuous string of pictures as we approach the subject. Or we could simply rotate the camera while taking
pictures of the same scene.

When shooting animations, switch your camera to the lower
resolution because GIF animations work best as small animations with lots of frames. This approach will also allow
you to capture more images during a single session.

Tripods are almost a necessity for animated GIFs of objects.
You won't be able to do a good object animation without a
steady tripod.

PUTTING TOGETHER AN ANIMATED GIF

Once you've snapped a collection of photos, download them and clean them up a bit. To clean up an animated GIF, you might want to remove backgrounds from an object (of course, it's best to shoot object animations with a white background to make this easier) or simply run some sharpen and despeckle filters.

 Whatever filters you run, make sure you apply the same filters to all your photos to maintain uniformity. JASC's Batchmaster is a great program for applying multiple filters to a group of photos, as is Equilibrium's DeBabelizer.

Now that your photos are ready to be assembled into an animation, we'll need a special program that lets us actually create the animated GIF. Microsoft recently debuted a nicely done animated GIF program for Windows called Microsoft GIF Animator (shown in Figure 11.1), and you can use GIF Builder for the Mac. For demonstration purposes, we're going to use GIF Construction Set from Alchemy

Figure 11.1
Microsoft's GIF Animator.

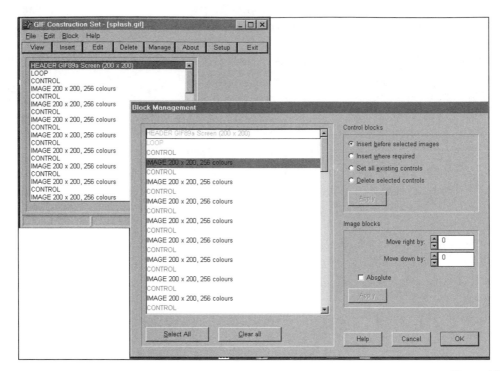

Figure 11.2
Alchemy Mindworks's GIF Construction Set.

Mindworks (shown in Figure 11.2), which is one of the most popular animated GIF-creation programs. This product is also contained on the CD-ROM included with this book.

Step 1 Gather your photos together

The first step is to save all your photo frames. You can "preconvert" them to GIF format if you want, or let your animation program do it for you. Remember to use an adaptive palette when outputting to GIF format. Place all your images in the same directory and use a sequentially numbered file naming approach to identify the order in which they will be displayed. This will make it much easier to assemble the GIF later.

Step 2 Run GIF Construction Set

When you use GIF Construction Set, you have two main routes to take to assemble your animated GIF. First, you can run the built-in Wizard, which is the quickest route, or you can begin assembling the GIF step-by-step. Let's run the Wizard to see how that works. In many cases, if you've organized and sequentially named your photos, this can be a really fast way to produce your GIF. Here are the prompts:

1. **The Wizard Asks:** Do you want to create an Animated GIF for a Web page?

   Explanation: We're creating this for a Web page, so the answer, of course, is yes.

2. **The Wizard Asks:** Do you want the GIF to loop indefinitely or just once?

   Explanation: Most of the time, you'll want to choose "indefinitely," but for situations like an opening title sequence for a Web site, you might choose to run the animation only once.

3. **The Wizard Asks:** Is this a Photorealistic Image, A Drawn Image, or Text?

   Explanation: GIF Construction Set is being quite handy here. There are many ways to arrange the color palette for a GIF file. Here, GCS is basically trying to determine the best way to do this. Of course, since these are digital camera pictures, we'll select "Photorealistic."

4. **The Wizard Asks:** How much delay do you want between images?

   Explanation: Animated GIFs work by cycling through frames one at a time. Each frame can have a distinct time delay before the next frame is displayed. Time is counted in hundredths of a second. While each frame gap can have a different delay, to keep things simple, the Wizard asks you for a uniform delay. You can later go back and specify different delay times where you might need them. Of course, for animations, you'll usually want a uniform delay rate anyway.

5. **The Wizard Asks:** Select Files.

   Explanation: Now you simply click the Select button, then choose the first graphics file to be included. Keep choosing files until you've chosen every frame that you want to include. Then click the Done button. *Note: You must choose at least two frames before you can continue to the next part of the Wizard.*

6. **The Wizard informs you** that your animation is complete.

   Explanation: Click the Done button.

Step *Fine-tune and improve your animation*

3 After running the Wizard, the GIF Construction Set returns you to the main editing window, where you can test your animation and add any fine tuning. Let's quickly run through the options here. Then, it will be up to you to explore the program in more depth on your own.

An animated GIF file in GCS can contain any of the following elements:

- Images

- Comments

- Loop commands

- Controls

- Plain text

Images are always GIF-formatted when they're output by GCS, but during compilation, they can be of several different file types. Comments are composed of text that is embedded in the file but is not shown during playback. A loop command tells the GIF Animator player to loop the animation endlessly. Controls allow you to set the timing delay between each image or to wait for user feedback. The Plain Text type (unlike a comment) will display text within the animation during playback.

Here are the basic GCS commands:

View: Test your animation.

Insert: Use to insert (at any point in your animated GIF script) any of the major elements of an animated GIF file.

Edit: Allows you to edit the details of the current selection in the script box.

Delete: Removes the current selection in the script box.

Manage: Launches you into a block management window (see the help documentation for more information).

Setup: This button opens a window of major settings that control overall aspects of animated GIFs.

Focus on small imagery for animated GIFs. Otherwise, your final result can be an extremely large file. The best animated GIFs are small in overall size but have lots of frames for smooth animation. A good animated GIF can be created with a file size of less than 50 K if you work the individual frames' image sizes down far enough.

Two new books are devoted to the art of creating animated GIFs. Check them out for more information:

GIF Animation Studio: Animating Your Web Site by Richard Koman (O'Reilly & Associates, 1996, ISBN 1-56592-230-1)

GIF Animation Web Magic With CD by Shamms Mortier (Hayden Books, 1997, ISBN 1-56830-353-X)

IMAGE MAPS

An image map is a collection of icons or images, each of which is a hyperlink to a different Web page. When the user clicks on part of the picture, the browser checks to see if that area is linked to a Web address, and, if so, the browser sends the user there. Digital photos can make great image maps.

There are two types of image maps: *server side* and *client side*. Server-side maps respond by initiating a CGI script when users click on a linked region. A CGI script is a special program that executes a collection of non-HTML Web browser commands. In contrast, a client-side image map includes all of the coordinate-link information in the page's HTML code. The name of the desired page is determined by the browser, which then requests that page for immediate display. Client-side maps are not only faster than server-side image maps, but they also cut down on server requests and thus are quickly becoming the dominant form of image map.

There is yet another way to categorize image maps—by map styles. There are two flavors of image map styles: NCSA and CERN. We won't spend time differentiating the two here (there are other books and Web pages for that). Simply ask your Webmaster or hosting company which style to use—most servers use NCSA image maps.

 If you want to learn more about image maps, check out the Imagemap Help Page located at www.ihip.com.

Creating An Image Map

To create an image map, we need two critical pieces—the graphics image and an image map editor. There are many image map editors, but for demonstration purposes, we're going to use Mapedit from Boutell.Com, Inc. This widely used image map editor is available for Windows and Unix. You can find Mapedit at the following address:

Mapedit

Boutell.Com, Inc.
P.O. Box 20837
Seattle, WA 98102

Phone: 206-325-3009

Fax: 206-325-3009

Web address: www.boutell.com/mapedit/

Mapedit is very easy to use. When you load the program, it will prompt you for the name of a map file, and ask you whether that file is an NCSA or CERN map and what image file you wish to load. First, give it the name of the HTML page. If that page doesn't exist, Mapedit will create it for you (later, you can cut and paste the code into whatever page you really wish to locate the image map on) and then choose the graphic.

Once you've responded to these prompts, the editing begins. Simply choose a drawing object—circle, rectangle, or polygon—from the toolbar and outline the area you want to create a link from. After you've set the size, Mapedit prompts you for the URL name (the Web address) and then lets you enter some comments that will pop up when the cursor moves over that section of your image.

From this point on, you can test your map, edit changes, and create adjustments to the areas you've outlined. If you find Mapedit useful, be sure to register it. The demonstration version expires after 30 days of use. An example of Mapedit is seen in Figure 11.3.

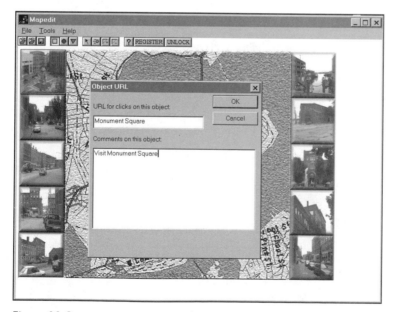

Figure 11.3
Mapedit in action.

Other Editors

Mapedit is truly one of the best editors available, but other good ones are available as well. You might check out Web Hotspots, located at www.cris.com/~automata/order.htm. Or, if you're a Mac enthusiast, check out WebMap by Rowland Smith at home.city.net/cnx/software webmap.html.

CREATE A WALKING ADVENTURE

In Chapter 3, we showed you some screen shots from a simple walking adventure we created using a digital camera and the Web. Armed with our digital cameras, some simple artwork, and a plan, we can create cool walk-throughs of houses, neighborhoods, or any other area we wish to show to the rest of the world. Here's what you can do:

Step 1 *Sketch a plan*

On paper, create a simple map of your neighborhood, house, or some other structure. If you have a local map, use that. Try to think ahead of time where you will position yourself to take pictures and of what images you want to shoot. Then label everything—you can even label file names on the map.

Step 2 *Shoot, shoot, shoot*

Armed with your map, head out to shoot your walking tour. If you want to be fancy, create branching points in your map—places where viewers actually need to choose to go one way or the other. Also, look for objects you can zoom in on. Later, you can create image maps from different pictures and allow people to click on them to examine the images at a better resolution. You might also record sounds of the area, or jot down some notes on a piece of paper.

Step 3 *Assemble your photos on your hard drive and code your HTML pages*

After you've downloaded all your photos from the camera and adjusted the images in your image editing software, you'll want to begin assembling the pages for your Web site. We can't spend the time teaching you how to do this with HTML code. See the HTML section in this chapter for recommended books and software on HTML. Briefly, though, we'll provide the following tips for designing your Web tour.

Step 4 *Keep everything viewable on one screen*

The best walking tours are those where you confine the pictures and any buttons (such as arrow bars) on one page. For our demo, we used a resolution of 1024×768, which admittedly is cheating. Run your browser in 800×600 mode and, if you can load a page completely with no need to scroll, you've got a good setup.

Step 5 Create an introduction with a map to guide the user

For your walk-through, on your home page use a nice map of the area. You might even turn it into a clickable image map. Give people a good idea of the geography of the area they'll be touring. If you can, provide a constant link back to this page for easy navigation while viewers are touring your photos.

Step 6 Label links well

You'll notice in our demo that we tell the user where they'll be headed with each button.

QuickTime VR And Surround Video

Now let's move from the simple to the advanced. The apex of Web development and digital photography is a technology called Video VR. Apple pioneered the creation of this technology with QuickTime VR. Now, Apple has some competition from Microsoft and Black Diamond Consulting with their cooperative release of Surround Video.

The basic premise of VR technology: You can create a 360-degree photo that, when displayed on a Web page or in an application, allows the user to scroll around a 360-degree view. If you were to do this as one flat image—which you can do by simply stitching a series photos together like we did in Chapter 9—you would get a fun result, but the image would contain misalignments and warping errors. A Video VR software engine actually smooths out the picture on the fly so that, at any given moment, the user sees essentially what one would see if viewing the scene without a camera.

Web developers of all sorts are using Video VR to create incredible walking tours. There is even a special style of QuickTime VR, called Object VR, that allows you to photograph around an object, horizontally and vertically 360 degrees, so that users can view the object from any direction.

One way to create a walking tour is to simply render a scene with advanced 3D editing and animation software. However, because Video VR technology uses actual photos, the realism of a scene is incredibly high. In addition, the cost of creating a VR scene in this manner is actually lower when you consider the time, expertise, and equipment that would be needed for cutting-edge 3D rendering.

What follows is a primer of what you need to acquire and what you need to know about QuickTime VR and Surrround Video to be able to utilize your digital camera with this new technology.

In the future, look for cameras from Apple and others that will have built-in capabilities to help you automate the production and output of QuickTime VR scenes. Many in the industry are talking about including such features in their future camera products.

QuickTime VR

Apple Computer, Inc.
1 Infinite Loop
Cupertino, CA 95014

Phone:	408-996-1010
Fax:	408-974-2113
Web address:	quicktime.apple.com

There are two specific things you need to produce a QuickTime VR scene with your digital camera: an advanced panoramic tripod or one of Kaidan's specialized VR rigs, and the Apple QuickTime VR Developer Kit, which is available from the Apple Developers Catalog. The Apple Developer Catalog is available at www.devcatalog.apple.com

The QuickTime VR kit costs around $500 and comes with two huge binders of information, all the software you need, and a videotape that will further walk you through the development process. The manual is exceptionally well written and includes lots of tips and figures that guide you through every possible option.

QuickTime VR Development Overview

You can make three different kinds of QuickTime VR scenes.

Single-Node Panoramas/Partial Or Full

A single-node VR scene is called a panorama and denotes that there is one viewpoint—that is, one specific location from which you shot the scene. Not every scene needs to be a full 360-degree picture; you can create a scene of any range.

Multi-Node Scenes

A multi-node scene is called a VR scene by Apple, and is much more advanced than a plain panorama. In this implementation, a user can actually move to various spots that link to a panoramic display. Multiple panoramic displays can be linked to create one contiguous movie.

Object Movies

As we explained earlier, object movies are VR scenes in which the camera moves around an object, shooting it from all the major vertical and horizontal sides, thus allowing a user to rotate the object for a variety of views. An object movie requires a special object camera rig, like those made by the VR rigmasters at Kaidan.

The Basics Of Shooting For QuickTime VR

After you've mapped a full scene or chosen a single panoramic spot, you're ready to set up your tripod and rig and begin shooting. Most panoramic rigs have clickable positions, which are separated about every 10 to 15 degrees and make it easy to perfectly capture a scene. Kaidan also makes motorized rigs that can automatically move through a scene. One caveat: A 15-degree implementation of a 360-degree panorama means you are taking 24 shots. Make sure your camera supports up to 24 shots or greater; otherwise, you'll have to have a laptop handy for downloading. You'll want to shoot your images at 640×480 or greater resolution for decent output. So, switching to lower modes isn't recommended.

With object movies, Apple recommends a black backdrop, as opposed to the white background we mentioned earlier. Taking the time to use a good black backdrop is useful because it removes shadowing from an object, and gives the object a "floating in space" look that is complementary to the way a QuickTime VR object scene works. If black is not going to work for contrast reasons, try another solid color.

Apple recommends using as high quality a camera as you can find, and many top VR scenes are created with digitized 35 mm camera pictures converted to Photo CD format. Even so, we've seen very acceptable results from Apple QuickTake cameras and with newer cameras like the Olympus 300L. With 1024×768-resolution cameras becoming increasingly affordable, the results will get markedly better.

Additionally, with QuickTime VR of any kind, planning is really key. Especially with multi-node VR scenes, you'll need to plan for the time required to capture images in optimal conditions (especially if you're outdoors where lighting is constantly changing) and for the time required to make a map of each node shot. It takes time to learn how to complete these tasks efficiently and effectively. Expect some erratic results until you've worked through a few image efforts.

Tip   Shoot outdoor scenes at midday, when the sun will be least likely to create unwanted shadows.

Stitching The Scene

After you've created all of your shots, it's time to open them within Apple's QuickTime VR authoring software so that you can build them into a scene. The software is fairly straightforward. It asks you for the photos, assembles them into a scene, lets you make some adjustments, and, if you're creating a panorama, allows you to set some hotspots as well (which can be set to launch other Web pages or other VR scenes). Finally, the program outputs the result to a file.

Viewing QuickTime VR

To view a QuickTime VR scene, a user's system has to have QuickTime and the QuickTime VR plug-in installed and configured so that the Web browser can launch them. The latest version of Netscape Navigator includes this software as part of its main package. Microsoft Internet Explorer users currently have to download QuickTime and the VR plug-in from Apple's QuickTime Web site. After this software has been installed, the user's browser will run a VR scene automatically when it is encountered.

SURROUND VIDEO

The biggest drawback of QuickTime VR for Windows is that you can't edit QuickTime VR scenes on a Windows machine—you can only view them. Fortunately, Black Diamond and Microsoft have teamed up to create Surround Video, which is the Windows-based answer to QuickTime VR. In other words, the videos can be developed on a Windows-based PC.

The basic process of creating a Surround Video scene is similar in outline to QuickTime VR. So, instead of rehashing the basics, let's cover some Surround Video specifics. To author a Surround Video scene, you need to order the Surround Video SDK, which is available directly from Black Diamond.

Surround Video SDK

Black Diamond Consulting
195 Hanover St., Suite 22
Portsmouth, NH 03801
Phone: 603-430-7777
Fax: 603-430-7778
Web address: www.bdiamond.com

This kit contains four components: the Surround Video Editor, the Surround Video API, the Surround Video Link Editor, and the Surround Video Internet Control, which is what you distribute to users to view the files within their browsers.

Note: You can download an evaluation version of the Surround Video SDK from Black Diamond's Web site at blackdiamond.com/.

Viewing A Surround Video Scene

Surround Video viewing works slightly differently from QuickTime VR. Black Diamond has created an ActiveX control for Surround Video that can be downloaded to a browser that supports ActiveX controls automatically. Netscape users who are using a non-ActiveX browser (though future Netscape versions will support it) can download a compatible plug-in from Black Diamond's Web site.

The Differences Between Surround Video And QuickTime VR

As Surround Video has started to become popular on the Web, many people are beginning to ask questions about which to use (SV or QTVR)—especially Windows-oriented developers who find it appealing to have a Video VR editor available on their development system. This isn't an easy question to answer. At first blush, the situation actually seems quite easy to resolve—QuickTime VR requires a Mac to create. Therefore, no Mac, no choice. Surround Video, however, is not nearly as widely used as QuickTime VR. QuickTime VR is somewhat more robust in some ways, too, with object movies and multiple node movies being among its more powerful features.

However, Surround Video is coming on strong these days. A PowerMac version is in the works for the spring of 1997, which will make it the first cross-platform development kit—which hopefully will push Apple to finally move QuickTime VR development to Windows as well. Black Diamond also claims that their smoothing routines are also superior to QuickTime's, something we've yet to confirm, but certainly worth checking out. Surround Video is also designed to work easily with a host of Windows programming tools.

In summary, it's difficult to determine which package will ultimately win out—both could easily last. For now, our bet goes to QuickTime VR, simply because it has had such a long lead time in terms of market presence.

WEB GRAPHICS: FURTHER READING

Some excellent books have been published recently on creating graphics for the Web. We especially recommend those by Lynda Weinman, who has written several good books. Her *Coloring Web Graphics* will be of special interest to digital camera owners.

Designing Web Graphics by Lynda Weinman (New Riders Publishing, 1996, ISBN 1-56205-532-1)

Designing Web Graphics 2 by Lynda Weinman (New Riders Publishing, 1997, ISBN 1-56205-715-4)

Coloring Web Graphics by Lynda Weinman (New Riders Publishing, 1996, ISBN 1-56205-669-7)

You can read all about Lynda's awesome graphics books, and then some, at her Web site (www.lynda.com).

THE ART OF HTML AND WEB PAGE EDITING

So far in this chapter, we haven't discussed *HTML*, which is the language you use to create Web pages. HTML stands for Hypertext Markup Language. However, there's considerably more to learning HTML or creating Web pages than knowing the meaning of HTML.

To be honest, we need to wiggle out of explaining HTML in detail here because we don't have the space to do it justice. Besides, hundreds of books on HTML are available, and there are dozens of excellent HTML editors available, which actually make it unnecessary to learn HTML. Even so, we should provide you with some basic HTML information so that you're steered in the right direction.

Let's start with a recommended book. Coriolis (the publisher of this book) has an excellent guide to the basics of HTML and then some:

The New HTML &Netscape EXplorer by Urban Lejeune (The Coriolis Group, 1996, ISBN 1-883577-91-8).

There is also some really good HTML information to be found directly on the Internet. Here are a few Web sites that provide excellent HTML tutorials:

The NCSA Beginner's Guide To HTML

www.ncsa.uiuc.edu/General/Internet/WWW/HTMLPrimer.html

For anyone just getting started with HTML, this is probably the best place to visit first.

Novice HTML

www.microsoft.com/workshop/author/howto/novice.htm

Offered by Microsoft, this is a well-done beginner's guide to HTML.

Paul's Design Guide To HTML 3.0

www.sirius.com/~paulus/html30.html

Here you'll find an excellent collection of links to all sorts of helpful tutorial sites on HTML.

Microsoft's Guide To HTML

www.microsoft.com/workshop/author/newhtml/htmlr020.htm

Another Microsoft offering, this is a very comprehensive guide to all the HTML syntax and Microsoft's extensions to HTML (especially useful with the Microsoft Internet Explorer browser).

HTML Editors

When it comes to creating a Web page, it really helps to have a good HTML editor (some are so good you don't need to even learn HTML). We recommend the following basic HTML editors if you are new to HTML.

Claris Homepage (Mac and Windows)

www.claris.com

This is a very solid editor from Claris Corporation and is available for both Windows and Macintosh. It's a very good choice for beginners.

NetObjects Fusion (Mac And Windows)

www.netobjects.com

For the more ambitious comes NetObjects Fusion. This editor is very easy to use, but is a little more advanced in scope than Claris Homepage. Fusion allows for very precise placement of graphics on a Web page, something that's difficult to do by hand for beginners. NetObjects offers much more, though, as its $400+ price tag suggests. If you're planning on doing some serious cool Web sites or photo gallery work you might want to check out this package.

At least a dozen more HTML editors are available, but there are also some excellent Web page editors available online from shareware vendors. Here are three popular ones.

HotDog Professional (Windows)

www.sausage.com

HotDog is one of the best HTML editors around for Windows. You can download a 30-day trial version directly from Sausage Software's Web site.

BBEdit (Mac)

http://www.barebones.com

Among Mac enthusiasts, BBEdit is king of the hill when it comes to Web design. Check out the trial version at the Barebones Web site.

The Syntax Of HTML Imagery

Before we send you off in search of more HTML wisdom, we'll take you on a brief mini-tutorial of HTML, especially the ins and outs of the <IMG> (image) HTML tag. As you learn HTML, you'll pick up a lot of additional basics, but for digital camera owners, the most important HTML tag is <IMG>.

You need to use the <IMG> tag in order to place an image on a Web page. If you're using a good HTML editor, it will handle much of this tag's options for you. But sometimes you'll need to tweak an <IMG> line by hand. Let's look at a well-stocked <IMG> tag and dissect its contents:

```
<IMG SRC="Gallery1.JPG" ALIGN=RIGHT ALT="First Photo in Gal-
lery " BORDER=0 HEIGHT=300 WIDTH=200 HSPACE=10 VSPACE=10
LOWSRC="lowgall.GIF" TITLE="Lighthouse"
```

SRC: Inside the quotation marks that follow the SRC attribute, you place the Web file name (and the Web address if the image is located in a different directory) of the picture you want displayed.

ALIGN: With the align attribute, you can denote the alignment of text that surrounds the image. All of this is fairly self explanatory. Note that with the LEFT attribute, the picture is aligned against the left margin and text flows around it on the right; with the RIGHT attribute, the picture is aligned against the right margin, with the text flowing around the image on the left.

ALT: Within the quotation marks following the ALT=, you can define an alternative text display that is shown while the image loads or if the image is unavailable or not able to be viewed by the user's browser.

BORDER: The number following the BORDER= text denotes how thick the border should be around a hyperlink or picture. Most designers set this to 0 for no border.

HEIGHT and WIDTH: By telling the browser the dimensions of your image, it can load a Web page faster. It does this by blocking off an area, as defined by the HEIGHT and WIDTH attributes, even before the image is loaded. Consequently, the page loads faster because the browser doesn't have to determine how big an incoming image will be. Most editors will automatically insert the dimensions for you, but if not, you should absolutely do this.

You can also use numbers other than the true size of your image if you want the image to be reduced or enlarged when it is displayed. For example, if your photo is 300×200, but you specify 600 and 400 as the height and width in your <IMG> tag, it will draw the picture at double the size of the original.

You should note, though, that for optimal results you should enlarge or reduce the actual image before you place it on a Web page.

HSPACE and VSPACE: These attributes specify how much extra vertical and horizontal space should reside between text and your picture, as measured in pixels.

LOWSRC: Some browsers will look first for a LOWSRC attribute in an <IMG> tag. The file name contained within the quotation marks is supposed to be a very low-resolution or small file size version of your image, which can be loaded quickly before the browser proceeds to load the more complex version of the image. If you opt to use this feature (most don't), our advice is create a simple black-and-white (two color) GIF, which results in a very fast-loading LOWSRC image.

TITLE: On some browsers, this will place title text near your image.

Two Additional HTML Tags

ISMAP: By placing an ISMAP command in your <IMG> tag, you are telling the browser that this is an image map. See your image map software for more help in developing image map code.

USEMAP: This command is used to specifically identify an image map known as a *client-side* image map. See your image map development software for more help in developing image maps.

Note: For more information about authoring your first Web pages, see the "How To Build A Home Page" section in Appendix A.

Having Fun With Your

Digital Camera

12

There's no point in owning a digital camera if you don't have fun with it. Simply taking and viewing digital photos can be entertaining enough. However, when you add some fun software with great pictures, you can really create excitement. In this chapter, we'll show you some of the more interesting and entertaining ways to use your digital camera and your digital photos.

CREATING A VIRTUAL JIGSAW PUZZLE

David P. Gray has created a great Windows application that can take a fun digital photo and turn it into an electronic jigsaw puzzle. This application, Jigsaws Galore, is included on the CD-ROM. The program will run for 30 days. After that, if you want to continue playing with this wonderful program, you'll need to register it.

You can order Jigsaws Galore from:

David P. Gray
Gray Design Associates
P.O. Box 333
Northboro, MA 01532
Web address: www.dgray.com

To use Jigsaws Galore with your digital photos, just follow the simple steps we've provided below.

Step 1 Convert your photo to a BMP image

Converting a photo to a bitmap is easy, and you can do it quickly with Paint Shop Pro (also included on the CD-ROM). Simply run Paint Shop Pro and open the file you want to turn into a jigsaw puzzle. Then, choose the Save As option from the File menu. When the Save As dialog box appears, type a new name and, below that, choose BMP/OS2 Bitmap as the file type from the drop-down list, as shown in Figure 12.1.

Step 2 Convert your bitmap to a jigsaw file

After you've saved your image as a BMP file, run Jigsaws Galore. When the program is running, select Open from the File menu, then select your BMP file. This will put the application into puzzle-creation mode, where you can define the characteristics of the puzzle.

Step 3 Design your puzzle

After you've loaded your file into Jigsaws Galore, you have several options for creating the puzzle, as shown in Figure 12.2:

- Pieces. Choose the number of pieces that your puzzle will contain.

- Oddness. Choose how irregularly shaped the pieces will be, on a scale of 0 to 10. It should be noted that a setting of 3 to 7 is best. A setting of 10 can produce holes in your puzzle or sometimes make it impossible for pieces to fit together.

- Generate. After you've set the number of pieces and the oddness level, click on Generate to see what the puzzler comes up with. Keep clicking until you're satisfied with the result. Then click on Save. At that point, you can test your puzzle.

- Scale/Original. The check box in the lower-right-hand corner lets you choose between a scaled image or the original size of the BMP file.

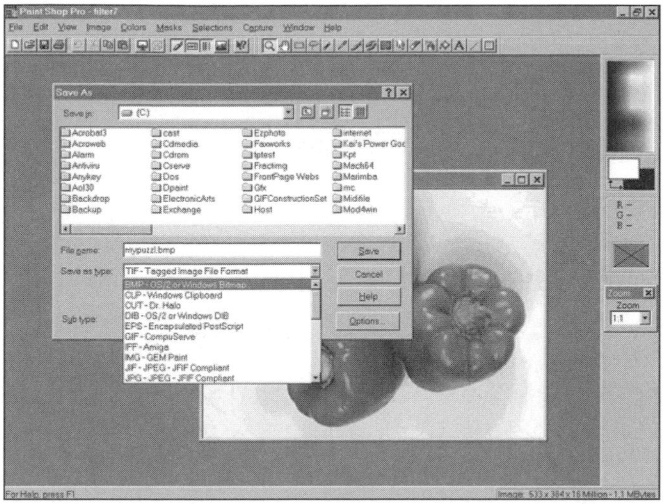

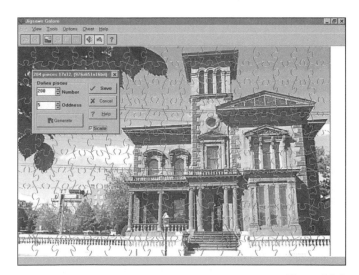

Figure 12.1

Save your image as a BMP for use with Jigsaws Galore.

Step **Put your puzzle together**

4

As shown in Figure 12.3, it's so easy to play with Jigsaws Galore that we're not going to give you step-by-step instructions on how to use it—it's all drag and drop. Here though, are a few tips:

- Create pictures with lots of colors and good detail so that each piece will be distinct enough to make it fun, rather than frustrating, to put the puzzle together. One unique idea is to create a black-and-white line art version of your puzzle picture.

Figure 12.2

Designing your puzzle.

- When you put the puzzle together, keep your desktop neat. It's easy to place pieces on top of each other, resulting in a jumbled mess. Use the edge-arranging feature to constantly clear up space.

- As the puzzle comes together, and if you have space, increase the size of the pieces by using the scaling feature. This makes the shapes and details more distinct, which in turn makes it easier to identify pieces that fit together.

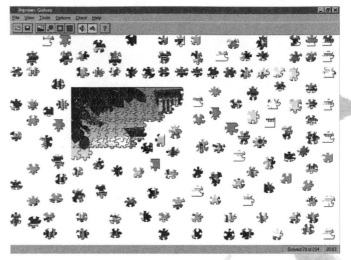

Figure 12.3
Putting together your completed puzzle.

- If you're putting together a puzzle that has a lot of light pieces, switch to a dark background to bring out the shapes better.

Step *Distribute your puzzle*
5

Only registered users are allowed to distribute puzzles via the Internet, so make sure you register the software with Gray Designs first. Read the documentation supplied with Jigsaws Galore for more information.

FUN WITH GOO

In the computer industry, we use the term "killer app" to describe a program that is so unique it can create an entirely new industry or set a certain technology on fire. Well Goo, from MetaTools, is the "killer app" of digital photography.

When we show Goo to our friends, they go nuts. In fact, Goo is an awesome party entertaining device. Snap pictures of people and then morph and smudge them in Goo. The laughter you'll generate can be infectious.

Although you might already have Goo, yours might be what is known as the "OEM" version, which is a scaled-down version of the product. The OEM version will definitely give you a good idea of what the complete package has to offer, but get the full product as soon as you can. Here are some tips and tricks for using Goo....

Shooting For Goo

Goo lets you download images directly from your camera; however, not every camera is supported. So, you might need to save images first with your downloading software. Goo accepts imagery at a starting resolution of 360×360. After you've downloaded a picture, crop it directly to the input size of Goo so that you have maximum control of the image. Place objects and faces onto a white background for maximum effect and clarity.

Goo is certainly great for use with head shots, but don't hesitate to Goo other things, like cars, hands, pets, and anything else that entertains you. A good place to begin is with weird faces. For example, Gooing Figure 12.5 is far more fun than plain old Figure 12.4.

Goo Features

Goo has two main components, which MetaTools calls "rooms." In the Goo Room, you can morph, twist, shape, and smear a picture into all sorts of interesting results. In the Fusion Room, you can take two pictures and turn them into one. The OEM version of Goo doesn't include the Fusion Room.

Figure 12.4
You can still have fun morphing this shot with Goo...

The Goo Room

In the Goo Room, several tools are available. Take a look at the two rainbow sets of icons located in the upper-left corner of the window. The first set, shown in Figure 12.6, includes the main effects:

Figure 12.5
...but this shot is a better Goo candidate.

Figure 12.6
The Goo Room provides the main effects.

- Reset. Pressing this button will return the image to the original frame in the strip.

- Grow/Shrink. When you use this option and circle an image clockwise, Goo will grow that portion of the screen (awesome on eyeballs!). A counter-clockwise painting motion will shrink that portion of the screen (try this on noses!).

- Move. Want to move one piece of a picture to another? Use this option.

- Smear. This is the finger-painting feature of Goo. It pushes parts of your picture around as if they were parts of a thick oil painting. Smear is great for stretch effects and is among Goo's most-often-used features.

- Smudge. This works like Smear, but shows less detail.

- Nudge. This option also works like Smear, but provides finer detail.

- Mirror Toggle. When you use this feature, it will cause any of Goo's effects to take place in multiple, symmetrical areas of your picture.

- Smooth. This option cuts down on the "jaggies" or artifacting that can result when you smear, smudge, or nudge your image.

- UnGoo. Went too far in modifying a certain area of your picture? Rubbing an UnGoo brush on your picture returns that specific area to its original state.

The second group of effects is only found in the full-scale version of Goo and is shown in Figure 12.7:

- Reset. Pressing this button will return the image to the original frame in the strip.

- Bulge. This button applies a convex or concave effect, which causes the picture to bulge out or punch in from the center of the picture.

- Twirl. Use this feature to create a rotation effect; it's akin to creating a whirlpool in the middle of your image, twisting it like spaghetti around a fork.

- Rotate. This option rotates the picture, but keeps the entire image intact.

Tip

As the user's manual points out, one cool combination is to twirl an image partially one way while rotating it in the opposite direction.

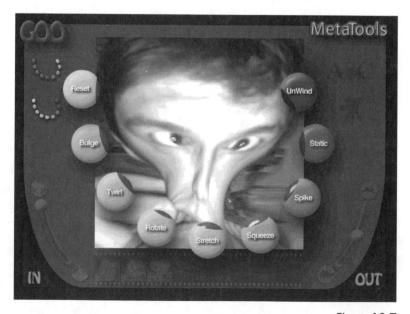

Figure 12.7

Goo's second set of manipulation features is found only in the full retail version of the product.

- Stretch. When you apply this option, Goo stretches the image vertically or compresses it down when the image is stretched horizontally.

- Squeeze. From fat head to fat jaw, the squeeze feature sends a rippling bulge through your picture; it's like squeezing a tube of toothpaste.

- Spike. When you apply this option, Goo shoots out a series of "spikes," which smear out from the center of the image.

- Static. This feature sends a varying degree of static distortion throughout the image.

- UnWind. These items work together with the slider bar (located in the lower-left corner of the Goo window). Choose an UnWind option, then move the slider to see the effects.

Adding Text And Playing Movies

Two icons appear in the upper-right corner of the Goo window. The ABC icon (not available in the OEM version) adds text to a Goo picture, and the movie player icon plays an animation of your Goo work. The slider in the lower-right corner (the one with the tortoise and hare icons) controls the speed of the playback.

When you use Goo, concentrate on making a few key changes between frames. You can achieve more interesting results by avoiding radical changes between key frames. Instead, build the entire effect over a series of three to four key frames. Also, perform some image processing on your photos first. Why give Goo a straight shot? Instead, run some funky filters on the image first. For instance, try Photoshop's Glowing Edges filter.

The Fusion Room

In the Fusion room (shown in Figure 12.8), you can choose two pictures to load. Then, by painting on the large canvas in the center, you can combine both images into one fused form. Below each picture are four icons, which control the rotation of the picture, the way each image is loaded, and let you determine which picture is the base picture.

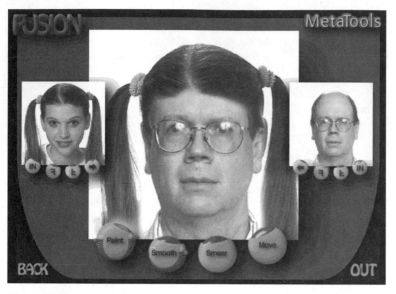

Figure 12.8
Goo comes with a collection of stock images, or you can use your own in the Fusion Room to make a hybrid picture from two images.

At the bottom of the fusion canvas are four icons, two of which have sliders attached for fine-tuning control:

- Paint. This option transfers imagery onto the fused canvas.

- Smooth. Use this button to smooth out "jaggies" and artifacts caused by the fusion process.

- Smear. This is yet another fusion process, but with this feature, you must smear in one picture or smear out another.

- Move. Sometimes, two pictures don't match up as well as you want them to. By using Move, you can better align the two picture elements within the fused picture by moving all the elements of one picture until you are satisfied with the new positioning.

Inputting And Outputting With Goo

After you've completed your Goo masterpiece, you can output it as a picture, save it as a digital video animation file (AVI for Windows users, QuickTime for Mac users), or save it as a Goovie. A Goovie is much smaller than an AVI file, since only the key frames are used. However, you'll have to save a Goovie as a QuickTime or AVI movie in order to share it with non-Goo users. If you want to put your images on the Web, you can do so by using a digital video output or by converting those digital video files to animated GIFs, as demonstrated in the project showing how to place Goos on the Web.

You'll probably quickly discover that Goo is picky about file sizes. Specifically, Goo will crop and reduce every photo to a 360×360 image. From there, you can output the image to any size—with the exception of AVI files, which are output as a series of 360×360 frames. Individual pictures, though, can be saved at any size.

Morphing Images

Unfortunately, Goo doesn't allow you to make a morph animation. True, you can use Fusion to create a combination picture, but that's not the same as a genuine morph animation—which is more complex. To create a cool morph from our digital photos, we need a special program. Several morphing programs are available and most share similar features. For demonstration purposes, we're going to use Morph from Gryphon Software (shown in Figure 12.9) because it's available for both PCs and Macs.

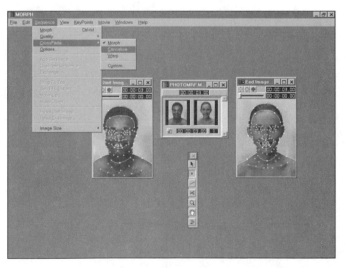

Figure 12.9
Gryphon Software's Morph in action.

Here's where to get Morph:

Gryphon Software Corporation

7220 Trade St.
San Diego, CA 92121
Phone: 619-536-8815
Fax: 619-536-8932
Web address: www.gryphonsw.com/morph/index.html

Using Morph: An Overview

To morph an image, we need to supply some information that will tell the software how to transition from one object to another. You provide this information by matching key points of one image to the key points of another image. For example, you might place some points around the lips of a subject in one picture. As you do this, the software places points in the same coordinates on the destination picture—except that may not be where the lips are in the destination picture. In this case, you then adjust the second set of key points until they align properly around the subject's lips in the destination picture. This alignment of objects "teaches" the software how to create a morph. You can also connect points to form lines, which can create even more precise alignments. As a general rule, the more you outline and align the two different pictures, the better the morph animation will be.

After you've completed the outlining process, you need to select the way in which the animation will be rendered. You do so by selecting the number of frames and by setting the video file output options. When you're satisfied with the results, process the morph. The program will draw each frame as needed and build the digital video file. *Voila!* You now have a morph.

 Looking for a nice still shot? Have Morph output a single frame (from any of the frames in the animation) and save that.

USING MORPH: STEP-BY-STEP

Step 1   Load the source and destination pictures

In this tutorial, we'll morph two faces—a popular way to use Morph. If you morph objects that are similar, you make it much easier to place key points. You should also choose pictures that are similar in size. You load images by choosing from the Read Start Image or Read End Image Sequence menu,—don't select File|Open as you might think (this is used to load a previously made Morph file).

Step 2   Outline the key points

From the menu bar, choose the small square that denotes that you want to add key points to the imagery. Then, choose one of the two pictures and outline the key features with several points, much like you would do if you where creating a connect-the-dots picture. When you're satisfied that you have enough points, look at the second picture to determine how closely it aligns with the first image. Chances are that the two don't align perfectly. So, you'll need to adjust the key points on the second image. Choose the arrow from the menu bar. Then, click on any point on the second image. The point should turn red. Using the first picture as a guide, look at where the point should be in the second picture, and then drag that point to the appropriate spot on the second image. Figure 12.10 shows a first batch of points being laid out. Notice how they're mismatched on the second figure of the woman. Figure 12.11 has both sets lined up. We'll need a lot more than this to get a good morph.

After you've aligned all the points, look again at the second image to see if there are any additional locations where you want to add key points. If so, be sure to align them properly on the first image, just as you just did with the original batch of points. Now you should have lots of points on both images, all aligned.

Step 3   Connect major outlines

Once you've created enough points to satisfy yourself, connect some points into lines to create clear definitions of some areas, such as the overall outline of a face, or the outline of a smile. Do this by selecting the line tool and then, with the cursor, click on a point, drag it to another point, and click on this second point. Morph will draw a straight line between the two points. From here, you can select another endpoint or find a new beginning point for another line. To start a new beginning point, click anywhere on the picture, but *not* on an existing point. This simple procedure deselects the previously selected point and lets you start fresh.

Once you've got a straight line, you can switch back to the highlight tool (the arrow) and drag the line by the white middle points to bend it into a perfect contour of the face. You don't have to connect every key point for your morph to be successful. However, where you have large contiguous outlines, it makes sense to connect them with lines. All of this can be seen in detail in Figure 12.12.

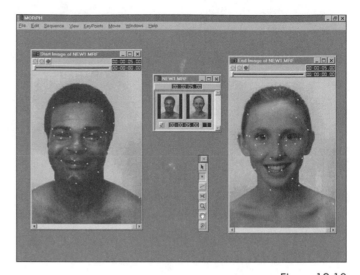

Figure 12.10
The first batch of points for a morph.

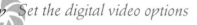

Step 4 Set the digital video options

Once you've established your key points, and lines, you're ready to render the morph. This is fairly easy. First, set the options that describe the movie.

The most important option is the length of the movie, which determines the number of frames that Morph will create. You specify the length by increasing or decreasing the time counter of the Start Image. The time counter is found in the upper-right corner of the Morph window. When you click on the top half of any part of this counter, you increase the time; clicking on the bottom half of the counter will

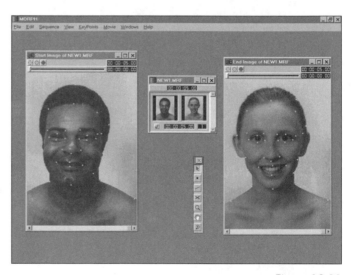

Figure 12.11
Lining up points for a morph.

reduce the time. Be sure to look at the mouse pointer, which will change to tell you what direction you're moving the time. Also, you can click to increase each time element separately. That is, you can click on the minutes portions to increase/decrease minutes, click on the seconds portion to increase or decrease seconds, and so forth. Our recommendation is to set the seconds within three to six seconds. If you go beyond that, you'll make it more work to render the video and more difficult because the longer the morph is, the more detailed it has to be—

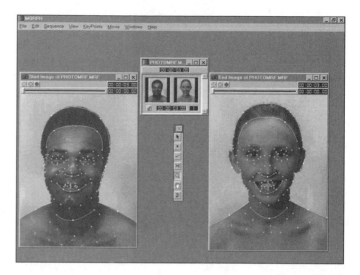

Figure 12.12
Connecting the outlines with lines.

or people will notice inconsistencies, because you'll need many more points in your morph. Finally, more than six seconds can eat up a lot of space, especially if you're thinking about displaying this morph on the Web.

With the length now set, you can turn your attention to the Sequence menu. Here, you'll find a menu item labeled Options. Click on Options to display a dialog box that will let you choose some styles for your digital video. You can find a picture of this box in Figure 12.13. The first option in this dialog box determines whether the end image of the frame possibly plays or plays not at all. Many times you want to ensure that the last frame of your video is absolutely the same last frame you've defined for your morph. If you don't do this, you might not end up with that exact frame of the video—the results might not be perfect. This is important if you might be letting that last frame of video stay on screen after it has played. This is really an issue of perfection and for the most part, we can ignore this option—we're far more interested in the second set of options, which deal with timing. Here, we can choose what sort of rate of change the

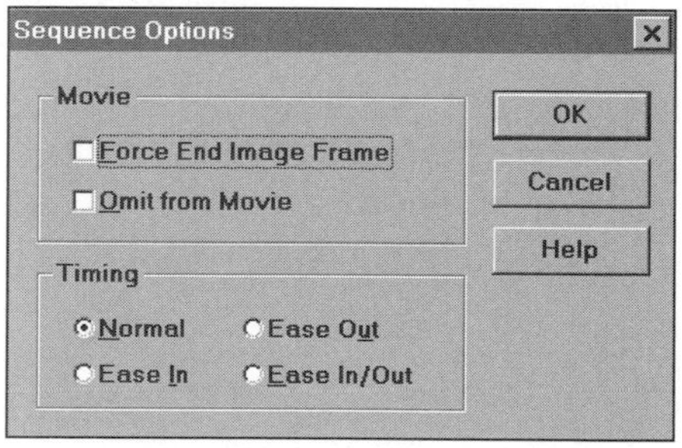

Figure 12.13
The Sequence Options box for Morph.

video will go through when it plays. Normal is fine, but you can also choose to have the video "ease in," "ease out," or both. Experiment with these options to find the results you like best.

Finally, we need to check and set our video codec, which determines the actual format of the digital video. (Codec stands for compress/decompress.) From the File menu, choose the Compression item. This brings up a dialog box that lets you choose the compression scheme (we used Cinepak) and the format—either QuickTime or Video For Windows (essentially an AVI file). We can also set the color depth to 8, 16, or 24 bits. Finally, we can choose the overall quality and the frames per second. We set this to the highest quality and at 15 frames per second.

Step 5 Render the video

Now you're ready to render the movie. From the File menu, choose Save Movie As. When the dialog box appears, type in a name for your movie and click on OK. Morph will now render the movie. You can play back the movie by opening it with a video player or with Morph. Choose File|Open, and then find the digital video file you just rendered. Morph will load and play the file.

> *Note: The grid lines that appear in your morph (if it is made with the demo version of the program) are removed when you upgrade to the registered version.*

Step 6 Isn't there more?

In this chapter, we've only outlined some of Morph's fundamentals. Keep in mind that Morph is a powerful program and can do much more than we've described. Morph comes with a good online manual, so we urge you to explore this program to discover new possibilities. You can also place your Morphs on the Web or turn them into animated GIFs (just output 10 to 24 key frames to your animated GIF maker, or use the VideoCraft animated GIF maker, which we demonstrate in the "Placing Goos On The Web" section near the end of this chapter).

Even More Fun Awaits!

We've made a jigsaw puzzle, we've explored Goo, and we've even created a morph. You might think this is about as much fun as anybody could expect to have with digital photos, but you'd be doing yourself and your photos a disservice. There's still more fun to be had. Take a quick look at two other interesting programs.

Art Song By David Strohbeen

David Strohbeen has used his knowledge of music, fractals, and other math to create Art Song—a program that transforms graphics art into music. The program scans a bitmap (including a digital photo) at various points and coverts the RGB values of the area into MIDI notes, which the program then plays back in various styles—as defined by the user. Although the results aren't exactly Beethoven, Art Song is worth experimenting with. Visit the Fractal MusicLabWeb site operated by Strohbeen, and click on Software to download the latest version of Art Song. This site can be found at:

members.aol.com/strohbeen/fml.html

Kodak's Email Picture Postcards

In a previous chapter, we explained how to send your pictures over the Web. But there's even more fun to be had. Specifically, Kodak is trying to make the process even simpler and snazzier with their Picture Postcard Software (shown in Figure 12.14). The product makes it easy to snap a picture with your Kodak (or other camera), download it, attach some text and an email address, and send it to friends and family via the Internet. The program was still being tested when we tried it. However, the final product should be available by the time you read this. You can find out more about Picture Postcard at:

www.kodak.com/daiHome/postcard/

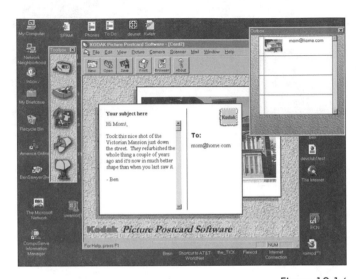

Figure 12.14

Kodak's Postcard Software makes it easy to send people fun picture postcard email.

PLACING GOOS ON THE WEB

The Goo manual is basically a brochure that highlights the program's features—it's not much of a help document. One of the features that the manual describes is the ability to output Goo animations for use in other media, like Web pages. It's an interesting concept, so let's do this ourselves!

The biggest problem with outputting a Goo animation onto your Web site: The only output options provided by Goo are as a digital video file or as something called a "Goovie," which is a very compact file that contains the key frames the Goo software requires to create the complete frames of the animation on the fly. Until MetaTools creates a Web player for Goovies, we can't use that format. And even though we can upload digital video files to the Web, their size can be huge, which means it will take a lot of time for users to download. Another problem with digital video files is that the two major formats—AVI and QuickTime—require different players for Web viewing, and not everyone has these players at their disposal. Frankly, animated GIF is a much more accessible format for Web users. So, we need to find some simple way to turn a digital video file of a Goo movie into a fun, animated GIF. Here's how.

Step 1 Create a Goo animation

First, we must create a source Goo animation. It's okay to use lots of frames, but it's better to create a nice, fluid yet short animation. Ideally, create an animation that begins and ends with the same image. Goo up an image and then return to it to its normal state. This makes the video loopable.

Step 2 Output the animation as an AVI file

To output your animation as an AVI file, you must choose a codec type and quality. Choose 100% as the quality, and Cinepak or Indeo (Cinepak is easiest) for the codec (again, a codec is simply a file compression method).

Step 3 Change the video size

Now that we have created our video file, we need to optimize it before we convert it to a GIF animation. All we need to do here is reduce the dimensions of the video. By default, Goo outputs a video in 360×360 resolution, which is way too big for a small-sized GIF animation. In addition, by reducing the dimensions, we can use more frames and the color reduction will be less noticeable. We recommend reducing the video to an 80×80 image size. To do this, we need a program that will easily let us convert image sizes. We chose a simple AVI Editor, available as shareware, called Personal AVI editor from a Denmark-based company called FlickerFree Multimedia.

Personal AVI Editor

FlickerFree Multimedia Products A/S
Hobrovej 479, Box 7115
DK-9200 Aalborg SV
Denmark

Phone:	(+45) 98189787
Fax:	(+45) 98186889
Web address:	www.flickerfree.com

Step 4   *Convert to animated GIF*

To create an animated GIF from an AVI file, you can use either of two good products. One is Microsoft's GIF Animator, which will read an AVI file. The problem with this program is that it requires you to do a lot of fine tuning to remove enough frames to achieve a decent file size. A better program is North Coast Software's VideoCraft GIF Animator.

VideoCraft GIF Animator is a video-editing package that includes loads of animated GIF features. The product is offered as shareware, so surf on over and download this wonderful program. The best feature of VideoCraft: You can easily specify what frame rate you want for your animated GIF (4 to 8 is best). Also, VideoCraft can reduce the AVI file to a 16-color palette, which can give you extremely small files (and the quality will still be good).

After we used VideoCraft on a simple test run of a 2 MB GOO file, we ended up reducing it to a good animated GIF of about 80,000 bytes.

VideoCraft GIF Animator

Andover Advanced Technologies, Inc.
532 Great Road
Acton, MA 01720

Phone:	508-635-5300
Fax:	508-635-5326]
Web address:	www.andatech.com

Making Money With Your

Digital Camera

13

People who want to earn extra income are often told the best place to start is with a hobby. If you make pottery for fun, why not sell it? If you travel to exotic places, why not try some freelance travel writing? However, only those who are skilled at their hobby can expect to make any money at it.

No one wants to buy an ugly, cracked bowl.

No newspaper or magazine will purchase a poorly written article, whether it is about an African safari or an afternoon at the mall.

The same principle holds true for digital photography. Anyone can try to sell his or her digital images, just as anyone can try to sell film photographs. However, professional photographers make money because they do quality work. If you are not a professional, that doesn't rule you out. A company that needs digital images, but doesn't have a lot of money to spend, might consider an amateur freelancer as a cost-cutting measure. Still, you had better be good.

Becoming good enough to sell your images means lots of practice and, just as importantly, spending time and money on photography classes. It also involves purchasing the right equipment. Entry-level digital cameras usually will not be good enough to provide the quality and resolution needed to sell your images. In other words: Selling digital images as a hobby can be an expensive proposition.

Even if you do decide to invest in a quality camera and photography classes, it will take some time to establish the contacts needed to make money. The income you earn will probably be meager, but if you earn enough to pay for your hobby, it can be worth it. Okay, we've broken the news to you that you aren't going to get rich selling your photographs. On to the good news: There *are* opportunities to sell your images if you approach the task professionally.

A DIGITAL WORLD WILL PAY FOR DIGITAL PHOTOGRAPHY

Most photographers currently try to make money with digital images by simply converting their existing photo collection into digital format. However, as the world of graphic design becomes increasingly digital—and as art directors become increasingly familiar with digital camera imagery and output—you can expect to see a demand for photographers who can do "digital work" directly. Especially now, with the increasing need for high-end imagery on the Web. Photographers who can bypass the scanning process and shoot photos directly with medium- and high-end digital camera equipment can often meet clients' needs faster and with better quality results than by converting printed photos into digital format.

If you're going to take the trouble to set up a digital studio, you might as well do it properly. You'll not only need to purchase the right hardware and software, you'll need to know how to use it—and use it well. That means becoming as familiar, and comfortable, with products like Photoshop and various plug-in filters as your clients are. Your clients will expect you to have the computer expertise to support their work. Some photographers who shoot with digital cameras don't really want to master digital-imaging software, and simply subcontract this work. That's becoming a bad idea—and a costly one. As your clients become more savvy about the digital photography process, they're going to expect *you* to answer their questions and respond to new deadlines, not some service bureau that you hire to do touch-up work.

If you're serious about making money from your digital photos, you'll need to buy an exceptional digital camera. Most professionals that we've spoken with use Kodak's 420-460 series of cameras, or use cameras from Leaf, Dicomed, or Phase One. The Kodak cameras are among the strongest-selling in the 35 mm category, while Leaf, Dicomed, and Phase One excel at photos in the 4×5 category.

DIGITAL STOCK PHOTOGRAPHY: THE MAJOR WAY TO TAKE STOCK

Stock photography is the business of selling existing photos to publishers and other companies that want to select from a collection to meet specific needs. In that sense, stock photography differs from working with clients. When you work directly with clients, *they* tell *you* what they want you to shoot. With stock photography, you present your existing portfolio to customers, and they select any photos that meet their current needs. When you sell your images as stock photography, you usually aren't selling your images outright. Instead, you retain all copyrights, and grant customers the right to publish your work in exchange for a royalty or licensing fee. Some photographers elect to sell their work outright to a stock photography company, which in turn grants licensing rights to customers. Sometimes, a combination approach is used, where a stock photography company agrees to sell your photos, while both you and the company split the licensing fees that customers pay.

There are three major categories of stock photography. You can:

- Generate high-quality clip art, which might be sold through various clip-art companies

- Create traditional stock photography, which is usually sold through a stock photography clearinghouse or agency

- "Go it on your own" by setting up shop on the Web and, via direct marketing methods, license or sell your images directly

Stock Photography Archives

In any case, generating stock photography is a major way for many photographers to earn money. However, stock photography archives have exploded in growth and the competition has become intense. Some agencies only accept photos from established professionals. But other stock photography houses have been reluctant to go the digital route. That's where companies that specialize in digital imagery can step in, and where you stand to have the best opportunity to make money. At least for now....

The market for digital stock art and images is growing rapidly, and will continue to grow, thanks to the proliferation of Web sites that need artwork in addition to other companies that realize the convenience, speed, and flexibility in acquiring and processing digital images.

If you purchase or license a digital image from an agency's Web site, you can download and access the image minutes after you complete the business transaction. If you order a photo from a traditional stock photography house, you can wait a week or more before receiving the photo via mail. Plus, you can be held accountable for additional charges if the image is not returned or is returned damaged.

Microsoft founder Bill Gates has realized the opportunities available with digital images stored online. He has started Corbis (see Figure 13.1), a separate company that is building an enormous digital image archive. You can view this on the Web at http://www.corbis.com. Corbis licenses images to magazines, Web sites, and other publishers and artists. Although Corbis is only one of many stock photo archives, it is one of the few that is trying to

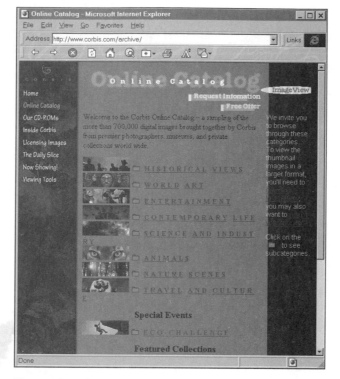

Figure 13.1

You can browse and order imagery from Corbis directly from their Web site.

promote an all-digital format. However, Corbis is still working to convert film via scans into digital works. Their executives hope they can soon start accepting quality digital camera work—and that means opportunities for digital photographers like yourself.

Digital Clip Art

Some companies specialize in providing high-quality, stock photography. Some examples include CD-ROM archives, such as Corel's (**www.corel.com**). Others are online archives, such as Art Today (**www.arttoday.com**). Some companies provide both services, such as PhotoDisc (**www.photodisc.com**). In most cases, these products are usually stock photos aimed at desktop publishers or multimedia developers. PhotoDisc has been extremely aggressive at building specific types of photo collections aimed at a niche audience—like Web developers.

Many of these companies will accept submissions from freelancers. Before approaching one of these companies, however, you need to do some research. Find out what types of images they are looking for (don't submit sports photos to a company specializing in nature images). Try to find out if you have the equipment and expertise required to meet the company's standards. And try to find out exactly who makes the decision regarding which images the company purchases. You want to route your queries to the right person; otherwise, your efforts could go unnoticed.

Most clip art is sold on CD-ROMs or via the Internet through automated retailing systems. Often, these companies are looking for specific compilations of material, so providing a cornucopia of imagery for a variety of categories might not be as appealing as a specialized selection. Check first, but many companies that use clip art are also looking for imagery that looks good at low resolutions—especially if the collection is meant for Web developers.

Going It Alone

It isn't easy, but you may want to try setting up your own stock photography archive from which to sell your photos.

This approach may or may not work. Most photographers who do this tend to be very good at marketing themselves, as well as taking good photographs. They're aggressive and continually looking for new ways to sell their work. It's important to ask yourself whether you fit into this category. And be honest: if you're not good at marketing yourself, will you be wasting time and expense trying to sell your images on your own? These individuals also tend to set up such ventures as supplements to their agency stock work. This can also be a good way to generate assignment-based work.

Some more advice:

- Focus on a unique category of images: Check out the larger archives, see what they have, and offer something different. We'll suggest some online archives to look at later in the chapter.

- Be different, but not too different: Be sure there is a market for your images. This doesn't take sophisticated market research, just some creativity and common sense.

- Set up shop online: Establish your archive on the World Wide Web so that potential customers can easily access your catalog of images. If you are focusing on lower-end users, make it possible for your customers to buy images with credit cards and make images available in both single and collection form. If you are targeting a niche or professional clientele, you'll want to negotiate a price and be paid by check.

- Protect your work: Consider using a watermarking filter on your imagery to protect your images against unlawful use by Web browsers.

- Consider buying a custom pricing package: Custom pricing software can help you determine pricing for your stock photos when you're not working through an agency. You can find some leads on these types of products at Joel Day's awesome stock photo resource page on the Web, mentioned later in this chapter.

ASSIGNMENT WORK

We mentioned assignment work earlier in this chapter. We didn't dwell on this category, but it's worth a closer look. At present, it is a little easier to break into assignment work with digital cameras than to get into stock photography. Numerous sites on the World Wide Web actively solicit digital images from freelancers. And, while most of the larger online newspapers use their own staff photographers, some of the smaller newspapers may accept freelance submissions. The AP is currently staffing many of their photographers with digital cameras—and is always looking for stringers. Granted, the pay isn't great, but it's a great way to break into the business.

In fact, because most daily newspapers now have their own Web sites, the number of available outlets for soliciting work is staggering. In addition, thousands of desktop graphics designers around the world are increasingly working with digital photographers. With their seasoned computer skills, these artists understand that higher-end digital cameras provide more-than-capable digital imagery to support their own work.

Online newspapers and desktop publishers aren't the only outlets available for soliciting your services. Browse the Web and check out some

sites that interest you or that match your photographic specialty. With the enormous number of Web pages available, if you do good work and are persistent, eventually one site might bite.

To acquire assignment work, you must first put together a good portfolio. Second, you need to be as savvy as possible about technology issues and trends so that you feel confident enough to answer any questions your potential clients might ask. Finally, you'll need to do a lot of leg work to both advertise and network. You should make phone calls until you find enough desktop graphics artists who need photography partners and are looking for (or accepting) digitally generated imagery.

PORTFOLIOS ONLINE

Another way to display your images on the World Wide Web is through advertisers such as Portfolios Online (**www.portfolios.com**), a Web directory of visual artists and communications professionals (see Figure 13.2). Portfolios Online is divided into 10 categories:

- Photographers

- Animators

- Multimedia craftsmen

Figure 13.2
The Portfolios Online Web site.

- Copywriters

- Art directors

- Advertising agencies

- Graphic designers

- Illustrators

- Industrial designers

- Surface designers

- Fashion designers (future category)

For $199 a year, subscribers can display 6 portfolio thumbnail images, each of which can be enlarged for a closer look. For an additional $100, you can display 12 images, any of which can be replaced for $15 per image. Resume and contact information can also be posted. And if a client has a Web site, a free hypertext link to it is provided.

You can also set up your own site on the Web for much less, but Portfolios Online is selling a single destination that art directors and other potential clients can return to without having to continually search the Web for photography collections. This site is a destination and your site isn't, so it's hard to see them constantly searching the entire Web versus a few select sites.

PHOTOGRAPHS OR PRODUCTS?

As we've already explained, just because you own a digital camera doesn't necessarily mean that you can make money from your photos. However, if you have a creative and entrepreneurial mind, or if you consider yourself a "semi-pro hobbyist," a digital camera can open up new avenues for both fun and revenue.

In other words, think beyond the conventional arenas of stock photography and shooting photos for clients. There are other ways to use and sell digital images. For instance, consider CD-ROM-based multimedia. This is still a tough business to break into, but people who've put together niche CD-ROM products have been very successful in selling them directly or via a Web promotion. For instance, perhaps you've taken your digital camera on a trip to an exotic site and snapped hundreds of photos. Consider putting together a travel book on CD-ROM. Or maybe you're an expert on antiques and have snapped hundreds of pictures of antique furniture. Why not consider putting together a CD-ROM about that? The key is to consider what you have a strong knowledge about or interest in, and then use that as the focus for shooting and marketing your images.

A few more examples: Perhaps you could create a calendar of awesome digital art. Or how about creating and marketing a line of funky greeting cards? Photographers typically try to make money by selling just their photographs. However, if you consider the niches that are available on the Web, or that are suitable for adapting digital photos, you can create entirely new markets for your work .

RESOURCES FOR PROFESSIONAL DIGITAL CAMERA WORK

While researching this chapter, we uncovered several resources that can show you how to earn money from your digital photography efforts.

The STOCKPHOTO Page

This site, at **www.s2f.com/STOCKPHOTO/,** was created by stock photographer Joel Day. For digital photography wannabes and other up-and-comers, it's about as good as the Web gets. The site is packed with excellent information on how to be a successful stock photographer. There is an excellent FAQ on the subject, pointers to useful sites, addresses and contacts for almost every stock photo company in the world, and information on key software for stock photographers.

Other Stock Photo Resources

Stock Connection
110 Frederick Ave. Suite A
Rockville, MD 20850
Phone: 301-424-2455
Fax: 301-309-0941

Marketing Stock In The Digital Environment is a book by stock photography experts Jim Pickerell and Andrew Child. It covers many of the important issues that photographers in the digital age need to know about, especially regarding the ins and outs of selling photographs. The authors' Web site at www.pickphoto.com/ includes descriptions and links to several services and information that may be of interest to stock photographers.

This book sells for $25 plus $3 postage and handling.

Index Stock
126 Fifth Ave.
New York, NY 10011
Phone: 212-929-4644
Fax: 212-633-1914
Web address: http://www.indexstock.com/

Index Stock is a leading stock photo company. Their Web site contains extensive resources for stock photography, with some discussion about stock photography and its future. There are also several white papers and advice sections that can help you to become a better stock photographer.

Index Stock, like many of their peers, hasn't yet begun accepting digital-only pictures. Until that time, the information provided here is still useful for those pioneering in digital camera stock photos.

PhotoDisc, Inc.
2013 Fourth Ave.
Seattle, WA 98121
Phone: 206-441-9355
Fax: 206-441-4961
Web address: http://www.photodisc.com

PhotoDisc is an exciting up-and-comer in the emerging digital stock industry. Their stock photos are aimed at Web developers as well as desktop publishers. Like Corbis, PhotoDisc is moving toward complete digital camera stock but still hasn't pushed into digital camera acquisition. Still, PhotoDisc has put together some promising multimedia CD-ROM packages, and this site is a good resource for their focus on multimedia and Web developers.

Camera Manufacturers:

A Reference Guide

14

No real digital camera enthusiast is going to use the same digital camera forever; some may even buy two or three just to have access to different cameras for different situations (for instance, one for road trips, one for Web work, one for high-end publishing work). Regardless of why or when you decide to purchase a new camera, this chapter is for you.

What follows is a roundup of all the major manufacturers and their cameras, complete with very brief introductions of the camera models each company was producing as of December, 1996. Certainly, many models and brand names will continue to be sold for some time, but we've included manufacturers' Web pages and phone numbers to help you find out about any changes or new models.

In this chapter, we won't describe every feature of every camera. We've mostly noted a camera's image resolution and a few other key features (such as LCD screens) to help you understand the basic camera design. To find out more about a particular camera, take a look at the camera company's Web page (if they have one).

In addition, you can expect other electronics and technology companies (like Sharp, JVC, and Panasonic; and a host of traditional camera companies) to enter the digital camera market soon.

For the most part, expect high-end cameras to cost between $5,000 and $50,000; mid-range cameras to cost between $1,000 to $5,000; and low-end cameras to cost between $250 and $1,000. Another point to note is that cameras dubbed "studio cameras" usually require direct hookup to a computer at all times. Most high-end cameras fall into this category, except for those that have internal hard drives or accept Type III PCMCIA hard-drive memory cards.

Tip

Even if you're not yet ready to buy your next camera, an afternoon spent surfing the camera sites and the manufacturers' sites can be useful. Many offer camera operation tips, and some offer free software that can be compatible with your existing camera. The technology is progressing so rapidly that it's smart to stay abreast of the latest developments.

AGFA

Bayer Corp./AGFA Division
100 Challenger Road
Ridgefield Park, NJ 07660
Phone: 201-440-2500
Fax: 201-440-5733
Web address: www.agfa.com

AGFA ActionCam

Web page: www.agfahome.com/products/prodfam/actcam.html

A high-end 1-shot camera with 1528×1148 resolution, the ActionCam uses Type III hard disks for storage (114 images) and features a 28 to 80 mm zoom lens and autofocus. Other features include auto exposure, auto and remote flash triggering, shutter speeds between 1/2 second and 1/2000 second, and FotoTune color management software.

AGFA StudioCam

Web page: www.agfahome.com/products/prodfam/studiocam.html

Another high-end camera, the StudioCam is a tethered scanning camera that features a resolution of up to 4500×3648 with zoom and manual focusing. The product includes AGFA's FotoLook, FotoTune, FotoFlavor software, and Adobe Photoshop.

AGFA ePhoto 307

Web page: www.agfahome.com/products/ephoto307.html

The ePhoto 307 is AGFA's low-end point-and-shoot camera with 640×480 resolution. AGFA PhotoWise and Adobe PhotoDeluxe are included.

Figure 14.1

AGFA's ActionCam captures up to 24 images per minute.

APPLE COMPUTER, INC.

1 Infinite Loop
Cupertino, CA 95014
Phone: 408-996-1010
Web address: www.apple.com

Apple QuickTake 150

Web address: product.info.apple.com/productinfo/datasheets/im/quicktakewin.html

The QuickTake 150 is currently Apple's main camera. It's a low-end point-and-shoot camera with up to 640×480 resolution, with a built-in flash and close-up lens.

ARCA-SWISS

442 West Belden Lane
Chicago, IL 60614
Phone: 312-248-2513

Arca-Swiss TrueCam

The TrueCam is a three-shot, tethered, high-end studio camera with a 1512×1162 resolution.

ASSOCIATED PRESS

50 Rockefeller Plaza
New York, NY 10020
Phone: 212-621-6904
Fax: 212-621-1784

NC2000E

Web address: 204.80.115.38/kodak/

This camera is manufactured specially for AP photographers by Kodak, and is a sister camera to Kodak's own 420 model. The camera is a high-end 35 mm attachment for Nikon N90S, has 16 MB of memory, and can shoot consecutive frames (2.25 frames per second) at 1280×1024 resolution. The camera also features an internal microphone for recording annotations. AP photographers can purchase this directly from The Associated Press.

CANON USA, INC.

One Canon Plaza
Lake Success, NY 11042
Phone:　　　　516-488-6700
Email:　　　　info@canon.com
Web address:　www.usa.canon.com

Canon EOS DCS 3

Web address: www.usa.canon.com/cameras/digitalcamera.html

A high-end one-shot add-on camera with 1268×1012 resolution. The EOS DCS 3 can take pictures at 2.7 frames per second, and offers full compatibility with Canon EF lenses. The add on is manufactured by Kodak for Canon, which places it on their EOS-1N camera.

Canon EOS DCS 1

Web page: www.usa.canon.com/cameras/dcs1.html

A very high-end camera, the EOS DCS 1 is Canon's top-of-the-line camera, with maximum resolution of 3060×2036. It shoots one frame per second and uses the Canon EOS-1N body.

Canon PowerShot 600

Canon's low-end camera features 832×608 resolution, a timer, 1 MB of memory, and a built-in microphone. It uses PCMCIA cards.

CASIO, INC.

570 Mt. Pleasant Ave.
Dover, NJ 07801
Phone: 201-361-5400
Fax: 201-361-3819
Email: info@casio-usa.com
Web address: www.casio-usa.com

Casio QV-30

Web page: www.casio-usa.com/html/products/qv-30detail.html

The QV-30 from Casio features 480×240 resolution, an LCD screen, and video output to a TV.

Casio QV-10A

Web page: www.casio-usa.com/html/products/qv-10adetail.html

Another low-end camera from Casio, the QV10A has 480×240 resolution, an LCD screen, video output, and comes with Adobe PhotoDeluxe.

Casio QV-10

Web page: www.casio-usa.com/html/products/qv-10detail.html

This is a low-end camera with resolution of 480×240 and an LCD screen.

Casio QV-100

Web page: www.casio-usa.com/html/products/qv-100detail.html

With 640×480 resolution, the QV-100 features a slightly higher resolution than Casio's other cameras, but still includes the LCD screen.

CHINON AMERICA, INC.

615 Hawaii Ave.
Torrance, CA

Figure 14.2
*The Casio QV-100 has 4 MB flash memory and can store from
64 (fine) to 192 (normal) images.*

Phone: 310-533-0274
Fax: 310-533-1727

Chinon ES-3000

A low-end point-and-shoot camera with 640×480 resolution, the Chinon
ES-3000 includes a built-in flash and a power zoom lens. The product works
with PCMCIA cards for removable storage.

CONNECTIX CORPORATION

2655 Campus Drive
San Mateo, CA 94403
Phone: 415-571-5100
Fax: 415-571-5195

Connectix makes the QuickCam series of digital cameras. The products
are desktop cameras used for video conferencing or Web cams, and are
meant for direct connection to your PC.

Connectix Color QuickCam

Web page: www.connectix.com/connect/cqchome.html

The Color QuickCam is optimized for indoor lighting and features a 640×480
resolution. Telephoto, wide-angle, and close-up lenses are available.

DICOMED, INC.

12270 Nicollet Ave.
Burnsville, MN 55337
Phone: 612-895-3000
Fax: 612-895-3258
Email: info@dicomed.com
Web address: www.dicomed.com

Dicomed is one of a handful of companies that manufactures at the cutting edge, high end of the digital camera market.

Dicomed DDC 7520

Web page: www.dicomed.com/products.html

This high-end camera features a whopping 6000×7520 resolution. An internal 1-GB hard drive is used to store imagery.

Dicomed BigShot 3000

Web page: www.dicomed.com/bigshot.html

The BigShot 3000 is a 3-shot camera that features 4096×4096 resolution.

Figure 14.3
Dicomed's ProSeries camera backs allow for full viewing range.

Dicomed BigShot 4000

Web page: www.dicomed.com/bigshot.html

The BigShot 4000 also features resolution of 4096×4096, but is a 1-shot camera.

DuPont Printing And Publishing

380 Allwood Road
Clifton, NJ 07012
Phone: 201-916-1317
Fax: 201-612-5933
Web address: www.dupont.com/print

Crosfield C130

Web page: www.dupont.com/print/products/scanfilm.html

This is a high-end scanning camera with 3072×2320 resolution.

Dycam, Inc.

9414 Eton Ave.
Chatsworth, CA 91311
Phone: 818-407-3960
Fax: 818-407-3966
Web address: www.dycam.com

Dycam 10-C

Web page: www.dycam.com/r10-c.html

This is a low-end camera with zoom, wide-angle, and close-up lenses available, and with 640×480 resolution. The camera features PCMCIA cards for removable storage.

Dycam Agricultural Digital Camera

Web page: www.dycam.com/adc.html

A digital camera specifically made for agricultural photography, the Dycam ADC photographs visible red and near-infrared light that reflects off plants. Images can be analyzed with Dycam software for categorization in any of three specific vegetation indexes.

EASTMAN KODAK

343 State Street
Rochester, NY 14650
Phone: 716-724-4000
Web address: www.kodak.com

Kodak DCS 460

Web page: www.kodak.com/daiHome/DCS/range.shtml

One of Kodak's high-end 35 mm cameras, the DCS 460 features 3060×2036 resolution, and PCMCIA storage. It uses a Nikon N90 body and accepts all F-mount lenses. The camera shoots one frame per second.

Kodak Professional DCS 420

Web page: www.kodak.com/daiHome/DCS/range.shtml

This is another high-end camera, featuring a 35 mm body and 1524×1012 resolution, PCMCIA card support, and an internal microphone.

Figure 14.4
The Dycam has the option of close-up and super-wide-angle lens adapters.

Kodak Professional EOS-DCS 5

Web page: www.kodak.com/daiHome/DCS/range.shtml

A high-end camera with 1524×1012 resolution.

Kodak Professional DCS 465

Web page: www.kodak.com/daiHome/DCS/range.shtml

The DCS 465 digital camera back is compatible with medium format and 4×5 view cameras. It's a high-end studio camera with 3060×2036 resolution, PCMCIA cards for storage, and an internal microphone.

Kodak Digital Science DC50 Zoom

Web page: www.kodak.com/daiHome/DC50/indexDC50.shtml

Kodak's top-of-the-line low-end camera, the DC50 is one of the more popular low-end digital cameras around. It features a 756×504 resolution, PCMCIA card support, zoom and close-up lenses, and auto focus.

Kodak Digital Science DC40

Web page: www.kodak.com/daiHome/DC40/INDEX-DC40.shtml

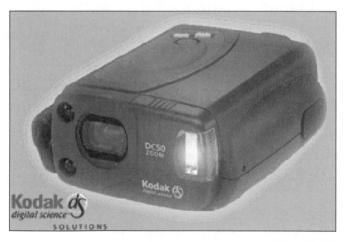

Figure 14.5

Kodak's DC50, a relatively low-end camera, features a zoom lens, flash, and a Timer LED (which enables you to take time-delayed shots).

Just below the DC50 is the DC40, which offers the same 756×504 resolution but doesn't have the power zoom or close-up lenses.

Kodak Digital Science DC20

Web page: www.kodak.com/daiHome/DC20/index.shtml

The DC20 is the lowest priced digital camera around. It sports 493×373 resolution, but in order to keep the camera's cost down, Kodak elected not to include flash or an LCD screen.

Kodak Digital Science DC25

Web page: www.kodak.com/daiHome/DC25/

Kodak's newest low-end camera, the DC25 is a sort of "DC20+," featuring the same 493×373 resolution, but with removable CompactFlash memory cards, an LCD screen, built-in flash, and it comes with photo software and Kai's Power Goo.

EPSON AMERICA, INC.

20770 Madrona Ave., D1-04A
Torrance, CA 90509
Phone: 310-782-0770
Web address: www.epson.com/home.shtml

Epson PhotoPC

Web page: www.epson.com/graphicarts/cameras/photopc

The point-and-shoot PhotoPC has a resolution of 640×480, a built-in flash, and upgradeable memory. A second model was recently released that includes an LCD viewfinder.

FUJI PHOTO FILM CO., LTD.

555 Taxter Road
Elmsford, NY 10523

Phone: 914-789-8100

Web address: www.fujifilm.com

Fujix DS-7

The DS-7 has a maximum resolution of 640×480, an LCD screen, and re-movable storage through solid state, floppy disk cards.

Fujix DS-220

The mid-range Fujix-DS-220 features a major power zoom lens, PCMCIA card support, and 640×480 resolution. An optional LCD at-tachment is available.

Fujix DS-505/DS-515

Web page: www.fujifilm.co.jp/eng/505/indexe.html

The DS-505 and DS-515 are high-end cameras with 1280×1000 resolu-tion, PCMCIA card support, and a 35 mm Nikon camera body. The DS-505 shoots up to 1 frame per second and the DS-515 shoots up to 3 frames per second.

Figure 14.6
The DS-505 is one of Fuji's high-end cameras.

Fujix HC-2000

This high-end camera features PCMCIA cards and has a resolution of 1280×1000.

KanImage, Inc.

11-05 44th Drive
Long Island City, NY 11101
Phone: 718-482-1800

KanImage Digital Photography System

This high-end studio scanning camera has a resolution of 4608×3480.

Leaf Systems, Inc.

8 Technology Drive
Westborough, MA 01581
Phone: 617-275-5150
Fax: 508-836-5599
Web address: www.scitex.com

Leaf CatchLight

Web page: www.scitex.com/leaf/products/CatchLight/CatchLight.html

A high-end camera with a 2048×2048 resolution, the CatchLight is a 1-shot studio camera that requires connection to a PC.

Leaf DCB II

Web page: www.scitex.com/leaf/products/DCB2/leafdcb2.html

The Leaf DCB II is a high-end, 3-shot studio camera with a resolution of 2048×2048.

Leaf Lumina

Web page: www.scitex.com/leaf/products/Lumina/Lumina.html

This is Leaf's mid-range scanning studio camera, which has a resolution of 2700×3380.

MegaVision, Inc.

P.O. Box 60158
Santa Barbara, CA 93160
Phone: 805-964-1400
Web address: www.mega-vision.com

MegaVision T2

This is a high-end, 3-shot studio camera with a resolution of 2048×2048.

Minolta Corporation

101 Williams Drive
Ramsey, NJ 07466
Phone: 201-825-4000
Fax: 201-818-3590
Web address: www.minolta.com

Minolta RD-175

A high-end, 1-shot camera utilizing 3 CCD chips for a 1528×1145 resolution, the Minolta RD-175 has PCMCIA card support and uses a traditional 35 mm camera body, which accepts all other AF-series lenses.

Dimage V

Minolta's low-end digital camera, the Dimage V sports 640×480 resolution, removable storage via solid state disk drives, and an LCD screen.

Nikon, Inc.

1300 Walt Whitman Road
Melville, NY 11747-3068
Phone: 516-547-4200
Web address: www.klt.co.jp/nikon

Nikon E2 Series

Web page: www.klt.co.jp/nikon/EID/Digital_Cameras/E2/index.html

These high-end cameras are based on a Nikon 35 mm camera and work as one-shot field cameras. They support PCMCIA cards; and can take pictures at one frame per second (E2N), three frames per second, or even seven frames when in a compressed "burst mode" (E2NS). The cameras have a resolution of 1280×1000 and feature a video output port.

Coolpix 100

This is a digital camera specially designed for laptop users. It can directly attach to a PCMCIA card slot. The camera has a resolution of 512×480 and a built-in flash.

Olympus America

2 Corporate Center Drive
Melville, NY 11747
Phone: 516-844-5520
Email: info@olympusamerica.com
Web address: www.olympus.com/digital

Olympus D-200L

Web page: www.olympusamerica.com/digital/docs/digproduct.html

The D-200L is a low-end point-and-shoot camera with 640×480 resolution, built-in flash, and an LCD screen.

Olympus D-300L

Web page: www.olympusamerica.com/digital/docs/digproduct.html

The D-300L, also a low-end camera, is identical to the 200L except it features a higher resolution (1024×768), plus a few extra focus features.

PHASE ONE UNITED STATES, INC.

24 Woodbine Ave., Suite 1
Northport, NY 11768
Phone: 516-757-0400
Fax: 516-757-2217
Email: info@phaseone.com
Web address: www.phaseone.com

PhotoPhase Plus

Web page: www.phaseone.com/brochures/ppp/Welcome.html

The PhotoPhase Plus camera back is a high-end scanning camera that works with common 4×5 studio cameras. The PhotoPhase Plus sports a hefty 5000×7200 resolution.

Phase One Studiokit

Web page: www.phaseone.com/brochures/sk/Welcome.html

The Phase One Studiokit is a reasonably priced high-end system that offers a digital camera back, a couple high-end filters, soft light boxes, and powerful but easy-to-use software. The package works with any 4×5 camera.

PowerPhase

Web page: www.phaseone.com/brochures/powerphase.html

A very high-end camera back for medium format cameras, the PowerPhase features 7000×7000 resolution.

Figure 14.7
Phase One Studiokit is a great digital start for the professional studio photographer.

POLAROID CORP.

549 Technology Square
Cambridge, MA 02139
Phone: 617-386-2000
Fax: 617-386-3118
Web address: www.polaroid.com

Polaroid PDC 2000/60, Polaroid PDC 2000/40, Polaroid PDC 2000/T

Web page: www.polaroid.com/digcam/digcam.html

Poloroid makes several different designs of their mid-range PDC 2000 camera. They all sport 1600×1200 resolution, built-in flash, and a 38 mm lens. An optional 60 mm lens attachment is available. The differences between the three models are the sizes of their internal storage.

RICOH CORP.

475 Lillard Drive
Sparks, NV 89434
Phone: 702-352-1600
Fax: 702-352-1615
Web address: www.ricohcpg.com

Ricoh RDC-1

Web page: www.ricohcpg.com/rdc.html

The RDC-1 features 768×576 resolution, zoom, an (optional) LCD screen, and can record single images or up to 4 seconds of video and sound per PCMCIA card. Still shots can also be augmented with sound.

Ricoh RDC-2

Web page: www.ricohcpg.com/rdc2.html

Ricoh's newest version of the RDC series features 768×576 resolution and an optional LCD screen, and can record single images, a continuous series, or up to 10 seconds of video and sound per PCMCIA card. Still shots can also be augmented with sound.

Figure 14.8
The RDC-1 is the first digital camera to record motion scenes with sound.

Scanview, Inc.

330A Hatch Drive
Foster City, CA 94404
Phone: 415-378-6360
Fax: 415-378-6368
Email: info@scanview-inc.com

Scanview Carnival 2000S

The high-end Scanview Carnival is a one-shot, 2048×2048 resolution camera with single and multishot modes. It's designed to connect to existing medium-to-large-format camera bodies, and is a studio camera requiring a computer to store imagery as it is captured.

Sega

255 Shoreline Drive, Suite 200
Redwood City, CA 94065
Phone: 415-508-2800
Fax: 415-802-3063
Web address: www.sega.com

Sega, the large video game company, recently debuted their digital camera, which is to be released this year. The low-end camera will work with both PCs and the Sega Saturn. Reportedly, it will also allow you to input pictures of your face (or anything else, for that matter) into various Sega games. Sega also offers a netlink device to use for email and Web browsing, and the camera software will also allow you to download pictures to Sega Saturn memory cards. This product certainly foreshadows a time when digital photos become an integral part of people's game experience.

Sony

550 Madison Ave.
New York, NY 10022-3211
Phone: 1-800-472-SONY

Figure 14.9
The DKC-ID1 digital still camera.

Fax: 212-833-6938

Web address: www.sony.com

Sony DKC-ID1

Web page: www.sel.sony.com/SEL/bppg/new/index.html

A mid-range camera, the DKC-ID1 features 768×576 resolution, 12× zoom lens, an LCD screen, removable PCMCIA cards for storage, and infrared data transfer.

Sony DKC-5000 CatsEye

Web page: www.sel.sony.com/SEL/bppg/epp/stills.html

The high-end DKC-5000 is a studio camera with 3 CCD chips to give you a 1520×1144 resolution.

Appendix

A

Around The World In 80 Minutes: A Quick Guide To The Internet And Web

Throughout this book, we've supplied Web addresses of camera companies, software companies, photographers, and other individuals and companies that we think can help you get more out of your digital photography experience. But we haven't lost sight of an important fact: Just because you own a digital camera doesn't mean you're an experienced Web surfer. You might not yet even have an Internet account. Or maybe you've done a bit of exploring on the Web but are still confused about what's available or how to use the Web more efficiently. And as a digital camera owner, you're probably going to want to post some of your photos on the Internet or even create your own Web pages to make your photos accessible to the world. But you might be in the dark about how to go about these tasks. So, let's clear up the confusion once and for all, and answer your questions regarding the Internet and the World Wide Web.

What's The Difference Between The Internet And The World Wide Web?

We hear this question a lot. Because people talk about the Internet and the World Wide Web (we'll just call it the Web from here on) as two distinct entities, it's easy to understand the confusion. But the truth is that the Internet and the Web are not separate—any more than a car and its engine are separate. And that's exactly how you should view the Web and the Internet. First, a bit of history is in order.

A Brief History Of The World Wide Web

The Internet began in the 1960s as a joint effort between the U.S. Government and various research groups at universities throughout the world. In fact, if we can say that anything good came of the Cold War, it would have to be the Internet. The government was concerned that a nuclear attack by the Soviets could wipe out a major defense installation. At the time, computers were networked among different government facilities in what could basically could be considered a chain. And if one link in the chain was to be broken, the entire network would literally come crashing to the ground.

The solution? Use ordinary telephone lines to link computers across the country and even around the world. Then, develop a standard set of rules, or protocols, that different computers could use to talk to each. Any computer that was operating the software that applied these rules could have access to any other computer that used compatible software. At first blush, it seems hard to believe that the Department of Defense would want to have any part of such an arrangement. After all, if any computer can talk to any other computer around the world, how can there be any security?

That's the most interesting part of the story. The creators of the Internet devised a plan so that even though one computer could link up with another computer, the second computer could limit access to its information if the first computer could not provide the correct password or other security information. And thus the Internet was born, although at the time it was called the ARPANET.

WHERE DO THE INTERNET AND WEB STAND NOW?

Well, the Cold War died a quick death in the early '90s, but the Internet didn't. By that time, thousands of governmental agencies, educational institutions, research groups, and corporations had joined this extremely simple, yet vast network of computers. And people quickly discovered the obvious: With the Internet, we have the ability to share or acquire information almost instantaneously—from anywhere in the world. So, the networking system that the U.S. Government has put into place has now become as public as the phone system. In fact, that's what the Internet is: a network of phone lines used to link computers, coupled with software to enable the computers to talk to one another. It really is about that simple.

And that leads us to the Web. Let's return to our car analogy for a moment. The engine is the component of a car that powers it. The rest of the car contains components for everything from sitting and steering to holding coffee cups. The Internet and the Web are a lot like that relationship. The Internet is the collection of phone lines, computers, and software that keep the whole operation puttering along nicely. In other words, the Internet is the engine. The Web, on the other hand, is what makes the Internet comfortable and fun to use. But the Web can be conceptually difficult to grasp at first, even though it's extraordinarily simple. The problem is that, like the Internet, the Web isn't a product, it isn't a thing, it doesn't exist in any one place, and it isn't controlled by any one person or company.

The Web began as the brainchild of an enterprising young man named Marc Andreessen, who observed that all of the information being exchanged on the Internet was in plain text form. And, he noted, the Internet was a bit difficult to use unless you knew a lot of arcane commands that are part of the Unix operating system. About 1990 (a bit earlier actually), Marc decided it was time to remove the Nerd Factor from the Internet. His solution was to create a user interface that would allow people to use the Internet more easily. Plus, this interface would allow people to view graphics on the Internet. The other major component of this interface was the ability to create *hyperlinks*. These were, and still are, items on screen that, when you click on them, take you to a different part of the Internet.

The result of Marc's effort became the world's first Web browser, called Mosaic. And because Marc was working for a government agency at the time, the browser became public property. Anybody who wanted to acquire and use Mosaic could do so free of charge. And that trend has continued into the present. The world's two most popular Web browsers (Netscape Navigator and Microsoft Internet Explorer) are free. But expect that situation to change soon.

The bottom line is that the Web is simply any site on the Internet that organizes its information so that it can be viewed by a Web browser. In other words: *a Web site is a computer that's connected to the Internet and stores information in a format that allows people to display the information in graphical form and with hyperlinks.* If you can digest that definition, you're ready to hear the most important fact: These days, information on almost all Internet sites is organized to support graphical display. So the Internet and the Web have truly become one—they are as inseparable as a car and its engine.

HTML Is Not A Four-Letter Word

Most people own and drive a car, but it's also true that a lot of people don't have the slightest idea what goes on underneath the hood. That lack of knowledge doesn't make it any more difficult for Mr. Klackney, for instance, to drive his car. However, it does prevent him from making his own minor repairs and even from carrying on an intelligent dialog with his automotive mechanic. The more Mr. Klackney decides to learn about his car, the better. He doesn't need to be an automotive expert, just a bit more mechanically savvy.

The same principle holds true for the Web. You can surf the Web night and day without ever understanding the fundamental way in which a Web page works. But if you want to get the most out of the Web, and especially if you want to create your own Web site, a little knowledge is essential. Not a lot of knowledge, mind you. A little will do.

Ask yourself this question: How does a Web browser (like Netscape or Internet Explorer) "know" how to display graphics and text for a Web site? In other words, how does the browser determine what a Web page should look like? In a word—HTML, which stands for Hypertext Markup Language. A lot of Web users run screaming whenever somebody mentions "HTML" to them. And for good reason. The first time you look at HTML code, your jaw will probably hang open in disbelief. HTML can look totally indecipherable.

HTML, though, is really simple in principle. It's nothing more than a collection of tags and commands that tell a Web browser how to format and display information. Most tags in HTML are in pairs and use slashes to tell the browser where one tag starts and ends. For instance, to tell a Web browser to display a word in boldface, you use the starting tag <B/> and the ending tag </B>. So, if we want Mr. Klackney's name to appear in bold on our Web page, we would encode it as:

```
Please call <B>Mr. Klackney</B> for more information.<P>
```

By the way, the <P> code tells a Web browser to create a paragraph break. Sounds simple, right? HTML really is that simple. It only begins to seem difficult when you consider that there are hundreds of HTML tags and commands. Who wants to memorize all that stuff? And do you really *need* to memorize "all that stuff" in order to create a Web page.

Fortunately, no.

There are literally dozens of HTML editor programs that automate the HTML encoding process. These packages allow you to define and format the content of your Web pages with a series of menus and dialog boxes. And while it's true that you can create a complete Web site (using an HTML editor) without ever learning a single HTML command, you can create a better Web site if you try to understand at least a few tags and commands. Why? Using an HTML editor is like finger painting with mittens on. You can create all of the basic shapes and designs you want, but if you want to provide some real detail, you need to use your fingers. Fine tuning a Web page needs to be done by hand—and that means adding a few specific HTML commands that aren't available from an HTML editor's menuing system. The good news is that you can create some dazzling Web pages with fewer than a dozen HTML commands at your fingertips. We'll walk you through the creation of a Web page later in this appendix. You'll be amazed at how simple the process is.

Joining The Internet

If you already have an Internet account, you might want to skip this section. On the other hand, if you're unhappy with your Internet service and feel like you need to know more before you yell at your provider or switch to another one, this section is tailor-made for you.

Only a few years ago, getting started on the Internet was an exercise in insanity. We know. We've lost plenty of hair, not to mention brain cells, trying desperately to make our computers Internet-ready. Today, though, getting into cyberspace is child's play. To begin, you need to find an *Internet provider*. This is a local company that leases high-performance phone lines, and lots of them, typically from a Baby Bell, like US West, Pacific Bell, NYNEX, etc. Unless you have direct access to one of these high-performance cables (called T1 and T3), you need to sign up with an Internet provider in order to use the Internet. A typical Internet subscription will cost you about $20 to $30 per month for unlimited access. The nice thing about the Internet is that you can visit Web sites anywhere in the world, anytime of the day or night, without incurring any long-distance charges. That's because your Internet provider really is "providing" you with something. You're getting access, through your provider's own leased lines, to the worldwide network of telephone cables and interconnected computers.

So, the first step involves opening an account with an Internet provider. It's not an easy step, though. In fact, choosing an Internet provider can be the most difficult part of getting connected to the Internet. You're an Internet novice, right? So how are you supposed to know which Internet provider to use?

The answer's easy: Ask around. In most parts of the U.S., and elsewhere in the world, there are several local Internet providers from which to choose. However, all Internet providers are not created equal. Some offer bargain-basement prices, but when you call for technical support, you'll discover that they truly are being run out of somebody's basement. Some providers overcommit by taking on way too many subscribers. The result is that it can be difficult—if not impossible—to get online during peak times of day, or that when you need technical support you find yourself on hold for an hour. So the only way to determine which Internet service to use involves talking to your friends, relatives, and co-workers who already subscribe to an Internet provider. Find out whether they are satisfied with their provider, how much they are being charged, how easy or difficult it was to install their Internet start-up software, how good or bad has the provider's technical support been, and so on.

But here's the difficult part. When you ask several people about their experiences with their Internet providers, almost all of them are going to express dissatisfaction. That fact has to do with the rapidly growing demand for Internet access and the relative newness of most Internet providers. No matter which company you sign up with, you're probably going to be dealing with a certain level of inexperience. Want to know the most foolproof way to find a good Internet provider? Locate one that is *not* currently taking any new subscribers. That means the company realizes what load it can handle, and has refused to overcommit by selling additional subscriptions. Then, get on this provider's waiting list. If you need instant Internet access, go ahead and sign up with another provider—just make sure you pay by the month and do not agree to a long-term contract. (You'll probably have to pay a $30 to $40 set-up fee, though.) Then, when your first-choice provider calls to let you know they can fit you in, cancel your other account.

Getting Started

The first thing you need before you can join the Internet community is a modem. If your computer already has a modem, you need to determine its speed. If the modem operates at 14.4 Kbps or slower, throw it out. Then buy a modem that operates at a speed of 28.8 Kbps or higher. You don't really need to know what the numbers mean. Just realize that the higher the number, the faster the modem. You'll want a fast modem to handle the graphics, sound, and other multimedia information contained on Web sites that you visit. After you've installed a modem, you're ready to go online.

We mentioned earlier that installing the software required to connect to the Internet—even after you've found an Internet provider—used to be a major headache. Not any more. When you talk to others about their set-up experiences with their Internet providers, take note of those who say that the installation was a breeze. That's exactly the way it should be. Subscribing to an Internet provider is literally a five-minute process that you can conduct over the phone. You give a sales representative your personal information and probably a credit card number, and the sales rep in turn gives you a user ID and a logon password. While you're on the phone, the sales rep will actually set up your account so that you have instant access to the Internet.

But hold on.

Remember that we said the Internet is a collection of phone lines and computers, *and* the software required to connect to these other computers. In reality, your computer probably already contains the software you need because Windows 95 and the Macintosh operating system (from System 7.5 on) both come with Internet software fully installed. Basically, you need two programs: First, you need a TCP/IP utility. Don't worry about the intimidating sounding acronym. Just realize that this is essentially the modem program that connects you to the rest of the Internet world. The second program you need is a utility that provides you with either a PPP or SLIP connection. Again, ignore the acronym. A PPP or SLIP program simply provides the *protocol* information required to identify and dial your Internet provider.

Again, Windows 95 and the Macintosh operating system include the TCP/ IP and PPP programs as built-in utilities. However, to connect to your Internet provider, your computer needs to know some technical identifying information about your provider's computer (called the *server)*. Specifically, your dial-up software needs to know your provider's phone number, Internet Protocol (IP) address, and domain name (called a DNS entry). You don't necessarily need to know what an IP or DNS is, but you do need to know that your computer needs this information.

Typically, all of the information that your computer requires to connect to your provider's server is supplied on a set-up disk that your provider will mail to you. You simply run the set-up program and the appropriate information is entered automatically into the networking utilities. Your provider might prefer to give you a dial-up phone number that essentially connects you to a simple bulletin board service. From there, you can select from menus to download the set-up software for your computer. If you're feeling really technically savvy, you can request all of the required settings directly from your provider's sales rep and then enter the information into the programs yourself. We don't recommend that approach. Let your provider's installation software do the work for you.

Logging On

After you've run your provider's set-up software, you should be ready to rock and roll online. The procedure for logging on is simple. We'll describe the approach for both Windows 95 and Macintosh users.

On both platforms, you can dial up your Internet provider simply by launching Netscape or Explorer. In Windows 95, the "Connect To" dialog box will appear when you launch the browser, as shown in Figure A.1. Your user name should already appear in the dialog box. (You would have defined this name when you ran the set-up program given to you by your provider.) At this point, simply type your password and press Enter (or click on the Connect button).

Alternatively, you can open the "Connect To" dialog box yourself. To do so, open the My Computer window, then open the Dial-Up Networking folder. Then double-click on the phone icon that represents your Internet connection to display the "Connect To" dialog box. If you find that you use

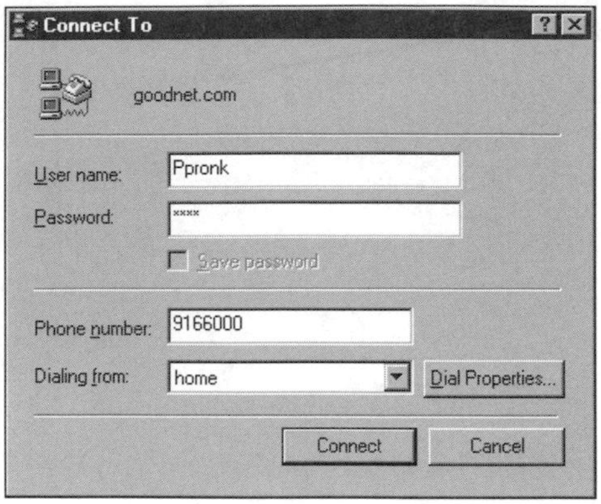

Figure A.1
The Connect To dialog box displayed in Windows 95.

this approach a lot, you might want to drag the phone icon to your desktop for easier access (or create a shortcut for it).

If you find that you get a busy signal frequently when you dial your provider, you can configure your dial-up program to redial the number repeatedly until it connects. To do this in Windows 95, open the My Computer window. Then, open the Dial-Up Networking folder. Next, click on the telephone icon that represents your dial-up connection (but don't double-click). Next, click on Connections|Settings. Then, specify the number of times you want the computer to redial before it gives up. You can enter a number from 1 to 9999. On the Macintosh, the Config PPP control panel will redial your provider by default whenever it receives a busy signal.

CHOOSING AND USING A WEB BROWSER

There are probably over a dozen different Web browsers available for free, but only two are widely used: Netscape Navigator and Microsoft Internet Explorer. One of your first tasks as a new Internet user is to select which browser to use to display Web pages. The decision might already be made for you, though. If you purchased a computer system or Windows 95 recently, Microsoft's Explorer browser will probably already be installed on your desktop. Look for the globe labeled "Internet." That launches Explorer.

Also, when you ran the set-up software given to you by your Internet provider, the software probably installed either the Netscape or Explorer browser. Depending on how the setup software works, the browser icon will either appear on your desktop or can be accessed from a folder.

Figure A.2 shows Adobe's home page displayed in both Netscape and Explorer. (Yes, you can actually run both browsers simultaneously and, yes, you can be online in both browsers simultaneously.) Other than the fact that the Netscape interface takes a bit more room near the top of the screen, there doesn't appear to be much difference between the two browsers, does there? In fact, even the interfaces that the two browsers use look extremely similar. So, what's the difference between the two?

The truth is, both browsers are quite comparable and provide almost identical services. Which one do we like better? It depends on what day you ask us. There are times when we want to use features that are specific to Explorer, and there are other times when we want to use features that are specific to Netscape. It's actually not a bad idea to download both browsers (they're both free, so why not) and try them both. That's really the best way to

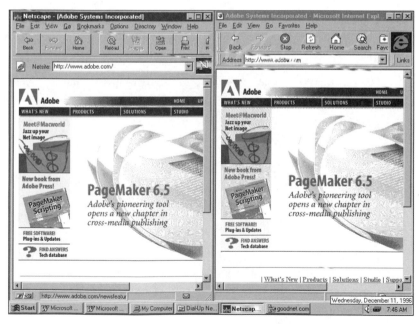

Figure A.2

The Netscape and Explorer browsers, displayed side by side.

determine which browser you prefer. In all honesty, we use both browsers and switch between them when we want to exploit different features.

In our view, Netscape's mail feature seems a bit easier to use than Explorer's. By the way, you can use both browsers to send and receive email. The first time you try to use the mail capability of either browser, it will prompt you to enter some information. You'll need to provide your real name, user name, and email address, and you'll also need to provide the name of your Internet provider's mail server. This is almost always the name of your provider preceded by the word mail and separated by a period. For instance, if the name of your provider is goodnet.com, then the name of your mail server is probably mail.goodnet.com. Your email address is your user name followed by your provider name, separated by an @ symbol. If your user name is rossp, and your provider is goodnet.com, then your email address is rossp@goodnet.com. It's that simple.

Both browsers are comparable in speed. Anyway, speed is a difficult thing to test, because you never know whether a delay is caused by your browser or by a server that you're passing through along the Internet. However, Microsoft has created some extended HTML commands that work in Explorer but not in Netscape (at least not currently). This is where Explorer might have an edge. At this writing, Netscape has about 75 percent of the browser market share. But Netscape had nearly a 90 percent market share before Explorer was introduced, so clearly Explorer is eroding Netscape's market. Now for the interesting part: Microsoft has recently released their FrontPage program, which allows you to create full-blown Web pages without the need to use any HTML directly. Instead, FrontPage creates HTML code based on the way you design a Web page. All you have to do is use menus, add text, and place images—your Web page is then ready to be placed on your provider's server. We'll show you how to do this later in this appendix.

The bottom line is that, by adding its own HTML extensions that only FrontPage can use, Microsoft encourages people to design Web pages that have features viewable only with the Explorer browser. It's a sneaky game that Microsoft is playing, but they're known for their ability to destroy competition through unique marketing strategies. The point we want to make is that the browser war is far from over. Again, we suggest that you try both Explorer and Netscape to see which one you prefer. In the following sections, we'll demonstrate some features of both browsers. We'll use a

Windows system to demonstrate; however, keep in mind that browser features for the Macintosh platform are nearly identical.

 It's amazing that so many savvy Web surfers, not to mention novices, are unaware of this little tidbit: You don't need to enter the http:// protocol when you enter a Web address for either Netscape or Explorer. The http:// part of the address is assumed. In fact, you don't even need to enter "www" if that's the first part of a Web address. Both browsers will automatically search for this part of an address if you don't enter it. For instance, the Web address for Coriolis Group Books is technically www.coriolis.com. However, if you simply type in coriolis.com, you'll get there, and just as quickly. The only time you need to enter a protocol is if you're going to a non-Web site, such as a newsgroup (news:) or an FTP site (ftp://).

Browsing The Web

Navigating the Web with Netscape or Explorer is really easy once you get the hang of it. To go to a Web site, type the Web address in the Location text box (called the Address text box in Explorer) and press Enter. One thing you need to know, though: In Netscape, the name of this text box switches from "Location" to "Go to" to "Netsite" depending on how you're using it. For now, don't worry about why this happens. Just be aware of it. As is true for any browser, just click on any underlined link to go to that site immediately. Images can also be used as links. If the hand pointer appears over any part of the Netscape or Explorer screen, then that part of the screen is a hyperlink—regardless of whether it's text or an image.

When you click on different hyperlinks, you'll discover that, oftentimes, you really don't want to be where the link took you. If that happens, you can return to the previous site by clicking on the Back button in the Toolbar. If you go back and then decide you want to return to where you've just been, click on the Forward button. Just practice using these buttons for a few minutes and you'll realize how easy it is to navigate the Web.

If you want to return to a Web site that you've previously visited during the current session, you can avoid the Forward and Back buttons by clicking on Go in the menu bar, and then highlighting the name of the Web site that you've previously visited. A neat feature of Explorer is that it stores previously visited Web addresses for 20 days (or longer or shorter if you specify differently). To view these sites in Explorer, click on Go in the menu bar, then click on Open History Folder. Then, locate the Web site you want to revisit and double-click on it. Netscape currently doesn't support this feature.

If you want to save specific Web addresses for later use, you can do so in Netscape by using the Bookmark feature. While you're at a particular Web site, click on Bookmarks in the Netscape menu bar, then click on Add Bookmark. That's all there is to it. Later, you can return to this site by clicking on Bookmarks, then clicking on the name of the Web site in the Bookmarks list. In Explorer, you can do the same thing by clicking on Favorites from the menu bar, then clicking on Add To Favorites. Explorer will give you the option of saving the Web address to a particular Favorites folder, which allows you to organize your favorite Web sites by different categories. Netscape offers a similar capability, but it's a little less intuitive to use than Explorer's Favorites feature.

Both browsers offer extensive search capabilities. This is probably the single most useful feature for new Web surfers. For instance, you might be aware that information exists on a certain topic, but you might not know where to find it. That's where *search engines* prove to be useful. Both browsers offer multiple search engines, which are actually servers (located throughout the world) that store massive databases of Web addresses and Web content. A search engine lets you enter one or more words to describe a topic, and then searches its databases to look for Web sites that have text that matches your search criteria. Where possible, use multiple words to narrow down your search. The Web is truly worldwide and consists of millions of sites, so you want to make sure your search locates specifically what you want, not a bunch of irrelevant Web pages.

To search for information using Netscape, click on the Net Search directory button to display a screen similar to the one we've shown in Figure A.3. You'll notice that Netscape (at least at this writing) offers links to five major search engines—Magellan, Excite, Yahoo, Infoseek, and Lycos. If you scroll down the page, you'll discover links to many other specialized search engines. Which search engine is best? That depends on what you're looking for. Each engine excels in a different way. You'll want to experiment

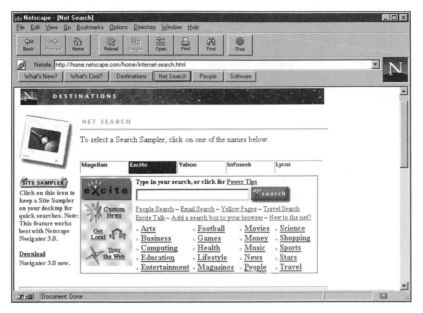

Figure A.3
The Netscape search screen.

with different search engines to discover the one (or ones) that works best for you. At this point, select a search engine. When the engine's dialog box appears, type the text for the topic you want to locate, then click on the Search button.

To search for information using Explorer, click on the Search button in the toolbar to display a screen similar to the one we've shown in Figure A.4. As the screen shows, Microsoft's search screen currently offers 10 search engines and some other, more specific search links. However, Microsoft has an annoying habit of changing this screen every few weeks, so expect your Explorer search screen to look different than the one shown in Figure A.4. To use this window, select a search engine, type the text for the topic you want to locate on the Web, then click on the Search button. Experiment with different search engines to find the one (or ones) that works best for you.

Reading And Sending Mail

As we mentioned earlier, both Netscape and Explorer provide a way for you to compose, send, and receive email. In Netscape, you access the Mail window by clicking on Window in the menu bar, then clicking on Netscape Mail. You'll then see a window similar to the one shown in Figure A.5.

Figure A.4
The Explorer search screen.

Composing messages, sending mail, and receiving mail are all pretty intuitive processes, so we won't delve into them here. To learn how to use Netscape Mail, you only need to spend perhaps 5 to 10 minutes exploring the various buttons and options.

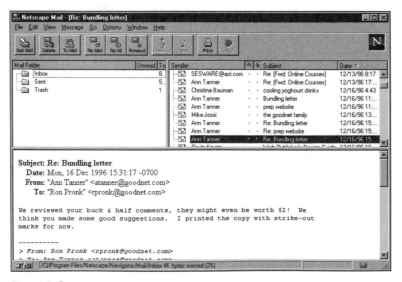

Figure A.5
The Netscape Mail window.

In Explorer, you access the Mail window by clicking on the Mail button in the toolbar, then clicking on either Read Mail or New Message. As a general rule, we click on Read Mail to display the window shown in Figure A.6. That way, we can check our new mail, and, if we want to reply or send new mail, we can do so easily from this window. Play around with the various buttons and options available in the Explorer Mail window. It will only take you a few minutes to become acclimated to these features.

Accessing Newsgroups

Newsgroups are a major part of the Internet. A newsgroup is a specialized area on the Internet that focuses on discussion of a particular topic for people who have a strong interest in that topic. Currently, there are more than 25,000 newsgroups, and the list grows every day. Although they're not technically part of the Web (because they only contain text and don't use HTML), newsgroups can be accessed easily from your Web browser. In both Netscape and Explorer, you access newsgroups by typing in the protocol "news:" followed by the name of the newsgroup you want to access. For instance, to access the Alfred Hitchcock newsgroup, you would type the following in the Netscape or Explorer text box:

news:alt.movies.hitchcock

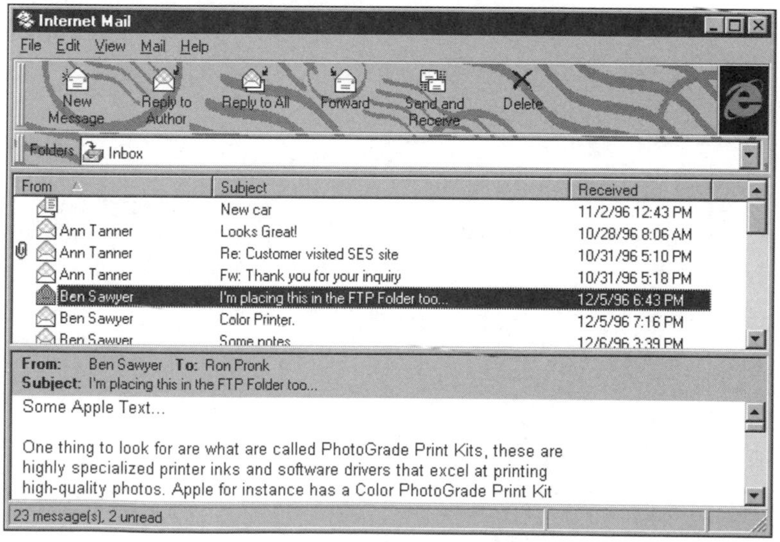

Figure A.6
The Explorer Mail window.

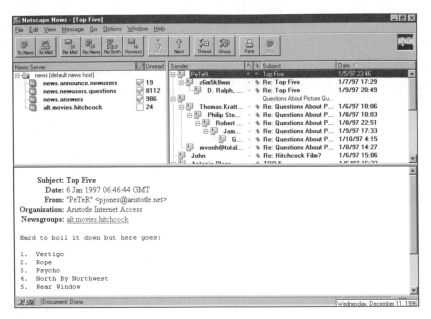

Figure A.7

The Alfred Hitchcock newsgroup contents, as displayed in the Netscape newsreader.
The newsreader for Explorer is almost identical to this one.

Notice that you don't need to put slashes after "news:" In fact, if you do, you'll receive an error message. Figure A.7 shows the newsreader window that Netscape displays when we access the Hitchcock newsgroup. The top portion shows messages that have been sent by newsgroup members. The bottom portion of the screen shows the content of a selected message.

Accessing FTP Sites

We're about ready to move on to the topic of creating your own Web pages. But before we do, we need to describe one last, and very important, part of the Internet—*File Transfer Protocol*, or *FTP* for short. FTP is a set of rules, or protocols, that Internet sites use to transfer files from one server to another. FTP sites are used to store shareware, Web pages, and much more. FTP sites exist to allow Internet users a convenient way to upload and download files from a centrally located site that can be accessed by multiple users. To be truly proficient on the Internet, you'll want to know how to make the most of FTP access.

Many FTP sites allow for what is called "anonymous login." That is, an anonymous FTP site is open to the public. Anybody can access it and no password is required to gain entrance. However, it's common courtesy to specify your email address when you log into an anonymous FTP site. Some FTP sites won't even let you in unless you specify your email address. You can visit anonymous FTP sites directly from your browser. Just type in the ftp:// protocol, followed by the site's FTP address. For instance, to access Coriolis's anonymous FTP site, we would type the following:

ftp://coriolis.com

It doesn't matter whether we use Netscape or Explorer to do this. The results would be the same. Figure A.8 shows the screen that results when we access the Coriolis FTP site. Notice that no graphics appear. An FTP site, technically, is not a Web page, although it is now possible to create hyperlinks for text in an FTP site, as Figure A.8 shows. However, it is not possible to display graphics from an FTP site. The major purpose of such a site is to provide a repository where users can send and receive files.

Other FTP sites are *secure.* In other words, if you don't have a password, you can't get in. If you want to log into a secure FTP site, you must use an FTP utility program. Neither Netscape nor Explorer provides a way to enter a user ID or password to a secure FTP site. On the Windows side, the most popular program for accessing secure FTP sites is called WS-FTP. The interface for this program is shown in Figure A.9. As you can see, you need to

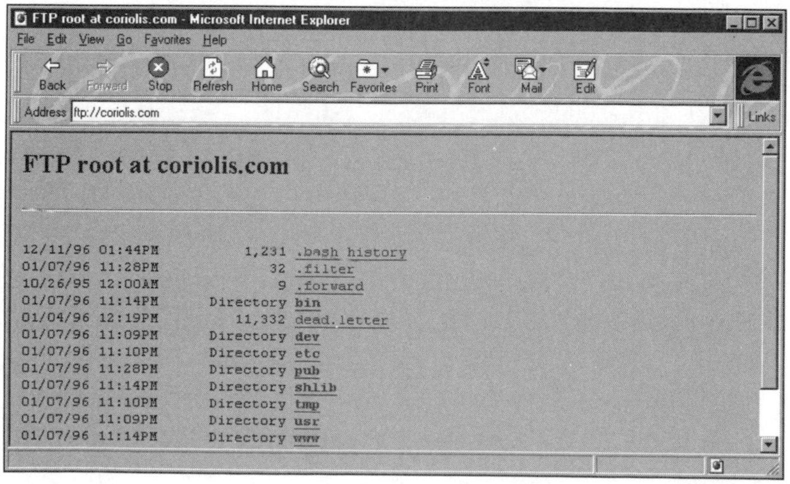

Figure A.8
The Coriolis FTP site.

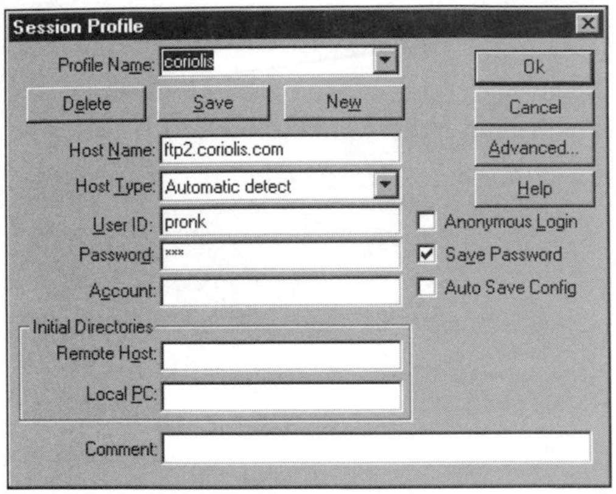

Figure A.9
The WS-FTP start-up dialog box.

enter a host name (the address of the FTP site), your user name, and your password. Also, enter a profile name at the top of the dialog box. This can be any name you choose. Whenever you create a profile name in WS-FTP, the program saves all of the logon information for that profile—including the FTP address, your user name, and password. So, once you've create a profile, you can simply highlight a profile name whenever you open WS-FTP, and the program will automatically insert all of the required information.

After you've entered this information, WS-FTP searches for the FTP site, and then displays its contents, along with the contents of your hard drive, as shown in Figure A.10. The contents of your hard drive appear in the pane on the left side of the window, while the contents of the FTP site appear on the right side of the window. To upload or download a file, simply click on one or more files in either pane, and then click on the left or right arrow in the middle to indicate in which direction you want the file transfer to take place. If you want to change the directory of your hard drive, you need to click on the ChgDir button, and then type in the full path (for instance, c:\digital camera) of the desired directory (folder).

On the Macintosh, the preferred FTP utility is called Fetch. When you launch Fetch on your Macintosh, you'll see the dialog box shown in Figure A.11. Your user name should appear by default. You need only type in the FTP site name and password, and then press Enter. Fetch will take you directly to the FTP site and the default folder

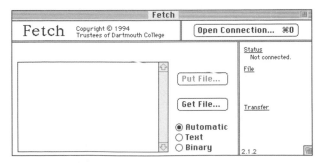

Figure A.10
The contents of an FTP site and a local hard drive, as displayed in WS-FTP.

CREATING YOUR OWN WEB SITE

Now we're ready to dig into the fun stuff. We could show you how to create a Web site using HTML tags and commands, but that would involve a lot of unnecessary work. As we've mentioned earlier, numerous HTML editors are available that will guide you through the Web site development process—without requiring you to enter HTML commands. However, even with the best HTML editor, you'll find it necessary to fine-tune your Web site with a few well-placed HTML tags and commands. For more information on using basic HTML tags, see the discussion near the end of Chapter 11.

Figure A.11
The contents of the Macintosh Fetch dialog.

In this appendix, we'll provide a brief example of creating a Web site using the most powerful HTML editor available—Microsoft FrontPage. Actually, it's not even fair to call FrontPage an HTML editor. It's really an HTML replacement. Let's take a look at how easy it is to create a personal Web site in FrontPage.

Defining A Home Page Template

FrontPage is actually composed of two major programs—FrontPage Explorer and FrontPage Editor. You use FrontPage Explorer to view the structure of your Web site, and you use FrontPage Editor to actually create and make changes to your Web site.

There are several ways to create a personal Web site with FrontPage. The easiest way is to use a FrontPage template. When you load FrontPage, it displays the blank Explorer screen shown in Figure A.12. From there, you click on File|New|New FrontPage Web to display the list of templates shown in Figure A.13. These templates provide basic Web page structures that serve different purposes—from creating corporate sites to creating personal Web pages. Double-click on Personal Web to display the Personal Web Page dialog box. Specify the path (location) where you want to store your Web page and type in a name for your Web page. Then click on OK to display the Web site map shown in Figure A.14.

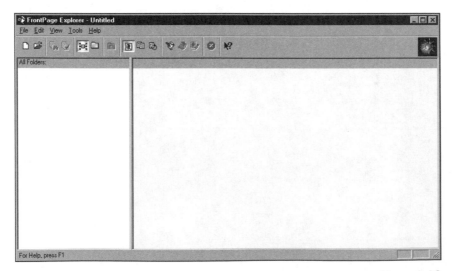

Figure A.12
The default FrontPage Explorer screen.

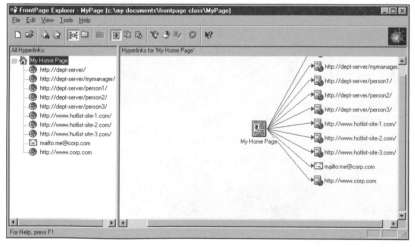

Figure A.13
Custom Web-development templates available within FrontPage Explorer.

We need to forewarn you that the Personal Web template is geared toward creating a page for corporate use. However, you don't need to abide by this. You can customize your Web site to contain anything you like, and you can disregard any components of the Web template or subsidiary Web pages that you don't want to use.

Figure A.15 shows the home page template that appears when you double-click on "My Home Page" in FrontPage Explorer. Keep in mind that this a template—a guideline. You can change any or all of the contents, depending on your needs. The existing hypertext links are suggestions. You can

Figure A.14
FrontPage displays a map of links for all related pages accessible from the home page.

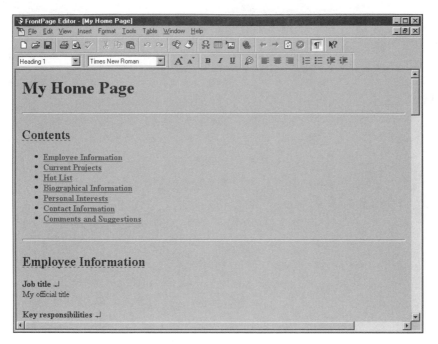

Figure A.15
The My Home Page template.

change these, too. To change a hyperlink, simply highlight the text for the link, and type over it with the new text that you want to use. Then click on Insert|Hypertext Link if you want to change the name and/or location of the link.

Figure A.16 shows some of the changes we've made in the template to customize it so it looks more like our own home page. We added an image at the start of the page, changed the title of the page, changed a few of the links, and added some custom text. We did all this by using FrontPage's menuing system and dialog boxes. We didn't need to type in any HTML tags. Although we don't have the space to describe how to use FrontPage in depth (that would require a separate book), we think that this introduction helps to give you an idea of how easy it is to create a Web page.

After you've completed the layout of your home page or Web site, you'll need to upload the files to the FTP site that your Internet provider uses to display personal Web sites. Your provider will give you a site name, user ID, and password that you can use to access this FTP site. Use WS-FTP (Windows) or Fetch (Macintosh) to upload your Web files to your provider's FTP site.

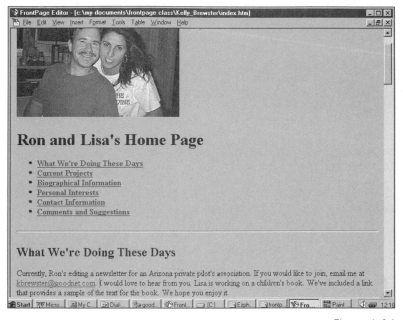

Figure A.16
A customized home page.

A common mistake made by many novice Web page developers is to reference images using their local hard drive paths. When you transfer images onto your provider's server, these paths will no longer make sense. So make sure you delete any such paths before you FTP files to your provider's server. This is an example of where a little knowledge of HTML code can help you. Figure A.17 shows how this situation can create problems. Notice the two "img src=" commands in the HTML code. You'll note that both commands point to an /image directory or folder. That folder exists on a local hard drive. When we move the images to our provider's Internet server, we need to delete that /image specification; otherwise, the server will try to look for images on a folder that doesn't exist. As a result, your Web site will display without any images. Again, make sure all "img src=" commands point to a file name only, not a path.

Deleting a file path is simple. Simply open FrontPage Editor, open the Web file that contains your Web page information, then click on View|HTML. The HTML source code for your Web page will appear. Delete any path information that appears next to "img src=" commands (leave the file name intact, of course), then click on OK to save changes to the HTML source code.

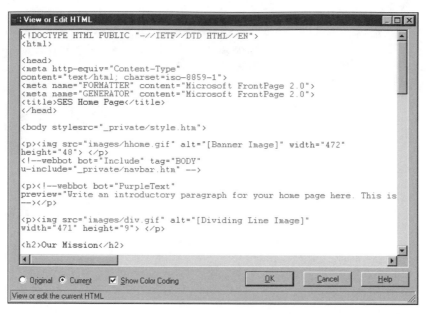

Figure A.17
Problems in HTML code.

In this appendix, we've attempted to explain the basics of using the Web. Of course, there are a lot of details involved in accessing Web sites and creating Web pages that we haven't been able to explain. But if you use this appendix as a rough guide, we think you'll find it easy to navigate the Web and to use an HTML editor to create your own Web page. As is true in all aspects of digital photography, the key lies in experimentation. Don't be afraid to try new things or to explore different options. That's where the fun is. And that's what we want you to do above all else—have fun!

Appendix

B

Advanced Photo System (See APS.)

AICP

The Apple Image Capture Platform is a software/hardware technology that incorporates a chip and programs designed to make digital cameras behave and function smarter, and to make them easier to use.

Apple Image Capture Platform (See AICP.)

APS

The Advanced Photo System is a specification that allows a camera to store information about a photo—not just the photo itself—when it is captured. APS is now being used in both digital and film-based cameras.

Bit Depth

The number of colors that a computer monitor can support. This value is based on the resolution that the monitor can support coupled with the amount of memory that is included on the video card. For example, 8 bit color can display 256 colors. Twenty-four-bit color can display 16.7 million colors.

BMP

This is Windows bitmap graphics format. A BMP is not scalable in any shape or form, so avoid BMP images like the proverbial plague.

Camera Companies

Oh, we could have tried to show off by listing them all individually in this glossary. But the truth is that all camera companies discussed in this book are mentioned in Chapter 14.

CCD

A microchip that records light passing through red, green, and blue filters within a digital camera so that the resulting image can be downloaded to a computer for editing and storage.

Charge-Coupled Device (See CCD.)

CMYK

Stands for Cyan, Magenta, Yellow, and Black—the four basic colors in any displayed image.

Compression

A technique in which a file is reduced in size so that it takes up significantly less space on a hard disk or diskette.

Corbis

A subsidiary of Microsoft that is being developed to provide and sell digital photos to Internet and other users.

Dots Per Inch (DPI)

The measurement of an image in terms of screen display or printer output. Monitors and printers output images as a series of dots. The more dots per inch, the better the quality of an image that's being output.

EPS

Stands for *Encapsulated PostScript*, a format that was developed by Adobe as a way to embed a PostScript file within other, non-Postscript files.

File Compression (See Compression.)

FlashPIX

A graphic format created by an alliance between Kodak, LivePicture, Microsoft, and Hewlett-Packard. It is based on an existing graphic format called IVUE, which stores imagery in such a way that the image can be manipulated extremely rapidly—even with relatively unsophisticated equipment.

GIF

Stands for Graphical Interchange Format, and refers to any image that's stored in this format. GIF was created (or at least absconded) by CompuServe and continues to be a popular format for storing images on the Internet.

HTML

Stands for Hypertext Markup Language. HTML is the required language for creating Web pages, but sophisticated Web-page editors are beginning to send HTML the way of Velociraptor eggs.

ISO/ASA

A ranking used to describe how sensitive and clean an image is. The lower the reading, the less likely the camera will introduce noise or graininess into the imagery.

Jaz Drive

An extremely high-density and removable storage media sold by iomega.

JPEG

Stands for Joint Photographic Experts Group, a consortium that created this popular image format to replace the outdated GIF standard.

Kai's Power Goo

A morphing program that's designed to convert digital photos into whatever is your preferred weirdness, from animals to zygotenes (go look it up).

LCD

Stands for Liquid Crystal Display. A crystal that, when combined with display technology, can show a detailed, full-color image, such as one that is displayed in the viewfinder of a digital camera so that the photographer can review the image prior to taking it.

LivePicture

A popular image-editing program that provides some powerful features for changing or improving digital images.

Lossy Compression

A technique in which an image is displayed with minimal color information to satisfy the way the human eye receives and records colors.

MCD Drive

From Nomai, this removable drive, which retails for about $580, stores 540 MB of data on each cartridge.

Megapixel

A term used to refer to digital photos produced from extremely high-resolution cameras, typically those that provide greater than 1000×1000 pixel resolution.

Morphing

The process of changing an image into something entirely different, and often entirely wierd. Morphing is another term for "fun."

PCMCIA card

A credit-card sized-add-on card that can add memory or other functionality to a computer or to a digital camera.

Photo CD

A technology developed by Kodak that allows standard photographic images to be scanned into a computer and stored on a CD for permanency.

PhotoDeluxe

A consumer-oriented image editor, by Adobe, that helps you to create calendars, greeting cards, and other popular designs from your digital images.

Photoshop

This is perhaps the most popular and versatile image-editing program available. Dozens of filters and plug-ins are available to extend the capabilities of Photoshop.

PictureIt!

An image editing program from Microsoft. This package is ideal for doing simple color correction and for creating greeting cards, calendars, posters, and other other popular items from your digital photos.

PK Zip (See WinZip.)

PNG

Stands for Portable Network Graphics, and is designed to be the successor to GIF graphics. This graphics file format uses a run-length compression scheme.

QuickTime (and QuickTime VR.)

QuickTime is a plug-in that allows both Windows and Mac users to view QuickTime-formatted movies—either on the Web or on their own personal systems. QuickTime VR is an extension of QuickTime that allows users to view three-dimensional virtual-reality videos on their computers.

Resolution

A measurement of the vertical and horizontal density of a digital image, based on pixels (or picture element). Each pixel represents a tiny dot on a computer screen or on a printout. The more dots that a picture can display or print, the higher its resolution and the better its visual quality will be.

Run-Length Encoding

A file compression format in which identical color information is stored and compressed together for later use.

Scanner

A device that can convert a flat image, such as a drawing or photograph, into digital form for display and use on a computer.

SRAM

A chip that stores digital information as light waves, rather than electrical signals. An SRAM chip can retain information in the absence of batteries or any other power source.

Static RAM (See SRAM.)

Stuff It

The most popular file compression utility for Macintosh computers. Don't have Stuff It? Here's where you can get it:

www.aladdinsys.com/index.html

Surround Video

A technology, similar to QuickTime VR, that allows you to view 3D movies on your computer.

TIFF

Stands for Tagged Image File Format, and was originally created by Aldus Corporation for use in storing and editing high-resolution grayscale images created with scanners.

TWAIN

A digital storage format that is used as a standard so that different hardware devices, from different manufacturers, can read or use images stored by a digital camera.

Vertex

The Vertex optical hard drive from Pinnacle Micro stores 2.6 GB on each removable, optical disk cartridge. At $1,500, the Vertex drive isn't cheap, but it's one great drive.

WinZip

The most widely used utility for compressing and uncompressing files. If you don't own WinZip, you need to get it—now. It's available on the Web at www.winzip.com.

Zip drive

A product of iomega, this is a removable storage medium that currently can store more than 100 MB of data on a disk that fits in the palm of your hand.

For More Information
on Kodak Digital Cameras:
www.kodak.com

Visit The
Digital Camera Companion
Web Site at:

www.coriolis.com/digital

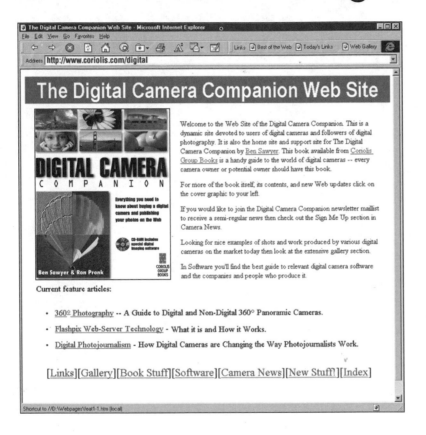

Coriolis plans to continually support the readers of *The Digital Camera Companion* and all digital camera owners with *The Digital Camera Companion* Web site, linked to our home page at http://www.coriolis.com/digital.

This site will offer camera news, new material, chapter updates, and useful links to other digital camera companies and software sites. Also, be sure to check out the gallery section where we'll post your own cool digital shots and neat digital photography ideas!